Ending the Cold War

New Visions in Security

Series Editor: Richard Ned Lebow

Ending the Cold War:
Interpretations, Causation, and the Study of International Relations
Edited by Richard K. Herrmann
and Richard Ned Lebow (2004)

Ending the Cold War

Interpretations, Causation, and
the Study of International Relations

Edited by

Richard K. Herrmann and Richard Ned Lebow

palgrave
macmillan

First published 2004 by
PALGRAVE MACMILLAN™
175 Fifth Avenue, New York, N.Y. 10010 and
Houndmills, Basingstoke, Hampshire, England RG21 6XS.
Companies and representatives throughout the world.

PALGRAVE MACMILLAN IS THE GLOBAL ACADEMIC IMPRINT OF THE PALGRAVE
MACMILLAN division of St. Martin's Press, LLC and of Palgrave Macmillan Ltd. Macmil-
lan® is a registered trademark in the United States, United Kingdom and other countries.
Palgrave is a registered trademark in the European Union and other countries.

ISBN 1-4039-6383-5 (hc)
ISBN 1-4039-6384-3 (pb)

Library of Congress Cataloging-in-Publication Data

Ending the Cold War / edited by Richard K. Herrmann and Richard New Lebow.
   p. cm.
  Includes bibliographical references and index.
  ISBN 1-4039-6383-5 — ISBN 1-4039-6384-3 (pbk.)
  1. Cold War. 2. World politics—1945–1989. 3. United States—Foreign relations—Soviet Union. 4. Soviet Union—Foreign relations—United States. 5. Disarmament. 6. Germany—History—Unification, 1990. I. Herrmann, Richard K.,
1925– II. Lebow, Richard Ned.

D843.E485 2004
940.55—dc22
   2003060900

A catalogue record for this book is available from the British Library.

Design by Letra Libre, Inc.

First edition: March 2004
10 9 8 7 6 5 4 3 2

Printed in the United States of America

Contents

Acknowledgments

This book is the product of team effort. All of the authors had a hand in designing the basic research strategy and participated in a series of oral history workshops. Beyond the oral history conferences, we conducted individual interviews in Russia, the United States, and across Europe. The first phase of the project involved collaboration between the Watson Institute at Brown University and the Mershon Center at Ohio and resulted in an oral history conference in Providence, Rhode Island, that featured key decision makers from the Gorbachev and Reagan administrations. We are grateful for the lead Thomas Biersteker, the Director of the Watson Institute, took in convening that meeting and appreciate the help his staff provided. We are especially grateful for the funding the Carnegie Corporation of New York provided to make that meeting possible.

The second, third, and fourth phases of the project involved oral history conferences in Moscow, Columbus, Ohio, and Wildbad Kreuth, Germany. These meetings were organized by the Mershon Center in conjunction with the Institute for General History at the Russian Academy of Sciences and the Geschwister-Scholl-Institut of the University of Munich. The Carnegie Corporation helped to sponsor these events and we are indebted to David C. Speedie and Patricia Moore Nicholas at the Corporation for their help. Oleg Skvortsov organized the meeting in Moscow and provided an indispensable bridge to former Soviet officials. Fritz Kratochwil and James Davis organized the meeting in Germany and provided access to important European leaders that was extremely valuable. We are grateful for their contribution.

In preparation for each of the oral history conferences, the Cold War International History Project and the National Security Archive complied collections of newly released documents relevant to the issues being discussed. These provided new information and helped to focus the discussion on critical missing pieces. We are grateful for the help provided in this regard by Thomas Blanton, William Burr, Christian Ostermann, and Vladislav Zubok. We also appreciate the help of the Anatoly Chernyaev and the Gorbachev foundation for the documents they made available for our meetings. Oleg Skvortsov conducted a series of interviews with former Soviet officials who came to oppose Gorbachev and we appreciate this as well.

Oleg Grinnevsky played a special role in this project, providing guidance and help navigating the Soviet side of the project. We thank him for the time he spent at the Mershon Center and for his valuable input and friendship. Raymond Garthoff also played a large role in making our conferences a success, providing his expertise and insight. Many other people gave generously of their time and expertise, attending our meetings, responding to our questions, and granting us interviews. Although none of them are responsible for whatever errors we may have made, all of them have our thanks and gratitude. We want to mention in particular in this regard Anatoly Adamishin, P. S. Akopov, O. D. Baklanov, V. I. Boldin, Richard Burt, Anatoly Chernayev, A. O Chubarian, Ilya Gaiduk, James Goodby, A.A. Gromyko, A. S. Grachev, Lynn Hansen, Vitaly Kataev, V. A. Kryuchkov, N. S. Leonov, Douglas MacEachin, Yuri Nazarkin, Dennis Ross, O. S. Shein, S. Tarasenko, James Woolsey, G. I. Yanaev, and D. T. Yazov.

Finally, we want to acknowledge the support of the Mershon Center. It made this project possible both by the generous financial support it provided and by the intellectually challenging atmosphere created by our Mershon colleagues.

Chapter 1

What Was the Cold War?
When and Why Did it End?

Richard K. Herrmann and Richard Ned Lebow

The end of the Cold War constitutes one of the most remarkable transformations of the twentieth century. Its peaceful and unexpected end
was a dramatic watershed, as was the collapse of the Soviet Union,
which followed in its wake. Both events had momentous and diverse consequences for hundreds of millions of people. The indirect consequences—unipo-
larity, accelerated globalization, and diminished fear of Armageddon—were
global and still reverberate through the societal groups, countries, and regions
that constitute the international community. Yet the end of the Cold War remains poorly understood. Even before critical parts of the historical record became accessible, the received wisdom in the United States was that the West
"won" through unrelenting pressure on the Soviet Union. In the former Soviet
Union, the end of the Cold War is most often attributed to "new thinking" and
is regarded as a triumph of ideas over dangerous and deeply entrenched institutional practices. The emerging evidence suggests that both interpretations are at
best only part of a very complex story.

The end of the Cold War poses a formidable challenge to international relations theory. Scholars of all persuasions failed to predict the possibility of such
momentous, let alone peaceful, change. In the aftermath, they struggled to find
explanations consistent with their theories and to make sense of the emerging
post–Cold War world. The Cold War might be described as a "mere data point"
that cannot be used to test or develop theories, but at the same time, the Cold
War's end has also been described as a "big bang" that created a new political
universe. The latter description appears closer to the truth given the response of

the discipline. Realism, especially neorealism, is on the defensive; new approaches and new substantive issues dominate the security agenda, and the nature and value of theory are widely contested. A better understanding of the end of the Cold War has important implications for all of these controversies.

The end of the Cold War has had important, although less revolutionary, consequences for the policy world. In Washington, the favorable outcome to that conflict was taken as confirmation of the earlier "lessons" of Munich—that peace could only be achieved through strength and a reputation for resolve. These beliefs continue to shape American security policy; they provide the principal justification for maintaining high levels of defense spending and were important underlying causes of the American crusades against Saddam Hussein and military intervention in the former Yugoslavia. Lessons can be a useful tool when they identify problems and strategies appropriate to them. They are counterproductive when they are based on a faulty understanding of the events that gave rise to them or are applied to situations where they are inappropriate. Another goal of our book is to subject these policy lessons to careful scrutiny by reexamining the historical interpretations on which they are based.

When Did the Cold War End?

The end of the Cold War, like its beginning, did not happen at an agreed upon time with a clear, commonly acknowledged event. Neither the beginning nor the end of this conflict can be marked in place and time outside of specific constructions and understandings of what the Cold War was. For some scholars the Cold War was an ideological struggle that began in 1917 and continued until the Soviet revolution was overturned, either with the renunciation of the constitutional privileges granted to the Communist Party of the Soviet Union in 1990 or with the dissolution of the Soviet Union in 1991. In a related understanding of the Cold War that also stresses ideological factors, the conflict ended, or at least abated in a serious way, in the late 1950s with Khrushchev's advocacy of peaceful coexistence between the social systems. Other constructions emphasize the geopolitical character of the Cold War, and characterize it as a struggle for influence between two emerging superpowers. In these understandings, the Cold War is usually seen to begin during the waning days of World War II or soon after, and to end between 1989 and 1991 with the contraction of the Soviet Union's sphere of influence and ultimate demise as a state.

In China, and in parts of the Third World, of course, there were always doubts about the reality of U.S.-Soviet confrontation, and a suspicion that the two superpowers were actually in collusion. In these constructions, the Cold War may have begun as both an ideological and geopolitical contest, but had by the 1960s evolved into at least a tacit, if not explicit, division of the world that served the imperial ambitions of both Washington and Moscow. The facade of intense competition was cultivated and exploited by the superpowers as an excuse to justify continued domination of allies and the extensive use of violence to preserve and extend their respective spheres of influence and control in the Third World.

In the conferences and interviews associated with this project, we encountered yet another construction of the Cold War that has many adherents in Moscow. In this reading, the Cold War was primarily driven by American determination to achieve global hegemony and destroy the countervailing power of the Soviet Union. Former Soviet officials and scholars who hold this view contend that Washington pursued an anti-Russian strategy throughout the post–World War II period, and has continued to do so after the collapse of the Soviet Union. They take umbrage at the notion that the Cold War ended in the late 1980s, insisting instead that the central causal forces driving this conflict became even more pronounced in the following decade. In the extreme version of this understanding of the Cold War, advanced by officials who opposed Gorbachev, the Soviet leadership and the post-Soviet Russian leadership lost their will to resist American hegemony, and their lack of resolve led to a collapse of Soviet capabilities.

Russians who construct the Cold War this way suggest that Russian-American relations are likely to become conflictual again, and may even take on global proportions if Russian power is revitalized and Washington adheres to its imperial and anti-Russian course. They suggest that future historians may look back on the 1990s as a mere hiatus in an enduring rivalry. Even if they are correct, the transformation of East-West that took place between 1985 and 1991 will still be regarded as a major development. And the explanations advanced for this transformation will have important implications for how we understand the prospects for peace and the factors that contribute to its creation and maintenance in Russian-American and other conflicts. For these reasons, we direct our attention toward the key turning points our authors identify as central to this transformation.

The End of the End of the Cold War

The Cold War in 1985

Although we concentrate on the 1985–1991 period, we do not see the transformation that occurred during these seven years as coming out of the blue. To the contrary, these developments were made possible by prior evolution of the Cold War, and some of these changes had been underway for years. When Ronald Reagan and Mikhail Gorbachev assumed office, the state of East-West relations—and superpower thinking about those relations—were very different than they had been in the 1950s.

Important changes had occurred in all relevant domains. The Soviet political system witnessed the end of Stalin's terror and the cult of personality, short-lived liberalization under Khrushchev, stabilization and then stagnation under Brezhnev, and a de facto interregnum under his short-lived successors. Washington and Moscow had fought costly and unsuccessful political-military campaigns in the Third World, America in Vietnam and the Soviet Union in Afghanistan. Both superpowers had lived through the immediate danger of nuclear confrontation in the Cuban missile crisis and had learned in the course of it that each superpower feared nuclear war as much as its rival. This recognition was a catalyst for efforts to pursue a detente that would stabilize mutual deterrence and contain the costs of competition in regional affairs. By 1985, strategic nuclear arms control agreements had been in place for more than a decade, and had powerful bureaucratic constituencies for and against it in both superpowers.

Both alliance systems had been transformed. With Hungary leading the way, some members of the Warsaw Pact pursued experimental economic programs, while others, most notably Romania, exercised increasing independence from Moscow in foreign policy. Most had experienced major challenges to the communist system in the form of workers' revolts (East Germany and Hungary), short-lived attempts at political liberalization from above (Hungary and Czechoslovakia), or opposition from a well-organized alliance of workers and the Roman Catholic Church (Poland). In East Germany, the political-economic picture was very different in 1985 than it had been in the early 1960s, when the Berlin Wall was hastily erected. With *Ostpolitk,* which began in the late 1960s, and the Helsinki Accords of 1975, the Western alliance had recognized de facto and then de jure both the Democratic Republic of Germany (GDR) and the territorial settlement the Soviet Union had imposed in Eastern Europe in the aftermath of World War II. Some scholars, Hans Morgenthau among them, considered the Cold War to be over.

Not everything was rosy. Hopes for an earlier end of the Cold War had been shattered. Expectations of regional disengagement, generated by the detente of the early and mid 1970s, were replaced on both sides by disappointment, renewed suspicion, and increased conflict. In Eastern Europe, the repression of the Solidarity movement in Poland produced discouragement and the pessimistic conclusion that peaceful change was still beyond reach. Arms control appeared more unattainable in the early 1980s, as Reagan's commitment to the Strategic Defense Initiative (SDI) prevented any further agreements between the superpowers and threatened to unravel the Anti-Ballistic Missile Treaty (ABM), long the cornerstone of strategic arms control.

The Importance of the Changes from 1985 to 1991

The analysis of only one stage of a long evolutionary process compels us to pose two cautionary questions: How important was the final stage, and How independent was it of previous stages or developments? There can be little doubt that the 1985–1991 period marked a radical departure in East-West relations. Ronald Reagan's first term as president witnessed an intensification of the Cold War, attributable to the president's bellicose rhetoric, support for the largest peacetime military buildup in American history, commitment to Star Wars, and efforts to engage the Soviets more actively throughout the Third World. Reagan's foreign policy raised fears of war in the Soviet Union, Western Europe, and among his opposition in the United States. And Moscow's brutal prosecution of the war in Afghanistan and suppression of the worker's movement in Poland heightened the concerns of Reaganites. No scholar or policy analyst predicted that seven years later, Ronald Reagan would walk arm and arm with Gorbachev at a Moscow summit, and dismiss with a chuckle his earlier depiction of the Soviet Union as an "evil empire." Reminded by a reporter of his earlier remark, the President explained that "I was talking about another time, another era."

The fact that events are unexpected does not preclude their being the outcome of trends that were underway for some time. In the aftermath of the Cold War, some realists claimed that this turn of events was readily explicable and even inevitable, something that none of them predicted, let alone thought possible at the time. William Wohlforth has rightly criticized such ex post facto confidence. He and coauthor James Davis review the most recent and reliable data on the Soviet economy and conclude that economic decline and the drain of military spending would sooner or later have required a radical rethinking of foreign policy. Although they argue that retrenchment and accommodation were the most rational responses to this predicament, they openly acknowledge that there were other choices, and that no choice was determined. Neither was the timing of retrenchment. Even if the Soviet Union and its command economy were doomed to implosion, both might have staggered on for some time to come.

Consider the possibility, as George Breslauer and Ned Lebow do, that a more conservative leader had been chosen in lieu of Gorbachev, and had introduced only minor economic and political reforms and had reduced tensions with the West without lessening Soviet control over Eastern Europe. The Soviet economic decline would have been gradual rather than precipitous. Holding the line on military spending, and better yet, cutbacks in the percentage of the national income devoted to the military-industrial complex, could have deferred a real reckoning well into this century. By then, the context of Soviet domestic and foreign policy choices almost certainly would have been very different. Nationalist unrest in the Soviet Union might have been more intense, especially along the southern frontier, and could have intensified leadership fears of falling dominoes. This in turn could have made it more difficult to let Eastern Europe go its own way. Gorbachev hoped that political upheavals in Eastern Europe would bring reform-minded communists to power who would become his natural allies. If tensions in the region had been acute and opposition to Moscow more overt, leaders in the Kremlin might have had no illusions about consequences of allowing reform, let alone openly encouraging it.

German unification could also have played out differently. Chancellor Helmut Kohl promised German voters that unification would not be a major financial burden for them, and many East Germans expected that it would quickly raise their living standards to the level of their Western compatriots. Reality was very different, with consequences that Germany is still struggling with more than a decade later, and from which other interested parties think they have learned important lessons. Interest in unification— as opposed to accommodation—has cooled off markedly in South Korea, and Indians privately express their fear that Pakistan will collapse. What if the Soviet Union had endured but North Korea had imploded and created a staggering economic, political, and human burden for the South? If ten years later, the former North Korea was a land of double-digit unemployment, civil unrest, and popular hostility toward the South, any West German leader faced with the prospect of unification might have been much more cautious than Kohl, and the German electorate more jaundiced, about the putative benefits of unification.

The situation would also have been different if Brezhnev had died earlier— say in 1978—and had been replaced, somewhat more implausibly, by a leader with an agenda similar to Gorbachev's. The Soviet Union would have bargained from a much stronger position; neither Afghanistan nor Star Wars would have clouded the agenda, and the Carter administration might have been responsive to a proposal that allowed Eastern European countries to choose their own political and economic systems without interference from Moscow provided they remained part of the Warsaw Pact. These hypothetical examples all suggest that the goals leaders seek, the strategies they choose, the response of important third parties, and their success or failure, are dependent on the broader political context. The variety of responses and possible outcomes to the structural dilemma the Soviet Union faced indicate that the final stage of the Cold War was important in its own right, and not merely the unfolding of events that would have taken place sooner or later with roughly the same results. It is not only appropriate but essential to inquire why and how the events of 1985–1991 led to the outcomes they did.

Four Theories in Search of the Cold War

The controversy surrounding the end of the Cold War is a continuation of a debate that began fifty years ago. Four generic explanations—material powers and capabilities, ideas, domestic structure and politics, and leaders—compete to explain the end of the Cold War as they did its origins.

Material Capabilities

Many realists conceive of the Cold War as a power struggle and the almost inevitable consequence of the power vacuum created in Central Europe by the collapse of Germany at the end of the Second World War. Some realists contend that the conflict assumed an added dimension because of the bipolar structure of the postwar world that transformed a regional conflict into a global one. Realists who embrace this latter conception argue that the Cold War ended when one of the poles (the Soviet Union) recognized that it could no longer compete. For them, Gorbachev's foreign policy was an attempt to extricate the Soviet Union from its conflict with the West on the best possible terms. The root cause of the Cold War and its demise was the rise and fall of the Soviet Union as a global power.[1]

Ideas

Other scholars conceive of the Cold War as primarily an ideological struggle. The Soviet Union and the United States represented incompatible social systems, and the clash between them was the continuation of a struggle between Leninist-style socialism and Western capitalism that began with the Bolshevik revolution in 1918. The ideology of both superpowers evolved over time. Indeed, according to one view of Soviet history, the USSR under Stalin more or less abandoned the ideal of world revolution altogether. But, different conceptions of society were still at the heart of the conflict, making it especially intense and enduring. No accommodation was possible until one of the sides renounced its ideology and began to adopt the political and economic values of its former adversary. From this perspective, learning by Soviet leaders was the underlying cause of the Cold War's end.[2]

Domestic Politics

Like quarks, this explanation comes in several flavors. Its core assertion is that Truman or Stalin—or both leaders—provoked the Cold War to solidify their domestic authority.[3] Some variants also stress the role played by domestic politics once the Cold War was underway. The "military-industrial complexes" of the superpowers are sometimes said to have profited from the conflict and kept it alive for parochial economic and political reasons.[4] Contenders for power (e.g., Khrushchev and Reagan), and allied leaders (e.g., Kim Il-sung, Ulbricht, and Chiang Kai-chek) are also seen as provoking confrontations to advance their local interests.[5] The Cold War ended, in this view, when Gorbachev shifted the basis of his domestic authority and needed to shift resources away from defense to reward a different set of constituencies. Some scholars contend that changing domestic coalitions in *both* superpowers were the root causes of the Cold War and its demise.[6]

Leaders

Some scholars acknowledge the foreign and domestic political constraints operating on leaders, but do not consider them determining. Leaders' choices also reflected their goals and subjective, and sometimes idiosyncratic, understanding of the environments in which they operated. Individual level explanations tend toward political psychology and the constructivist paradigm: the Cold War was—and is—what leaders and scholars made and make of it. More than a few Russian and American scholars attribute the Cold War to Stalin's expansionist goals and paranoia, which they contend he made self-fulfilling.[7] Others suggest that Gorbachev was equally successful in making his cooperative vision a reality.[8] If leaders' goals and understandings can influence and possibly transform international relations, the Cold War can be described as the emergence and ascendancy of different understandings of East-West relations.

Five Turning Points

At the outset of our project we convened a meeting of our authors to discuss and, if possible, reach consensus about turning points that led to the end of the Cold War. Most of the policymakers who attended our several conferences concurred with our choices. We define a turning point in terms of two properties. First, it must be a change of significant magnitude, not an incremental adjustment but a substantial departure from previous practice. Second, it must be a change that would be difficult to undo. Reversal, if possible, would require large expenditure of material and political resources and destroy or demand the reordering of previously established rationales, material assets, institutions, or relationships.

Both criteria, but especially the first, entail subjective judgments, and these judgments, of necessity, will be based on the underlying set of assumptions that scholars and policymakers bring to the question. Events and decisions are often ambiguous enough to allow diverse interpretations of their meaning or the motives of the actors involved. The Sino-Soviet split, a major turning point in the foreign relations of both countries, was not taken seriously at first by many American policymakers and analysts. Ronald Reagan maintained for many years that it was a calculated ploy on the part of Moscow and Peking to lure the United States into complaisance. Only in hindsight was it clear to all that the Sino-Soviet split was a set of turning points that marked the end of one pattern and the beginning of another. Gorbachev's foreign and domestic initiatives met a similarly divergent response. Public opinion in the West welcomed them, but many Soviet "experts" and policymakers were more cautious. When he assumed office in 1989, George Bush was still unconvinced of Gorbachev's sincerity.

We need to distinguish between contemporary judgments, and those of history. Sometimes they coincide; almost everyone agreed that the Soviet withdrawal from Eastern Europe marked a radical and all but irrevocable shift in foreign policy. On other occasions, their meaning is contested, or may be missed altogether. For our purposes both are relevant. The historical judgments we make are the basis for assigning turning point status to events and decisions. Contemporary judgments must also be taken into account to assess the consequences of these turning points for the subsequent course of resolution of the Cold War.

With these caveats in mind, our authors, after lengthy discussion, agreed on five turning points as critical to the end of the Cold War. We treat turning points as markers of the key changes we associate with the end of the Cold War, and as case studies in which to consider the plausibility of different explanatory narratives. Authors of turning point chapters begin by making the case for why the changes they are analyzing should be regarded as turning points. They go on to consider the plausibility of explaining this change in terms of the four generic explanations for the end of the Cold War. The five turning point chapters provide a rich terrain in which to evaluate both how and why this conflict ended.

The Rise of Gorbachev

Archie Brown writes about the first of our turning points: the appointment of Mikhail Gorbachev as General Secretary of the CPSU in March 1985. It brought to office a reform-minded leader who was open to new and revolutionary ideas. Given the hierarchical nature of the Soviet political system, Brown contends that the appointment of an unusually open-minded politician to the post of General Secretary was essential for any sustained program of reforms. The concentration of power in the office of the General Secretary allowed Gorbachev, once appointed, to make subsequent changes. One of these changes took place at the Nineteenth Party Conference in 1988, where the Communist

Party endorsed, against the better judgement of many of its officials, the pluralization of the political system through its decision to hold contested elections for a new legislature *and* the rights of allied states to decide for themselves the nature of their political and economic system. The freely contested elections of 1989 radicalized the society, brought new actors on to the political stage and gave the top-down, elite-driven process of change a mass-based element. They also were a catalyst for national separatist movements that would soon prove hard to contain.

Withdrawal from Regional Conflicts

Richard Herrmann's chapter addresses the second of our turning points: the Soviet withdrawal from Afghanistan. It was a retreat from a major military commitment and involved a major material redeployment and, more importantly, a change in the political line that would have been difficult to reverse without significant foreign and domestic costs. Herrmann also examines other regional conflicts—Angola and Nicaragua—that helped to derail detente in the 1970s and from which the superpowers withdrew in the late 1980s and early 1990s. In all these conflicts, Moscow and Washington backed away from commitments to their respective clients and the competitive use of force and moved toward commitments to resolving conflicts through the ballot box. The Gulf War, like the 1973 war in the Middle East, might have revived the Cold War. American policymakers regarded it as a major test of the value of the changes in the superpower relationship, and were satisfied with the Soviet role and outcome. Moscow, like Washington, was concerned with containing threats emanating from indigenous regional sources.

Arms Control

Matthew Evangelista writes about the turning point represented by arms control. He begins with the unilateral nuclear test moratorium and the offer to allow on-site monitoring announced by Mikhail Gorbachev in July 1986. This initiative constituted a precedent; the Soviet Union abandoned its longstanding opposition to on-site verification. Evangelista then examines the Intermediate-Range Nuclear Forces Treaty (INF), agreed to in December 1987. It too broke with precedent because it involved a disproportionate reduction in Soviet missiles and the Soviet acceptance, more-or-less, of the U.S. "zero option" position. It was followed by Soviet unilateral conventional force reductions and withdrawal from Eastern Europe announced in Gorbachev's December 1988 speech to the United Nations General Assembly. Evangelista argues that in one sense these developments marked the end of the Cold War in Europe because they removed the threat of a "standing-start" Soviet invasion of the West or major intervention in "fraternal" socialist allies. Evangelista concludes his chapter with an analysis of the evolution of the Soviet position during the Strategic Arms Reduction Talks (START). Here too there were breakthroughs—the Soviet decision in 1987 to acknowledge the Krasnoiarsk radar as a violation of the ABM Treaty and the Soviet decision to accept deep reductions under a START treaty in the absence of a U.S. commitment to the ABM treaty—that made possible the START agreement in 1991.

The Liberation of Eastern Europe

Jacques Lévesque analyzes what many regard as the most important turning point: the emancipation of Eastern Europe in 1989. Eastern Europe had always been the area of the utmost rigidity in Soviet foreign policy, with Moscow using direct armed force twice during the Cold War to preserve the tenure of a communist party there. The essential geopolitical role of Eastern Europe as a defensive *glacis* between the Soviet Union and Germany and Western Europe was no less important. The repudiation of the Brezhnev Doctrine was seen in Washington and other Western capitals as the litmus test of the credibility of Gorbachev's new foreign policy and a decision that once taken and implemented could not be reversed.

The Reunification of Germany

James Davis and William Wohlforth examine our final turning point: the reunification of Germany. The agreements achieved in arms control and regional conflicts, while important, were deeper versions of familiar detente-like easing of tensions. Hard-liners on both sides of the Cold War maintained that the fundamental character of the contest had not changed and that the emerging accommodation was still reversible. Davis and Wohlforth note that even as communist regimes in Eastern Europe began to tumble, Gorbachev still maintained his hopes for reform socialism and a new pan-European security system. However, once the terms of German unification were settled in the spring and summer of 1990, actors everywhere recognized that the Cold War would end. The outcome, moreover, sparked the first real, open, and concerted challenge to Gorbachev's leadership in Moscow, and reflected the unfolding American strategy for security in a post–Cold War Europe. Davis and Wohlforth observe that from a material perspective German reunification reflected, caused, and codified massive change in the distribution of capabilities; Germany's power increased significantly, while the Soviet Union's declined.

The Relative Importance of Each Turning Point

Some readers may object to our turning points because they appear to privilege the Soviet Union as the initiator and primary agent in the process that brought the Cold War to an end. Beth Fischer contends that Reagan's commitment to accommodation intensified in early 1984, before Gorbachev came to power, as a consequence of the Soviet Union's overreaction to the West's ABLE ARCHER nuclear exercise and the president's briefing on the country's strategic nuclear options, that is, its Single Integrated Operational Plan (SIOP). These events "primed" Reagan to initiate efforts to reestablish better communications with Moscow. Former Ambassador to the Soviet Union Jack F. Matlock, Jr. insists that he drafted the memorandum in the spring of 1985 that Reagan sent to Gorbachev that set their rapprochement in motion.[9]

None of our authors are persuaded by Matlock's claim, nor by the assertions of American triumphalists that Reagan's arms buildup and the Strategic Defense Initiative brought the Soviet Union to its knees and therefore qualify as key turning points. Our choice of turning points in no way precludes an examination of Reagan's important role in ending the Cold War. For the Cold War to end, both leaders had to desire this outcome, and it unfolded as the result of a process of interactions. Each of the turning points our contributors examine required some action by one or both leaders, as well as numerous third parties. By focusing our analysis on these turning points, we get a good series of snapshots that allows us to assess the roles of Reagan and Gorbachev, and how their pronouncements and behavior influenced the decisions that led to each of these outcomes.

We acknowledge that all turning points may not be of equal importance. We can imagine an end to the Cold War without Gorbachev or new arms control agreements. Some other Soviet leader at some future time might have sought and achieved accommodation. Arms control might have followed rather than preceded a collapse of Soviet influence in Eastern Europe, or have proven unnecessary if both sides in the aftermath of dramatic political change had begun unilaterally to remove their theater weapons systems and reduce their strategic arsenals. It is difficult to envisage an end to the Cold War without the unification of Germany, but if events in the Soviet Union and Eastern Europe had unfolded differently, East Germany, under noncommunist leadership, might have remained in existence for some time. It is harder to imagine an East-West accommodation without a Soviet withdrawal from Afghanistan, a general easing of support for anti-Western Third World client states and, perhaps most important, Soviet willingness to let the countries of Eastern Europe work out their own political destinies.

Our contributors reflect on the importance of their respective turning points and offer different judgments about them. Matt Evangelista makes the most modest claims about his turning point. He offers the counterfactual that a treaty on intermediate range nuclear forces (INF) was possible in the late 1970s if only Brezhnev had demonstrated a little more imagination and flexibility. But such a treaty would not have constituted a turning point in the end of the Cold War because it would not have represented a dramatic Soviet shift about the meaning and value of nuclear weapons and their delivery systems. Davis and Wohlforth make the most far-reaching claim for their turning point. They contend that the unification of Germany was the most important development between 1985 and 1991, and constituted the end point of the Cold War. And unlike some of the other turning points, it was not an artifact of hindsight or theoretical interpretation, but was regarded as momentous at the time by everyone involved as well as by the media and scholarly community.

Richard Herrmann considers Soviet withdrawal from Afghanistan, Angola, and Nicaragua to have been a necessary step for ending the Cold War. In their absence, progress toward ending the Cold War in other domains would have been far more difficult. Herrmann, nevertheless, acknowledges that arms control or the liberation of Eastern Europe might have come first, and could have been the catalysts for Soviet retrenchment in the Third World. He observes that Gorbachev introduced domestic political reforms before he achieved any breakthroughs in the Soviet relationship with the West, that these reforms paved the way for withdrawal from Afghanistan, which in turn facilitated reform. Jacques Lévesque makes a stronger claim for the emancipation of Eastern Europe. He considers it *the* turning point in the sequence of events leading up to the end of the Cold War. Soviet acceptance of political change in the region was not only a retreat from previous efforts to maintain control at all costs, but strong evidence for doubting Thomases in the West that Gorbachev and his circle were seeking new sources of legitimacy and new foundations for Soviet power.

The Cold War began as a struggle for influence in central Europe that quickly led to the division of Germany and the imposition of Soviet-style governments throughout much of Eastern Europe. Conflict became less acute in the late 1960s and 1970s after the United States and its Western allies reluctantly accepted, de facto and then de jure, division of Germany and the territorial arrangements that the Soviet Union had imposed after 1945. The Cold War ended when Eastern European states became free to choose their governments without Soviet interference and Germany was reunified. It is reasonable to privilege these two turning points, but with the recognition that the other turning points were instrumental in bringing them about. To be sure, events could have unfolded differently; arms control or withdrawal from Afghanistan could have come after a Soviet retreat from Eastern Europe and even the unification of Germany. In this case they would not have been turning points, but consequences of the end of the Cold War, as was the withdrawal of Soviet military garrisons from Germany and Eastern Europe.

Building Bridges Across Theoretical Divides

Our authors attempt to see how far variants of each of the four theoretical explanations for the end of the Cold War we have described can account for their respective turning points. They do not conceive of this exercise as a contest, but start from the premise that major turning points in international conflicts are almost always the product of multiple causes. The interesting question, therefore, is, What is the particular configuration of causes that lead to each of these outcomes? It may be that certain explanations are found in tandem and reinforce each other. Synergy may be created by more random combinations as well. By contrast, some combinations of causes may be cross-cutting and tend to cancel each other out. In this circumstance a turning point may require additional, idiosyncratic causes like accidents and confluences. Five turning points in the end stage of one international conflict are neither a sufficient nor representative enough sample to support any theoretical claims about the interaction among our generic causes. But it is a useful starting point for such an analysis, and productive of some propositions about the relationships among causes. These relationships in turn may point to ways of building meta-theory that bridges across discreet causes and levels of analysis. The case studies also allow us to make some judgments about the relative importance of agents versus structures and the role of contingency in ending the Cold War.

The search for a compound explanation for the end of the Cold War, and by extension for other conflicts, stands in sharp contrast to the more usual search for parsimonious explanations. We need to remember that parsimony is not an abstract or arbitrary criterion, but is determined by the nature of the case. Some phenomena may be explained by single causes, but others (e.g., the orbit of the earth, the spread of infections) have multiple causes that must be taken into account to explain a meaningful percentage of the variance. The end of the Cold War appears to be a case in point. Some realist accounts aside, none of the proponents of our four generic explanations claim that their preferred explanation is anything more than a starting point for analyzing the end of the Cold War. They acknowledge, sometimes only tacitly, the need to rely on one or more of the other explanations.

How Material Accounts Bridge to Other Theories

Some realist accounts assert that changes in the distribution of power lead ineluctably to changes in behavior. In the strongest formulation, this relationship is held to be independent of historical epoch, character of the political units involved, or the quality of their leadership. Leaders are assumed to understand the balance of power and its trends, and to respond appropriately. Like electrons, they are interchangeable conveyers of forces that exercise no independent influence on events. Less dogmatic realists offer weaker formulations that give primacy to structure but are not deterministic. Hans Morgenthau, the father of modern realism, espoused such a theory. He maintained that nuclear bipolarity could promote peace or encourage war; the outcome would depend on the moral qualities of leaders.[10] More recently, both Kenneth Oye and William Wohlforth have treated leaders' perceptions of the balance of power and its future trends as an important intervening variable.[11] Weak structural explanations build bridges to ideas, domestic structures and politics, and leaders, and, indeed, depend on them to impart subjective meaning to the balance of power and to explain variance under similar structural conditions.

How Ideational Accounts Bridge to Other Theories

All explanations based on ideas bridge to the other explanations.[12] Ideas are prompted by experience and environmental challenges, and in this way are related to structure. Perestroika and glasnost were a response to the economic stagnation of the Soviet Union and the belief that this was due to the restraining hand of unimaginative, unresponsive party and governmental cadres. The equally important conception of common security was developed as an alternative to confrontational policies that were seen as dangerous, expensive, and counterproductive.[13] In a more fundamental sense, the end of the Cold War and the subsequent collapse of the Soviet Union were due to widespread disenchantment with the Leninist model of society.[14] The ideas explanation relies on domestic politics and leaders to translate ideas into policies. Ideas need support in high places, and often among a wider public as well. Ideas depend on what John Kingdon has called "policy entrepreneurs" to bring them to the attention of policymakers who in turn use them to shape and influence the policy agenda.[15] This process has been well-studied in the Soviet context in the domain of security policy and arms control, where scientific elites and *institutchiki* are said to have been an important conduit of ideas to Gorbachev and his immediate advisors, who then seized upon them as solutions to policy or political problems.[16]

How Domestic Politics Accounts Bridge to Other Theories

The domestic politics explanation recognizes the importance of ideas but reverses the arrow of causation. Ideas sell policies, not motivate them. Politics is about power, but advocacy of appealing ideas helps office seekers gain power. Ideas are equally essential to coalitions. They form around interests, and in all but the most corrupt political systems, interests need to be justified to leaders, legislators, and other power brokers in terms of broader, shared interests or values. Ideas also help provide general direction and incentive to bureaucracies charged with policy implementation.

How Leadership Accounts Bridge to Other Theories

Through ideas, domestic politics and leadership bridge to structural explanations. Only the "great 'man' in history" approach denies the importance of structure. None of the scholars who emphasize the importance of leaders in creating or ending the Cold War endorse this formulation. Even in the case of Stalin, whose idiosyncratic influence is widely recognized to have been extraordinary, the debate is between those who maintain that the Soviet Union could have developed less violently and more democratically under a different leader, and their critics who contend that Stalin was the inevitable product of the terror-based political system created by Lenin. Political structure is the starting point for both sides.[17]

Our four explanations do not constitute distinct alternatives as much as they do different starting points for a complex and multilayered explanation. The controversy about explanations is really a dispute about the relevant point of entry into the problem. For scholars who believe that their preferred explanation accounts for much more of the variance than competitors, this is a significant decision. For those who see their explanation as essential but not necessarily privileged, the choice is one of intellectual appeal and convenience.

Counterfactual Thought Experiments

Historians and social scientists seek to understand the driving forces behind events; they usually do so after the fact, when the outcome is known. This process of backward reasoning and the "certainty of hindsight bias" tends to privilege theories that rely on only a few key variables.[18] Baruch Fischoff has demonstrated that "outcome knowledge" affects our understanding of the past by making it difficult for us to recall that we were once unsure about what was going to happen. Events deemed improbable are often considered "overdetermined" and all but inevitable after they have occurred.[19] By tracing the path that appears to have lead to a known outcome, we diminish our sensitivity to alternative paths and outcomes. We may fail to recognize the uncertainty under which actors operated and the possibility that they could have made different choices that might have led to different outcomes.

Political actors are particularly susceptible to the hindsight bias. The transcripts of the several conferences that the Mershon Center and allied institutions sponsored in conjunction with this book indicate that many policymakers, independent of their country or ideology, now see the end of the Cold War, the unification of Germany, and the collapse of the Soviet Union as more or less inevitable. But these same policymakers admit that they were surprised and even incredulous as these events unfolded. They further insist that the outcome of any decision or negotiation in which they personally participated was highly contingent. In conference discussions and later, over drinks or dinner, they told amusing stories of how clever tactics, the nature of the personal relationship between them and their opposites, or just sheer coincidence, often played a decisive role in shaping the outcome of negotiations.[20]

Scholarship is the unwitting handmaiden of the hindsight bias. Interpretations provoke counterinterpretations. Historians have proposed a wide range of intellectual, social, economic, and political causes for the fall of the Roman Empire, the French Revolution, and the origins of World War I.[21] Remove one or several of these putative causes and a half-dozen others still remain. Historical debate encourages the belief that major events and developments are massively "overdetermined."[22] One way to counter this hindsight certainty is to engage systematically and seriously in counterfactual thought experiments. George Breslauer and Ned Lebow employ this strategy to probe the importance of leaders in ending the Cold War. They invoke minimal rewrite counterfactuals to change the leadership in the United States (e.g., Hinkley's bullet kills Reagan) and the Soviet Union (Gorbachev is not elected General Secretary) to analyze the extent to which circumstances would—or would not—have compelled the same general foreign policies between 1985 and 1991.

Path Dependency

The years 1985–1991 were the endgame of the Cold War. In chess, an endgame follows opening and middle games, but not every game reaches this stage of play. The structure, strategy, and outcome of endgames are determined by the number of pieces on the board, their location, and who has tempo. Endgames are highly path dependent. The Cold War might have been also. Path dependency is a concept developed in the physical sciences that has been most widely used in economics among the social sciences. Its strongest formulation, most appropriate to evolutionary biology, asserts that what happens at $T + 3$ is entirely dependent on what happened at $T + 2$, $T + 1$, and T. If true, this would make meaningful cross-case comparison, the most common form of quantitative research in the social sciences, much more difficult. Comparisons could only be made among cases whose histories were similar in relevant dimensions. We use a more relaxed conception of path dependency here, which assumes only that the history of a conflict has a significant impact, and that the evolution and outcome of the conflict cannot be understood without taking that history into account.[23]

Path Dependency and Material Accounts

Strong structural explanations deny path dependency. When the power balance changes, leaders are expected to respond accordingly. Prior changes in the balance and past responses to them are irrelevant. Some realists acknowledge that actors do not always perceive power accurately, and weak structural explanations, as we have observed, emphasize the policy importance of perceptions. But they have made no attempt to explain perception with reference to the history of specific conflicts.

Path Dependency and Ideational Accounts

The ideas literature has long debated the relationship between ideas and the context in which they arise.[24] Structural explanations for ideas—Marxism is typical—consider them epiphenomena that have no independent existence apart from the structure that gives rise to them. Scholars who argue for the independent role of ideas in international relations acknowledge that they are to some extent context dependent. The environment provides stimuli to which people react, and also a social, political, and intellectual setting that helps shape how they react. But there is ample room for individual, group, and cultural variation.[25] Social concepts are generally nonfalsifiable, and, unlike concepts about the physical environment, can make themselves at least in part self-fulfilling. Leaders' beliefs that nuclear war should be avoided at almost any cost, and the recognition in the 1960s by each superpower that their adversary felt the same way, fundamentally transformed the character of the Cold War. So did Gorbachev's adoption of common security in leading to the end of the Cold War. To the extent that ideas and structures interact, any ideas-based explanation for the Cold War must to some extent be path dependent.

Path Dependency and Domestic Politics and Leadership Accounts

Domestic leadership explanations have not addressed the question of path dependency. They posit changes in leaders and coalitions that prompt changes in foreign policy, or changes in foreign policy by leaders anxious to maintain the support of coalitions and constituencies. But what produces coalitions and shifts in their membership or preferences? If these phenomena are random, we need not consider their origins, only their consequences. But to the extent that they are shaped by memories of prior leaders or coalitions, their politics and results, they are path dependent. The selection of Soviet leaders is a case in point. Khrushchev, a promoter of radical reform, was succeeded by Brezhnev, a defender of the status quo, who was followed after the short-lived leaderships of Andropov and Chernenko by Gorbachev, another radical reformer. This progression was not fortuitous. Brezhnev garnered support for his coup against Khrushchev by warning that the latter's "hare-brained schemes" threatened the privileges of office holders and perhaps the survival of the communist system. Brezhnev's orthodoxy reflected his personal preferences and his political need to maintain the support of the coalition that kept him in power. The latter all but precluded the possibility of major reform even though there was growing recognition among the leadership that the Soviet economy was performing poorly. The *zastoi* (stagnation) of the Brezhnev years and growing recognition within the elite that something had to be done about the economy paved the way for another reformer. By his own admission, Gorbachev's reforms were based on a careful reading of where and why Khrushchev had failed.[26] One of the challenges to domestic politics and leadership explanations is to root them in context to try to discover patterns associated with shifts in coalitions and leaders and the kinds of policies they espoused.

Path Dependency and Drawing Theoretical and Policy Lessons

The Cold War was path dependent in a much broader sense. American efforts to deter the Soviet Union through alliances, military buildups, forward deployments, and threatening rhetoric, represented the "lesson of Munich" and were implemented by leaders who had witnessed the failure of appeasement in the 1930s. Appeasement was a reaction to the horrors of World War I and the revisionist belief that gained wide credence in the 1930s, that Wilhelminian Germany might have been restrained more effectively by a policy of reassurance.[27] From Moscow's perspective, attempts to extend Soviet control as far West as possible were motivated in part by the expectation that World War III would have the same cause as World War II: a crisis of capitalism that would prompt a restored Germany, backed by the Anglo-Americans, to attack the Soviet Union.[28]

Path dependency is the starting point for the two final chapters. Ned Lebow and Janice Gross Stein use it as a benchmark to help distinguish what was idiosyncratic about the end of the Cold War from what it may have shared with other militarized disputes, and to assess the relative importance, causes, and contingency of the five turning points. The overall objective of this chapter is to build theoretical bridges across levels of analysis that are necessary to capture the complex causation of events like those between 1985 and 1991. Lebow and Stein frame this transformation as a nonlinear process.

Richard Herrmann in the final chapter looks at the policy lessons that are being drawn from the end of the Cold War and explores the inferential logics that underpin these lessons. He looks in particular at whether the processes by which lessons are drawn about the end of the Cold War are characterized by many of the shortcomings that plagued learning in previous historical cases. These include the tendency to minimize the role of contingency and path dependency and the inclination to conclude with excessive confidence that causal factors correlate with outcome factors. Herrmann also considers the writing of history as part of the contemporary political scene and acknowledges the possible effects contemporary purposes may have on the process of drawing of lessons from history. He discusses the strengths and limitations of the various strategies for warranting causal claims that are employed across the turning point chapters and concludes by identifying several additional strategies that might be employed to connect causal theories to empirical evidence.

The Evidence Available for this Study

Good social science requires explanation. Theories are incomplete if they do not specify the reasons why the outcomes they predict occur. They remain unsubstantiated even if the predicted outcome occurs because it could be the result of covariation and explained better by a different theory. Case studies are an ideal vehicle to show causation by documenting links between independent and dependent variables. The nature of these links varies as a function of the *explanans*. For structural theories that expect actors to react to the constraints and opportunities of the international or domestic environment, it is necessary to show that policymakers understood these constraints and opportunities and formulated the initiatives in response to them. For idea-based explanations, researchers must establish that policymakers were motivated by goals associated with these ideas, or framed the policy problem and their interests in terms of them. Leader-based explanations must demonstrate the connections between leaders' decisions and their goals, personalities, and subjective understanding of their environment.

The Soviet Union was one of the most secret societies the world has known, and it was not until the era of glasnost that Russian or Western scholars could gather the kind of evidence necessary to conduct meaningful case studies. The recent flow of evidence has encouraged high expectations about resolving some of the mysteries of the Soviet system and its leaders, and much of interest has come to light. But access to key archives is still restricted and uncertain, and pessimists in this field worry that the window of opportunity that we have been exploiting, which has already narrowed, may close in post-Yeltsin Russia.

The United States and European countries have also declassified many relevant documents, but others are likely to remain under lock and key for many years to come. Additional information comes from the many memoirs that key former officials, from Eastern and Western governments, have written describing the events leading up to the end of the Cold War and their role in them. Some of these memoirs include excerpts from hitherto unknown or still classified reports and memoranda.

Process tracing makes heavy requirements on data, and even in data rich situations it is difficult to document the motives and calculations of key actors. Documents are essential for process tracing, but recent studies of Cold War crises indicate that they can be incomplete and even misleading. The Soviet decision to deploy missiles in Cuba in May 1962 was shrouded in secrecy, and very few written records were kept by the handful of officials involved in its planning and initial execution. On the American side, President Kennedy deliberately avoided leaving any paper trail of his agreement to withdraw the Jupiter missiles from Turkey in return for withdrawal of the Soviet missiles from Cuba. In October 1973, Leonid Brezhnev made all the important decisions concerning Soviet Middle East policy in consultation with a small circle of advisors, and few records were kept of their deliberations. Process tracing of the decisions that led to the end of the Cold War must rely on oral as well as written evidence.[29]

With this end in mind, the Mershon Center collaborated with other institutions to generate additional evidence, oral and written, specifically for this book. The Center hosted two conferences on the end of the Cold War, and cosponsored two others, that brought together policymakers and scholars. The first of these conferences, organized by the Watson Institute and held at Brown University in May 1998, featured officials from the Reagan and Gorbachev administrations who played central roles in the 1983–1988 period.

In June 1999, Dr. Oleg I. Skvortsov, Head of the Oral History Project at the General History Institute of the Russian Academy of Sciences, in partnership with Mershon, convened a two-day meeting in Moscow that featured the most prominent former Soviet officials who opposed the foreign policy of Mikhail Gorbachev. Participating in the meeting, for example, were the former Head of the KGB, the former Minister of Defense, and the Former Vice President, all of whom played key roles in the unsuccessful coup attempt against President Mikhail Gorbachev.

In October 1999, Mershon and the Gorbachev Foundation hosted another conference that brought together top policymakers from the Gorbachev and Bush administrations to address important decisions and events leading to the end of the Cold War that transpired between 1988 and 1991. Special attention was devoted to arms control negotiations and regional conflicts in the recognition that arms control agreements and Soviet disengagement from Afghanistan were concrete turning points in the Cold War's end.

A fourth conference, organized and hosted by the Geschwister-Scholl-Institute of the University of Munich, and cosponsored by Mershon, met in Wildbad Kreuth, Bavaria. It focused on the European role in ending the Cold War, and on the events and decisions surrounding the unification of Germany. Participants included scholars and Soviet, American, German, French, and British policymakers.

The Mershon-sponsored conferences were recorded and transcripts were prepared, in Russian and English, for each of them. Copies of the transcripts are available on the Mershon web site [www.mershon.ohio-state.edu/] and from the National Security Archive. Mershon commissioned six interviews with prominent members of the Gorbachev opposition in preparation for our Moscow conference, and these interviews are also available at our web site. Our authors conducted their own interviews with former policymakers in the Soviet Union, the United States, and Western and Eastern Europe. Some of these policymakers attended one or more of our conferences, but for others, this was their first opportunity to go on record about events in which they participated or had inside knowledge. The National Security Archive prepared briefing books of newly released classified documents germane to the questions central to both the May 1998 conference at Brown and the October 1999 conference at Mershon. These documents are available though the National Security Archive.

We found from past experience that large conferences do not generate the kind of dialogue that is most useful for scholars. We accordingly proceeded in a more systematic manner to organize our conferences around particular controversies or gaps in our knowledge. Chapter authors met first to identify and reach a consensus on the key turning points of the end of the Cold War. They then prepared a list of questions about these turning points for which they sought answers for their respective chapters. The Moscow, Columbus, and Wildbad Kreuth conferences were organized around these questions, and the policymakers most likely to be able to answer them were invited to participate. The individual sessions were introduced and chaired by scholars who posed very specific questions to the policymakers. Contributors often followed up the panels with individual or small group discussions with policymakers to elicit more information. When feasible, we encouraged policymakers to bring relevant documents or make them available to scholars subsequent to the conferences.

The evidence now available is far richer and more complete than it was ten years ago, when policymakers and scholars first began to make competing claims about the causes of this transformation. However, new evidence from archives, interviews, and conferences will never produce a definitive "answer" to the question of what brought the Cold War to an end.[30] Nor is it likely that a consensus will form around any variant explanation, or combination of variants. An analogy to 1914 is relevant. The outpouring of documents and memoirs on the origins of World War I fueled rather than resolved controversy. But it also encouraged a more sophisticated debate by discrediting early, simplistic explanations (e.g., the Kaiser planned a war of aggression), and elicited more complex and nuanced explanations that built on evidence and insights from social science. By compelling scholars to specify different pathways to war, the *Kriegschuldfrage* also provided conceptual lenses and analogies that proved useful in understanding the Cold War and other conflicts. In sum, the decades-long debate over the origins of World War I, while still unresolved, was an important catalyst for the development both of international relations theory and foreign policy thinking. President Kennedy's reluctance to carry out an air strike in the Cuban missile crisis derived in large part from his earlier reading of Barbara Tuchman's *The Guns of August* and its portrayal of World War I as a case of runaway, mutual escalation. There is every reason to expect that rigorous study of the end of the Cold War, based on new empirical evidence, better specification, and even reformulation of existing explanations, their evaluation by means of an in-depth case study, and subsequently, by comparative analysis, will generate the same kinds of theoretical and policy insights into the process of accommodation.

Notes

1. Hans Morgenthau, in *Politics Among Nations,* 4th ed. (New York: Alfred Knopf, 1966), distinguishes between the onset of the Cold War in 1947 and bipolarity, which he does not believe was achieved until the mid-1950s at the earliest. Kenneth N. Waltz, *Theory of International Politics* (Reading, MA: Addison-Wesley, 1979), and "The Emerging Structure of International Politics," *International Security* 18 (Fall 1993), pp. 5–43; John J. Mearsheimer, "Back to the Future: Instability in Europe After the Cold War," *International Security* 15 (Summer 1990), pp. 5–56; William C. Wohlforth, "Realism and the End of the Cold War," *International Security* 19 (Winter 1994–95), pp. 91–129; Kenneth A. Oye, "Explaining the End of the Cold War: Morphological and Behavioral Adaptations to the Nuclear Peace?," in Richard Ned Lebow and Thomas Risse-Kappen, *International Relations Theory and the End of the Cold War* (New York: Columbia University Press, 1995), pp. 57–84, describe the Cold War and bipolarity as more or less coterminous. For a review of recent historical literature sympathetic to the realist conception of the Cold War, see Howard Jones and Randall B. Woods, "The Origins of the Cold War in Europe and the Near East: Recent Historiography and the National Security Imperative," *Diplomatic History* 17 (Spring 1993), pp. 251–76, and commentaries in the same issue by Emily S. Rosenberg, Anders Stephanson, and Barton J. Bernstein. For an overview see Michael Cox, "From the Truman Doctrine to the Second Superpower Détente: the Rise and Fall of the Cold War," *Journal of Peace Research* 27 (1) (1990), pp. 25–41.

2. Morgenthau, *Politics Among Nations;* Fred Halliday, *Rethinking International Relations* (Vancouver: University of British Columbia Press, 1994); Michael W. Doyle, "Liberalism and the End of the Cold War," in Lebow and Risse-Kappen, *International Relations Theory and the End of the Cold War,* pp. 85–108. Gaddis, *The Long Peace,* and Thomas Paterson, *On Every Front: The Making and Unmaking of the Cold War* (New York: W. W. Norton & Co., 1992), offer compound explanations of which the clash of visions

is part. For extreme statements of this position, see Adam Ulam, *Expansion and Coexistence: Soviet Foreign Policy, 1917–1973,* 2nd ed. (New York: Praeger, 1974); Francis Fukuyama, *The End of History and the Last Man* (New York: Free Press, 1992) and Douglas J. Macdonald, "Communist Bloc Expansion in the Early Cold War: Challenging Realism, Refuting Revisionism," *International Security* 20 (Winter 1995), pp. 152–88. For a Weberian analysis of the evolution of Marxism and its influence on Soviet foreign policy up through Gorbachev, see Stephen E. Hanson, "Gorbachev: The Last True Leninist Believer," in Daniel Chirot, ed., *The Crisis of Leninism and the Decline of the Left* (Seattle: University of Washington Press, 1991), pp. 74–99. The standard reference for the debate in the West on the role of ideology in Soviet foreign policy is R. N. Carew Hunt, Samuel L. Sharp, and Richard Lowenthal, "Ideology and Power Politics: A Symposium," *Problems of Communism* 7 (May-June 1958). For an overview of the historical debate on the role of ideology in the Cold War, see Stephen White and Alex Pravda, eds., *Ideology and Soviet Politics* (Basingstoke: Macmillan, 1988). For recent takes on ideology, see Martin Malia, *The Soviet Tragedy: A History of Socialism in Russia, 1917–91* (New York: Free Press, 1991); Odd Arne Westad, "Secrets of the Second World: The Russian Archives and the Reinterpretation of Cold War History," *Diplomatic History* 21 (Spring 1997), pp. 259–72; Robert D. English, *Russia and the Idea of the West: Gorbachev, Intellectuals, and the End of the Cold War* (New York: Columbia University Press, 2000).

3. John Lewis Gaddis, "The Tragedy of Cold War History," *Diplomatic History* 17 (Winter 1993), pp. 1–16; Vladislav Zubok and Constantine Pleshakov, *Inside the Kremlin's Cold War: From Stalin to Khrushchev* (Cambridge, MA: Harvard University Press, 1996), chs. 1–3, on Stalin. Frank Kofsky, *Harry S. Truman and the War Scare of 1948: A Successful Campaign to Deceive the Nation* (New York: St. Martin's Press, 1993), is the most extreme statement of this position for Truman.

4. For example, J. Garry Clifford, "Bureaucratic Politics" in *Explaining the History of American Foreign Relations,* eds. Michael J. Hogan and Thomas G. Paterson (New York: Cambridge University Press, 1991), pp. 141–50. Standard works that argue for the economic roots of American foreign policy and the Cold War include Lloyd C. Gardner, *Architects of Illusion: Men and Ideas in American Foreign Policy, 1941–1949* (Chicago: Quadrangle Books, 1970); Gabriel and Joyce Kolko, *The Limits of Power: The World and United States Foreign Policy, 1945–1954* (New York: Harper & Row, 1972); Thomas J. Paterson, *On Every Front: The Making and Unmaking of the Cold War,* rev. ed. (New York: W. W. Norton, 1992); Thomas J. McCormack, *America's Half-Century: United States Foreign Policy in the Cold War,* 2nd ed. (Baltimore: Johns Hopkins University Press, 1995.)

5. Zubok and Pleshakov, *Inside the Kremlin's Cold War.*

6. Thomas Risse-Kappen, "Ideas Do No Float Freely: Transnational Coalitions, Domestic Structures, and the End of the Cold War," in Lebow and Risse-Kappen, *International Relations Theory and the End of the Cold War,* pp. 187–222; Matthew Evangelista, "Transnational Relations, Domestic Structures and Security Policy in the USSR and Russia," in Thomas Risse-Kappen, ed., *Bringing Transnational Relations Back In: Non-State Actors, Domestic Structures and International Institutions* (Cambridge: Cambridge University Press, 1995), pp. 3–36; Robert G. Herman, "Identity, Norms and National Security: The Soviet Foreign Policy Revolution and the End of the Cold War," in Peter J. Katzenstein, ed., *The Culture of National Security: Norms and Identity in World Politics* (New York: Columbia University Press, 1996), pp. 271–316; Jeffrey T. Checkel, *Ideas and International Political Change: Soviet/Russian Behavior and the End of the Cold War* (New Haven, CT: Yale University Press, 1977).

7. Dimitri Volkogonov, *Stalin: Triumph and Tragedy* (New York: Grove, Weidenfeld, 1988), ch. 54; Zubok and Pleshakov, *Inside the Kremlin's Cold War,* pp. 47–53; David Holloway, *Stalin and the Bomb* (New Haven, CT: Yale University Press, 1994), pp. 253–72. On the

military lessons of World War II, see Raymond L. Garthoff, *The Soviet Image of Future War* (Washington, D.C.: Public Affairs Press, 1959).

8. Raymond L. Garthoff, *The Great Transition: American-Soviet Relations and the End of the Cold War* (Washington, D.C.: Brookings, 1994); Richard Ned Lebow and Janice Gross Stein, *We All Lost the Cold War* (Princeton, NJ: Princeton University Press, 1994), postscript.

9. The strongest statements for the view that Ronald Reagan deserves credit as the initiator of the overtures of conciliation that led to the end of the Cold War are found in Jack F. Matlock, Jr., *Autopsy on an Empire: The American Ambassador's Account of the Collapse of the Soviet Union* (New York: Random House, 1995), and Beth A. Fischer, *The Reagan Reversal: Foreign Policy and the End of the Cold War* (Columbia: University of Missouri Press, 1997).

10. Morgenthau, *Politics Among Nations,* pp. 347–49.

11. Kenneth A. Oye, "Explaining the End of the Cold War: Morphological and Behavioral Adaptations to the Nuclear Peace," in Lebow and Risse-Kappen, *International Relations and the End of the Cold War,* pp. 57–84; William C. Wohlforth, "Realism and the End of the Cold War," *International Security* 19 (Winter 1994–95), pp. 91–129.

12. The need to link ideas to other explanations is specifically acknowledged by Douglas W. Blum, "The Soviet Foreign Policy Belief System: Beliefs, Politics and Foreign Policy Outcomes," *International Studies Quarterly* 37 (December 1993), pp. 373–94, and Jacques Lévesque, *The Enigma of 1989: The USSR and the Liberation of Eastern Europe,* trans. Keith Martin (Berkeley: University of California Press, 1997).

13. Eduard Shevardnadze, *The Future Belongs to Freedom* (New York: Free Press, 1991); Anatoly S. Chernyaev, *My Six Years with Gorbachev,* trans. and ed. by Robert English and Elizabeth Tucker (University Park: Pennsylvania State University Press, 2000); Raymond L. Garthoff, *The Great Transition: American Soviet Relations and the End of the Cold War* (Washington, D.C.: Brookings, 1994); Checkel, *Ideas and International Political Change;* Robert Herman, "Ideas, Identity and the Redefinition of Interests: The Political and Intellectual Origins of the Soviet Foreign Policy Revolution," Ph.D. diss., Cornell University, 1996; Coit D. Blacker, "Learning in the Nuclear Age: Soviet Strategic Arms Control Policy, 1969–1989," in George Breslauer and Philip Tetlock, eds., *Learning in U.S. and Soviet Foreign Policy* (Boulder, CO: Westview, 1991); Sarah Mendelsohn, *Changing Course: Ideas, Politics and the Soviet Withdrawal from Afghanistan* (Princeton, NJ: Princeton University Press, 1998); English, *Russia and the Idea of the West.*

14. Fukuyama, *The End of History and the Last Man;* Fred Halliday, "International Society as Homogeneity: Burke, Marx, Fukuyama," *Millennium: Journal of International Studies* 21 (3) (1992), pp. 435–61; Michael Doyle, "Liberalism and the End of the Cold War," and Rey Koslowski and Friedrich V. Kratochwil, "Understanding Change in International Politics: The Soviet Union's Demise and the International System," in Lebow and Risse-Kappen, *International Relations Theory and the End of the Cold War,* pp. 85–108 and 109–26; John Mueller, "Realism and the End of the Cold War," in Mueller, *Quiet Cataclysm: Reflections on the Recent Transformation in World Politics* (New York: HarperCollins, 1995), pp. 27–39; Charles W. Kegley, Jr., "The Neo-Idealist Moment in International Studies? Realist Myths and the New International Realities," *International Studies Quarterly* 27 (June 1993), pp. 131–47; Alexander Wendt, "Collective Identity Formation and the International State," *American Political Science Review* 88 (June 1994), pp. 1–13.

15. Jack Walker, "The Diffusion of Knowledge, Policy Communities and Agenda Setting," in John Tropman, Robert Lind, and Milan Dluhy, eds., *New Strategic Perspectives on Social Policy* (New York: Pergamon, 1981), pp. 89–91; John W. Kingdon, *Agendas, Alternatives, and Public Policies* (New York: Harper-Collins, 1984). See also, Giandomenico Majone, *Evidence, Argument and Persuasion in the Policy Process* (New Haven, CT: Yale University Press, 1989).

16. Thomas Risse-Kappen, "Ideas Do Not Float Freely: Transnational Coalitions, Domestic Structures, and the End of the Cold War," in Lebow and Risse-Kappen, *International Relations Theory and the End of the Cold War*, pp. 187–222; Checkel, *Ideas and International Political Change;* Matthew A. Evangelista, "Sources of Moderation in Soviet Security Policy," in Philip E. Tetlock, et al., *Behavior, Society and Nuclear War* (New York: Oxford University Press, 1991), vol. 2, pp. 254–354, and "The Paradox of State Strength: Transnational Relations, Domestic Structures, and Security Policy in Russia and the Soviet Union," *International Organization* 49 (Winter 1995), pp. 1–38; Lévesque, *The Enigma of 1989*, pp. 38–41, and passim.

17. For recent works on Stalin that address this question, see Dimitri Volkogonov, *Stalin: Triumph and Tragedy* (New York: Grove, Weidenfeld, 1988); Robert C. Tucker, *Stalin in Power: The Revolution from Above, 1938–1941* (New York: Norton, 1990); Zubok and Pleshakov, *Inside the Kremlin's Cold War*, and Robert C. Tucker, "Sovietology and Russian History," *Post-Soviet Affairs* 8 (July-September 1992), pp. 175–96.

18. This point is also made by Philip E. Tetlock and Aaron Belkin, "Counterfactual Thought Experiments in World Politics: Logical, Methodological, and Psychological Perspectives," in Tetlock and Belkin, *Counterfactual Thought Experiments in World Politics* (Princeton, NJ: Princeton University Press, 1996), pp. 15–16.

19. Baruch Fischoff, "Hindsight is not Equal to Foresight: The Effect of Outcome Knowledge on Judgment under Uncertainty," *Journal of Experimental Psychology: Human Perception and Performance*, 1 (2) (1975), pp. 288–99; S. A. Hawkins and R. Hastie, "Hindsight: Biased Judgments of Past Events after the Outcomes are Known," *Psychological Bulletin* 107 (3) (1990), pp. 311–27. The tendency was earlier referred to as "retrospective determinism" in comparative-historical studies by Reinhard Bendix, *Nation-Building and Citizenship* (New York: Wiley, 1964).

20. Richard K. Herrmann and Richard Ned Lebow, "Policymakers and the Cold War's End: Micro and Macro Assessments of Contingency," to appear in the *Cold War History Bulletin.*

21. Alexander Demandt, *Der Fall Roms: die Auflosung des romischen Reiches im Urteil der Nachwelt* (Munich: Beck, 1984), p. 695, found 210 causes for the fall of Rome in the historical literature since 1600.

22. Paul W. Schroeder, "World War I as Galloping Gertie: A Reply to Joachim Remak," *Journal of Modern History* 44 (September 1972), pp. 319–45, reasons: "The fact that so many plausible explanations for the outbreak of war have been advanced over the years indicates on the one hand that it was massively overdetermined."

23. Stephen Jay Gould, *Wonderful Life: The Burgess Shale and the Nature of History* (New York: Norton, 1989). In economics, see Brian Arthur, "Competing Technologies, Increasing Returns, and Lock-In by Historical Events," *Economic Journal* 106 (March 1989), pp. 116–31, and *Increasing Returns and Path Dependence in the Economy* (Ann Arbor: University of Michigan Press, 1994); Robin Cowan and Philip Gunby, "Sprayed to Death: Path Dependence, Lock-In and Pest Control Strategies," *Economic Journal* 106 (May 1996), pp. 521–42; Throne Eggertsson, "The Economics of Institutions: Avoiding the Open-Field Syndrome and the Perils of Path Dependence," *Acta Sociologica* 36 (3) (1993), pp. 223–37; Eban Goodstein, "The Economic Roots of Environmental Decline: Property Rights or Path Dependence?," *Journal of Economic Issues* 29 (December 1995), pp. 1029–43.

24. See Max Weber, "The Social Psychology of World Religions, " in Hans Gerth and C. Wright Mills, eds., *Max Weber: Essays in Sociology* (New York: Oxford University Press, 1958); Quentin Skinner, "Meaning and Understanding in the History of Ideas," *History and Theory* 8 (1969), pp. 3–53, "Conventions and the Understanding of Speech Acts," *Philosophical Quarterly* 20 (1970), pp. 118–38, and "Some Problems in the Analysis of Political Thought and Action," *Political Theory* 2 (1974), pp. 227–303; Richard Rorty, *Contingency, Irony, Solidarity* (Cambridge: Cambridge University Press, 1989).

25. See, Friedrich V. Kratochwil, *Rules, Norms, and Decisions: On the Conditions of Practical and Legal Reasoning in International Relations and Domestic Affairs* (Cambridge: Cambridge University Press, 1989); Nicholas Onuf, *World of Our Making* (Columbia: University of South Carolina Press, 1989); Alexander Wendt, "Anarchy is What States Make of It: Social Construction of Power Politics," *International Organization* 46 (Summer 1992), pp. 391–425; David Dessler, "What's At Stake in the Agent-Structure Debate?," *International Organization* 43 (Summer 1989), pp. 441–73. For a much narrower take on the role of ideas, see Judith Goldstein, *Ideas, Interests and American Trade Policy* (Ithaca, NY: Cornell University Press, 1993), and Judith Goldstein and Robert O. Keohane, eds., *Ideas and Foreign Policy: Beliefs, Institutions and Political Change* (Ithaca, NY: Cornell University Press, 1993).

26. Author interviews with Georgyi Shakhnazarov, Vadim Zagladin, Mikhail Gorbachev, Moscow, May 1989.

27. On the Munich lesson, see Ernest R. May, " *Lessons" of the Past: The Use and Misuse of History in American Foreign Policy* (New York: Oxford University Press, 1973); Richard Ned Lebow, "Generational Learning and Conflict Management," *International Journal* 40 (Autumn 1985), pp. 555–85; Yuen Foong Khong, *Analogies at War: Korea, Munich, Dien Bien Phu, and the Vietnam Decisions of 1965* (Princeton, NJ: Princeton University Press, 1992).

28. Volkogonov, *Stalin,* ch. 54; Zubok and Pleshakov, *Inside the Kremlin's Cold War,* pp. 47–53; Holloway, *Stalin and the Bomb,* pp. 253–72; On the military lessons of World War II, see Raymond L. Garthoff, *The Soviet Image of Future War* (Washington, D.C.: Public Affairs Press, 1959).

29. Lebow and Stein, *We All Lost the Cold War,* pp. 9–14, for a fuller discussion of this problem.

30. This point is also made by William Wohlforth, "New Evidence on Moscow's Cold War: Ambiguity in Search of Theory," *Diplomatic History* 21 (Spring 1997), pp. 229–42.

Part I

Turning Points and Causes

Chapter 2

Gorbachev and the End of the Cold War

Archie Brown

Kjell Goldmann, in *A New Handbook of Political Science,* notes that from the mid-1950s to the mid-1980s, scholarship in international relations provided an "accumulation of explanations of the Cold War's persistence. . . . The sum was a powerful theory of international non-change."[1] After surveying a wide variety of international relations theory and outlining with the benefit of hindsight what actually happened during and after the end of the Cold War, John Lewis Gaddis is still more scathing: "What is immediately obvious . . . is that very few of our theoretical approaches to the study of international relations came anywhere close to forecasting *any* of these developments. One might as well have relied upon star-gazers, readers of entrails, and other 'pre-scientific' methods for all the good our 'scientific' methods did. . . ."[2]

Many scholars have tried to do in retrospect what they failed to foresee as a prospect, and this chapter is not the place to assess that already extensive literature. My intention is to discuss the immediate causes of the end of the Cold War and to argue that the selection of Mikhail Gorbachev as General Secretary of the Soviet Communist Party in March 1985 was of decisive importance. The idea that, if Gorbachev had not been chosen as party leader, some other member of the Politburo would have pursued essentially the same policies does not stand up to serious scrutiny. Clearly, Gorbachev alone was not responsible for the dramatic changes in Soviet policy that occurred over the next six and a half years. The argument about leadership is intimately linked to the importance both of institutions and ideas within the Soviet system—to the institutional power of the General Secretary and the fact that, to a greater extent than any other political actor, Gorbachev could determine key appointments and legitimize formerly heterodox ideas. While it was crucially important that there were Westernizing thinkers within the Soviet establishment on whose ideas Gorbachev could draw and some of whom he could promote to influential positions, it is no less fundamental that in the hierarchical Soviet system these people exerted influence only within restrictive limits until someone receptive to their ideas occupied the most powerful political office in the land.

The Choice of Gorbachev

There were a number of reasons why Gorbachev was chosen to be General Secretary, none of which had anything to do with the increased expenditure on armaments in the United States or in any perceived need to select a "soft-liner" in response to Ronald Reagan's hard-line policies.[3] Gorbachev's accession to the most senior party post was very much a product of Soviet domestic politics. Changes in foreign policy were not on the agenda of the top leadership when they chose Gorbachev to succeed Konstantin Chernenko. There was a certain path-dependence about Gorbachev's election as General Secretary, although that should not be interpreted deterministically, for fatal stumbles can occur even in the last twist of the path to the summit. Every General Secretary in the history of the Soviet Union was both a full (voting) member of the Politburo and a Secretary of the Central Committee at the point at which he became party leader. This meant that he had experience both of the party's highest policymaking body, the Politburo, and of its "general staff," the Secretariat, which also met regularly as a body and was charged with the implementation of policy as well as having special responsibility for the choice and supervision of the personnel of the party apparatus.

Mikhail Gorbachev had combined these two positions since 1980. Historically, at any given time there had been at least four people who were both full members of the Politburo and Secretaries of the Central Committee. However, when Gorbachev's predecessor, Konstantin Chernenko, died, there were only two such people—Gorbachev and Grigoriy Romanov. The latter, although a Politburo member longer than Gorbachev, had become a Central Committee Secretary (and moved from Leningrad to Moscow) only in 1983. Gorbachev, though younger than Romanov, therefore had been a senior Secretary for longer than the former Leningrad party boss. Accordingly, Gorbachev enjoyed party seniority, a real advantage in a system where hierarchy counted for much.

Gorbachev benefited also from the fact that, especially in the Brezhnev years, the Soviet Communist Party leadership had been allowed to grow old together. His comparative youth, by the standards of that era, ruled him out of contention for the party leadership when Brezhnev died, but by the time of Chernenko's death the fact that Gorbachev was only a week past his fifty-fourth birthday had become a distinct advantage. Public opinion, which counted for little in the unreformed Soviet Union, and, more importantly, opinion at regional and lower levels of the party apparatus was concerned that three Soviet leaders in a row had been obviously infirm. That had clearly been the case with Leonid Brezhnev from the second half of the 1970s until his death in 1982, with Yuriy Andropov throughout most of his fifteen months as General Secretary, and with Konstantin Chernenko throughout the thirteen months of stalemate separating Andropov's rule from Gorbachev's ascension. Most of the Politburo members were already of advanced years, and a younger man more likely to show vigor and provide a respite from state funerals was desired. True, Romanov was only in his early sixties and a possible choice from the point of view of age, but, as noted above, he had been in Moscow for less than two years and the vacancy came too soon for him.

Andropov had given Gorbachev extensive responsibilities and wanted him to be his successor. That was not because Andropov had any inkling that Gorbachev would turn most of Marxism-Leninism on its head and endorse pluralism within the Soviet political system and in the international Communist movement. It was, rather, because he saw Gorbachev as the most capable and intelligent member of a new generation of party leaders, the one best equipped to carry forward his own efforts to get the country moving again. Andropov, especially if compared with the long-standing and influential senior secretary, Mikhail Suslov, was an innovator within limits. He had gathered a team of talented reform-minded people around him in his days as a Secretary of the Central Committee before he moved to the Chairmanship of the KGB in 1967.[4] But fifteen years at the KGB had left their mark on Andropov, quite apart from the fact that his generational experiences were different from those of Gorbachev. Andropov approved of the economic reform that occurred in Hungary under the leadership of János Kádár and even provided valuable support in Moscow for the policies pursued by the Hungarians at times when some in the Soviet establishment viewed these as dangerous concessions to the market. It is very possible that, had Andropov lived longer, a partial economic reform involving market elements would have been attempted in the Soviet economy. What is certain, however, is that pluralizing political reform would not have been undertaken. Even such a far from root-and-branch critic of the Soviet system as Roy Medvedev was kept under close surveillance by the KGB throughout Andropov's General Secretaryship.

Andropov, when already mortally ill, had made an attempt to elevate Gorbachev above Chernenko in the party hierarchy. Although unable to attend the December 1983 plenary session of the Central Committee, he prepared a speech to be delivered on his behalf, and on the twenty-fourth of that month he added six paragraphs to it. The key passage occurred after he explained that in the near future he would not be able to chair meetings of the Politburo. Accordingly, he continued: "I would therefore request members of the Central Committee to examine the question of entrusting the leadership of the Politburo and Secretariat to Mikhail Sergeyevich Gorbachev."[5] Arkadiy Volsky, Andropov's aide, made a photocopy of Andropov's addition to his speech and handed the original over to Klavdiy Bogolyubov, the head of the General Department of the Central Committee and a strong Chernenko ally.[6] These new paragraphs, which would have conveyed to the membership of the Central Committee that Gorbachev was Andropov's personal choice to succeed him, were never read out. The decision not to include them was taken, according to Volsky, by Chernenko himself in consultation with two other senior members of the Politburo, the veteran Defense Minister Dmitriy Ustinov and the equally aged Chairman of the Council of Ministers, Nikolay Tikhonov.[7]

Andropov's extension of Gorbachev's responsibilities within the Secretariat meant that, even if he were not to succeed Andropov, he was in the strongest position to become de facto second secretary to Chernenko after the latter became party leader. As such he chaired the weekly meetings of the Secretariat while Chernenko chaired the Politburo. Since, however, Chernenko was often too ill to attend Politburo meetings, Gorbachev presided also over the Politburo on those occasions. Following the death of Andropov in February 1984, an attempt was made to put a stop to the rise of Gorbachev. Several members of the Politburo, led by Tikhonov, objected to Gorbachev becoming second secretary. Gorbachev himself has recalled that "Grishin and Gromyko resorted to delaying tactics, essentially supporting Tikhonov."[8] It was not so much that they feared Gorbachev at that stage as a dangerous reformer; rather, they feared him as a young and vigorous leader liable to sweep them aside. Allowing him to become number two to Chernenko, whose life expectancy was short, was virtually to concede the succession.

That the choice of second secretary had important implications was recognized by Gorbachev himself. He noted the competition to appoint a new second secretary after the death in 1982 of Mikhail Suslov, who had "played a stabilizing role, and to a certain extent moderated the contending forces." As Gorbachev observes: "The first question was who would replace him. Actually, it was a matter of who would be Brezhnev's successor, a 'second' secretary who, according to tradition, would eventually become 'first' and, under the incumbent General Secretary, gradually take over the levers of power and assume leadership."[9] Gorbachev makes clear that Brezhnev, although ailing, was still able to ensure that the second secretary would be someone acceptable to him. Given Konstantin Chernenko's long-standing closeness to Brezhnev, Chernenko was "undeniably a contender for the post of the 'second person.'"[10] Chernenko, according to Gorbachev, orchestrated Brezhnev's activities—or the public appearance of activity—while he, in turn, was being manipulated by "the exorbitant ambitions" of his group of apparatchiks who were "without any political credibility whatsoever." That there was no love lost between Chernenko's "group" and Gorbachev is evident from Gorbachev's phraseology. Thus, at several points during the first half of the 1980s a decision that divided the Soviet leadership could have gone the other way, probably preventing Gorbachev's ultimate succession to the leadership. One such crucial moment was Brezhnev's decision that Andropov would be "second secretary" while he himself remained General Secretary.[11] Had Chernenko been chosen then, the extension of Gorbachev's powers and responsibilities would surely not have occurred. The second critical moment was when Gorbachev was allowed to carry out the duties of second secretary following the election of Chernenko as General Secretary.

The opposition to this was such that Gorbachev was not formally chosen by the Politburo to be the most senior secretary and second-in-command to General Secretary Chernenko. Rather, it was eventually agreed, as a compromise, that Gorbachev would fulfill the functions associated with that position for the time being. As a result, he was before long the de facto second secretary. Gorbachev formally became second secretary only after Ustinov, in a personal meeting with Chernenko, persuaded the General Secretary that this was desirable.[12] Chernenko, however, long delayed Gorbachev's move into the room in the Central Committee building that had been occupied successively by Suslov, Andropov, and Chernenko during the period they had occupied the number two position within the party.[13] There was a definite reluctance on the part of the Chernenko camp to accord Gorbachev the status that would make his succession to the General Secretaryship appear automatic. Nevertheless, Gorbachev held on to the responsibility for overseeing the economy he had already acquired during Andropov's leadership and his supervisory role was significantly extended to include foreign affairs and ideology. Romanov also, as a result of the stalemate between the Andropov-Gorbachev and Chernenko camps that had prevented agreement on any new promotions to senior secretaryships, had a very wide range of supervisory responsibilities, embracing the military, military industry, the KGB, the Ministry of Interior, the Procuracy, and the Courts.

There were a number of "Kremlinological" signs during January and February 1985 that Gorbachev was, indeed, second only to Chernenko in the party hierarchy and well placed to succeed to the General Secretaryship, even though Grishin attempted to push himself forward by trying to emphasize his closeness to Chernenko.[14] Gorbachev's challenge to conservatism within the Soviet Communist Party was becoming increasingly clear, especially following a speech he delivered at a conference on ideology in December 1984. While not offering any innovative ideas on foreign or defense policy, it showed that Gorbachev was ready to break with some of the stale formulae of Marxism-Leninism. Indeed, such key terms of the later Gorbachev General Secretaryship as "perestroika," "acceleration," "glasnost," "the human factor," "self-management," and "commodity-money relations" (a euphemism for the still-taboo "market") were given an airing in Gorbachev's speech.[15] With this speech, Gorbachev, in a sense, "outed" himself as a reformer.

In castigating the "obsolete conceptions and stereotypes"[16] that he attributed to "some scholars," Gorbachev was in fact calling into question the orthodoxy of the time. He was in December 1984 putting forward views that he was now in a strong enough position to express and in which he firmly believed. Their appeal was to more than one constituency—the enlightened minority within the party apparatus and to well-educated professionals in the party intelligentsia. No one from either of those groups, however, had a vote in the Politburo and very few of them were members of the Central Committee. Thus, there was no causal relationship between Gorbachev's reformist speech and his election to the General Secretaryship three months later—unless it be the indirect one that the self-confidence Gorbachev demonstrated in making such a speech undermined the political will of his opponents. Indeed, if one looks at the composition of the selectorate, it is fair to say that Gorbachev was chosen *in spite of* his innovative thinking.

Essentially, Gorbachev was able to succeed to the General Secretaryship for two reasons. The first was that Andropov had advanced his career so far and so effectively that it was very difficult to prevent him becoming second secretary to Chernenko. This meant that Gorbachev himself controlled key levers of power as Chernenko was dying and in the crucial hours immediately after his death. Second, Gorbachev succeeded to the highest office because the conservative majority on the Politburo had no plausible alternative candidate to offer, although Romanov would have been their most logical one, especially in view of the precedent of the succession going to a senior secretary of the Central Committee. Even though Romanov was given no opportunity to compete for the General Secretaryship when Chernenko died, the conservative opponents of Gorbachev saw him, in retrospect at least, as a preferable alternative to the person they got. Thus, the former Soviet Vice President, Gennadiy Yanaev, observed that with Yegor Ligachev (who, however, was only a Secretary of the Central Committee, not yet a Politburo member, at the time of Chernenko's death) or Romanov there would still have been perestroika but without bloodshed.[17] The remark illustrates both the elasticity of the term "perestroika," since it is clear that neither Ligachev nor Romanov would have changed the fundamentals of the Soviet system, and dubious judgement, for Ligachev was far readier than Gorbachev to spill blood to avoid the secession of any republic of the Soviet Union.

Of more immediate relevance in the present context is the raising of Romanov's name as a possible alternative leader to Gorbachev. That proposal was not, however, made in the Politburo at the time. It is possible, as Jerry Hough has argued, that a Politburo majority feared that the Central Committee would, for once, revolt if they presented it with any name other than Gorbachev's.[18] Against that, the Central Committee itself was only marginally less conservative, if somewhat less gerontocratic, than the Politburo, and it may be doubted whether they would have broken with tradition and party discipline by rejecting the Politburo's choice of leader, whichever name that body had come up with. In the event, the Central Committee greeted with warm approval the Politburo's nomination of Gorbachev for the party leadership because they were seeking a new fillip for the stagnating Soviet economy and a revitalization of the party's role within the Soviet system. A majority of those who both in the Politburo and in the Central Committee voted unanimously for Gorbachev to become party leader on March 11, 1985, were certainly not looking for someone who would be a more radical reformer than Khrushchev. Several years later they were to be dismayed by the risks Gorbachev was taking with the Soviet political order (and with *their* careers) by undermining the pillars of the system.

Gorbachev himself took no chances when Chernenko died. He was later to be accused of indecisiveness, but there was nothing indecisive about his instruction to a politically bereft Bogolyubov to convene a meeting of the Politburo the same evening (March 10) on which Chernenko had died at 7:20 P.M. Thus, not all Politburo members were able to attend and the absentees included people who were not particularly well disposed toward Gorbachev. However, he used his institutional resources to the full to ensure that he *would* be the next party leader, even though he was also, among all the remotely conceivable candidates, the person who would have been the choice of the Central Committee (and, for that matter, the population as a whole) had they been given a free vote.

The key point, however, is that the selection of Gorbachev to be the new leader was, above all, a matter of Soviet domestic politics. External pressure played no part in the decision, and though Gorbachev was soon to demonstrate a remarkable capacity, especially given the Soviet context, to think the unthinkable, there is not a shred of evidence to suggest that the primary selectorate, the Politburo, endorsed him *because of* his "new thinking," which, in any case, on foreign and defense policy had not yet been revealed.

Structure and Agency

Gorbachev's role in the ending of the Cold War was intimately linked with that of the dismantling of Communist systems and, in particular, with the transformation of the Soviet political system.[19] As such, it raises in an acute form the issue of structure and agency. Is there a structural explanation sufficient to explain the massive changes of the late 1980s whereby if Mikhail Gorbachev had not become General Secretary of the Soviet Communist Party in 1985, some other holder of that office would have been constrained to pursue the same set of policies? Or was agency (in the shape of Gorbachev) of decisive importance in ending the Cold War and altering the character of the Soviet system with the unintended consequence of the breakup of the Soviet state? In addressing these questions, I naturally touch also, to varying degrees, upon questions raised elsewhere in this volume concerning the relative importance of leadership, ideas, shifts in the balance of power and in material capabilities as explanations of the dramatic change in the international system.

Although I argue that Gorbachev's role in ending the Cold War was crucial, and that he pursued policies that would not have been those of any politically conceivable alternative candidate for the General Secretaryship of the Central Committee of the Soviet Communist Party in 1985, it is no less essential to note the importance of *political structures* both as *constraints* upon and as *resources* available to a Soviet leader. While no sensible person would argue that structures wholly determine policy outcomes, it is not unreasonable to suggest that, in general, they impose limits on the range of policy options that may be considered. A purely structural analysis of Soviet foreign policy would surely have come to the conclusion—as most observers did before Soviet "new thinking" presaged new behavior—that it was literally unthinkable for a Kremlin leader to consider relinquishing Soviet control over Eastern Europe and to accept the reunification of Germany within the framework of a Western alliance.[20] Institutional constraints apart, open-mindedness was not a quality readily associated with leaders who had been molded by those structures. The notion of according the peoples of Eastern Europe the freedom to choose their political and economic system would simply never have entered the head of a Khrushchev, Brezhnev, Andropov, or Chernenko. They would have resisted with all the means at their disposal the "loss" of Eastern Europe. Gorbachev, in contrast, though he certainly did not set out with the aim of abandoning (as distinct from changing and improving) the Soviet relationship with Eastern Europe, was able to accommodate himself to such an outcome and to justify it.

There was nothing inevitable or preordained about the fall of Communism in 1989. If expectations in East Central Europe had not been raised in the way they were by Gorbachev and his allies in the Soviet leadership, even the *threat* of the use of force might have preserved Soviet hegemony in Eastern Europe for a few decades longer. Memories of the Soviet invasions of Hungary in 1956 and Czechoslovakia in 1968 were sufficiently fresh to ensure that opposition to the Communist regimes in Eastern Europe became massive and overt (for the first time since the rise of Solidarity in 1980, which ended with the imposition of martial law in 1981) only at the end of the 1980s. By then Gorbachev's utterances and actions had produced a growing confidence that the Soviet Union would not intervene militarily and thus make a bad situation worse for the citizens of East Central Europe.[21]

Institutional Constraints

Apart from the constraints of ideology and upbringing, there were three institutional factors that limited Gorbachev's scope for action in foreign (as well as domestic) policy. The *first* is that he was accountable during the first five years of his leadership primarily to the Politburo, which had unanimously elected him to the General Secretaryship.[22] Throughout the second half of the 1980s Gorbachev could attempt to *manipulate* opinion within the Communist Party and to *persuade* the Politburo—de facto the highest collective decision-making body within the state as well as the party—but he could not *dictate* policy. The General Secretary was accorded great authority within the party apparatus in order to uphold its interests, not to undermine them.[23] What the Politburo members had given, they could take away. Gorbachev's gradualism, in so far as it *was* gradual—for in Russian historical perspective his political evolution was quite rapid—was structurally conditioned. If Gorbachev had openly espoused in 1985 or 1986 policies he implemented in 1988 and 1989 his term in office would have been as short as Yuriy Andropov's and Konstantin Chernenko's, although its ending would have had more in common with that of Nikita Khrushchev, who was unceremoniously ousted from power in 1964. The party oligarchy, which elected Gorbachev as leader, had no inkling of how far he would be prepared to go in changing the fundamentals of the Soviet system or the pillars of Soviet foreign policy. Had this been clear to them at a time when everything could still be settled far from the public gaze, they would have removed this threat to their power and privileges.

Structural constraints upon a General Secretary in the field of foreign policy were imposed, *secondly,* by two of the most powerful institutions in the Soviet government—the Ministry of Defense and the KGB—as well as by the interests of the vast military-industrial complex and, less formidably, by the bureaucratic inertia of the Ministry of Foreign Affairs, the International Department and the Socialist Countries Department of the Central Committee. The Ministry of Defense and the KGB had, in the post-Stalin and especially post-Khrushchev period, been significant participants in the foreign policy-making process. As recently as 1979 the fateful decision to intervene militarily in Afghanistan had been taken by a small inner-group within the Politburo consisting of General Secretary Leonid Brezhnev, Yuriy Andropov (KGB Chairman), Dmitriy Ustinov (Minister of Defense), and Andrey Gromyko

(Foreign Minister).[24] It was entirely predictable that if and when there should be an attempt to remove Gorbachev from power, the KGB, military industry, and the defense chiefs would be part of it—as they were in the failed August 1991 coup in the persons of Vladimir Kryuchkov, Oleg Baklanov, and Dmitriy Yazov. When Khrushchev was removed, the KGB "was deeply involved from the beginning" in the plot.[25] The military stood aloof, but while they did not assist the Politburo[26] majority opposed to the party leader, neither did they offer any help to Khrushchev.[27]

A *third* and very important structural constraint on Gorbachev in the realm of foreign policy was a feature only of the *late* Gorbachev era. That was the growing independence and assertiveness, especially in 1990–91, of the union republics (the fifteen major national territories into which the Soviet Union was administratively divided). As the various republics acquired new authority as a result of contested elections and the salience of the "national question" in late Soviet politics, republican checks on the foreign policy–making prerogatives of the all-union authorities became a serious issue.[28] Of especial importance was Boris Yeltsin's determination to reduce the powers of the union center, to establish a distinctive Russian political identity and to become himself a major figure on the international stage. Andrey Kozyrev's appointment as head of the Russian Foreign Ministry in October 1990 began a process whereby that body gradually emerged as a serious political institution, eventually taking over from the Soviet Ministry of Foreign Affairs when the USSR itself came to an end in December 1991. Earlier that year, Gorbachev had visited Tokyo and had been prepared to seek a compromise with the Japanese over the disputed Kurile Islands.[29] But the Russian President, Foreign Ministry, and Parliament greatly circumscribed his scope for maneuver by insisting that these were Russia's islands and not Gorbachev's to negotiate away.

By 1991 relations between the Soviet Union (and subsequently Russia) and Japan were about all that was left of a Cold War that was undoubtedly over by 1990 at the latest. Indeed, former Secretary of State George Shultz insisted in his memoirs that it was over by the time he and President Reagan left office at the end of 1988 and quotes Margaret Thatcher voicing similar views in November of that year.[30] Certainly, by then Soviet doctrine no longer provided an ideological justification for the Cold War, but in the course of the following year that precept was put fully into practice as East European countries, one by one, acquired their independence. Since the Soviet takeover of Eastern Europe had been the main cause of the Cold War, and the division of Europe its most important manifestation over almost half a century, Soviet acceptance of the end of that hegemony in the course of 1989 surely marked the Cold War's end.[31] Thus, the three structural constraints upon Gorbachev's foreign policy initiatives outlined above are in declining order of importance as obstacles to the ending of the Cold War. Indeed, the constraints embodied in the third factor, while very real within the limited time period in which they operated, belong essentially to what was, globally (with Russo-Japanese relations the exception that proves the rule), a post–Cold War world.

Institutional Resources

The changes in Soviet foreign policy under Gorbachev cannot begin to be understood, however, unless attention is paid to *political structures* not only as *constraints* but also as *resources and opportunities* available to the leader of the Communist Party of the Soviet Union (CPSU) who, by virtue of that office, was the most powerful individual within the state as well as the party. The *first* point is that the CPSU remained markedly hierarchical, with a strong propensity to refer policy upwards to the General Secretary. No major innovation affecting the way the Soviet system worked and no important foreign policy initiative could be taken without consultation with the party leader. If anyone had the opportunity to give a lead in proposing radical change it was he. Given the deference accorded to the holder of that office, and the important fact that nothing was more crucial for an ambitious official than the opinion held of him by the *Gensek,* colleagues and subordinates would, in many cases, suppress their doubts about the wisdom of the leader's policies rather than openly challenge them, even in sessions of the Politburo. As Gorbachev's interpreter at the key summit meetings with Presidents Reagan and Bush, Pavel Palazchenko, put it in his sharply observant volume of memoirs: "Gorbachev was often able to take advantage of the old command system's methods, of the residual authority of the party and its general secretary, and of the fact that the conservatives did not immediately catch on to the consequences of the changes they were witnessing and taking part in."[32]

The mixture of Gorbachev's gifts of persuasion and the power and prestige of his position meant that senior colleagues were generally either carried along by his ideas or somewhat reticent in their opposition to them—often a mixture of both. As former Politburo member and Chairman of the Supreme Soviet of the Russian Republic, Vitaliy Vorotnikov, puts it in his memoirs: "During discussions in the Politburo of the projected reforms of Gorbachev I not infrequently had doubts about their essence and timeliness and argued and objected. . . . But in the end I often accepted the logic of his persuasion. In that lies my guilt. The thing is that I long believed in Gorbachev and rested my hopes in him."[33] At lower levels the theory and practice of democratic centralism meant that party officials had to implement—or, at a minimum, give the appearance of implementing—policies about which they had grave doubts. After 1988 that ceased to be the case in the Soviet Union. Gorbachev was increasingly openly criticized by members of the CPSU, including regional party officials, but that was merely evidence that the system had become different in kind. The strict discipline the party had traditionally maintained, alongside the great authority it accorded its leader (sedulously reinforced by the party-controlled mass media), meant that in his earliest years in office Gorbachev was, paradoxically, sustained by institutional norms of the Soviet system that he was in the preliminary stages of undermining.

Secondly, the fact that the Soviet Union was a major player in the international system—and that relations with it were, accordingly, high on the agenda of the chief executives of other countries, including the United States and the member states of the European Union—meant that the de facto chief executive of the Soviet Union was drawn into the foreign policy process whether he liked it or not. The very fact that the General Secretary became the highest-level interlocutor with the leaders of other countries and the ultimate negotiator on behalf of the Soviet Union put him in a position in which he had to be (a) thoroughly briefed on international affairs and to have at his disposal the expertise of the foreign policy network in Moscow; (b) given some scope for flexibility of response in his discussions with Western leaders; and (c) open to being influenced in the course of his firsthand experience of foreign countries and conversation with their leading representatives.

Of course, in the interaction between structure and agency, a great deal depended, and depends, upon the open-mindedness, intellectual grasp, and willingness to learn of the leader concerned. It was not least because these were qualities Gorbachev had in abundance that his personal contribution to the end of the Cold War became decisive. He has himself acknowledged the part played in his political learning process by involvement in international affairs. After observing how "ideological blinkers" had earlier prevented him from seeing "reality in all its many-sidedness and contradictoriness," he noted what a great contribution to his development had been made by "participation in world politics, cooperation with the greatest statesmen of the times, and relations with people who embodied the political and intellectual elite of the world."[34] Some of those who worked closely with Gorbachev, such as Anatoliy Chernyaev and Andrey Grachev, also observed the influence Gorbachev's meetings with foreign (especially West European) politicians had on his thinking.[35] Another long-serving Central Committee official, Karen Brutents (who was First Deputy Head of the International Department), noted in his memoirs that Gorbachev and his closest colleagues strove unceasingly to study the experience of Western countries "and of social democracy in particular."[36] Yet Gorbachev developed his ideas also in the course of discussion with more conservative Western politicians. His lengthy, but good-tempered, arguments with Margaret Thatcher were important, and Gorbachev was keenly interested in Western Europe generally—

much more interested, indeed, in the western than the eastern part of the continent. His first visit to Britain—in December 1984, just three months before he became Soviet leader—led him, he has observed, "to reflect on the role and place of Europe in the world."[37] Among his most important foreign partners during the years in which the end of the Cold War was being negotiated was American Secretary of State George Shultz. Gorbachev's principal foreign policy aide, Anatoliy Chernyaev, has observed: "For Gorbachev, Secretary Shultz was an extremely important and interesting interlocutor . . . in addition to their discussions about missiles and aircraft, there [were] from time to time important philosophical themes about mankind and its future in [their] conversations. . . . Gorbachev's words are, 'He helped me very much both in developing and in implementing my policies.'"[38]

A *third,* and very important, opportunity presented to a sufficiently bold General Secretary by Soviet institutional structures was the possibility of making a few key appointments that could alter, first, the *balance of influence* and, then, the *balance of power* within the Soviet foreign policy establishment.[39] In the former category the General Secretary had a free hand in appointing his personal aides and informal advisers. Thus, to take just one example, the replacement of the conservative Andrey Aleksandrov-Agentov, foreign policy aide of General Secretaries since Brezhnev's time, by the enlightened Chernyaev made a huge difference to the quality and nature of advice Gorbachev received. As distinct from the choice of aides (*pomoshchniki*), appointments to headships of major political institutions with an input to foreign policy required Politburo approval, but it was well understood that the General Secretary had to work closely with these people and that his opinion on appointments to those offices counted for more than anyone else's. The fact that when Gorbachev became General Secretary in March 1985 Gromyko had been Foreign Minister since 1957 and Boris Ponomarev head of the International Department since 1955 showed that, to say the least, changes in these posts were not made lightly and it required an exercise of political will on the part of the General Secretary to remove those party veterans. But again Gorbachev showed none of the indecisiveness often attributed to him in pushing through these changes. The fact that the officer holders were so aged made resistance by them or on their behalf the more difficult to mount.

Within a few months of taking office he had, to the surprise of Soviet insiders as well as Western observers, replaced Gromyko with Eduard Shevardnadze as Foreign Minister and within a year the veteran heads of the International Department and Socialist Countries Department of the Central Committee, Ponomarev and Konstantin Rusakov, by Anatoliy Dobrynin and Vadim Medvedev respectively. Gromyko had assumed that when he was eventually replaced, it would be by one of his senior subordinates in the Ministry of Foreign Affairs.

Gorbachev records: "When I mentioned Shevardnadze, Gromyko's first reaction was close to shock."[40] Gorbachev, however, refused to be deflected from his intention to appoint someone capable of looking at foreign policy with fresh eyes. He was justifiably confident that Shevardnadze would both share his general outlook and be *his* ally, whereas the more obvious candidates would be set in the ways of the Ministry of Foreign Affairs and beholden to Gromyko.

It took longer for Gorbachev to replace the Minister of Defense and Chairman of the KGB. When he did so, the newcomers were, only in the short run, an improvement over their predecessors. Gorbachev took advantage of the young West German Matthias Rust's unscheduled flight to Red Square in May 1987 to remove Sergey Sokolov as Minister of Defense and to replace him with Dmitriy Yazov. According to Dobrynin: "Yazov was far more obedient to Gorbachev than Sokolov, and thus Gorbachev accomplished a quiet coup. The new defense minister knew little about disarmament talks, and had nothing to do with them. . . . But the military establishment remained discontented with Gorbachev, and this would show time and again."[41] Yazov has said that "the issue is probably not that Rust flew in, but that Sokolov and Akhromeev had been in the opposition, so this was used as a pretext for making some staff changes. . . . [W]hen I was appointed minister, Gorbachev told me to get together with Shevardnadze immediately and find common ground with him on all the issues."[42] Kryuchkov endorsed that view, saying: "In the case of Rust, I came to the KGB leadership a little later and specially studied this problem in retrospect. Gorbachev used it in the traditional way, to strike a blow to the Ministry of Defense, which in his opinion was not wholly subordinate to him, and didn't carry out his will or follow his train of thought."[43]

Kryuchkov obtained his post of Chairman of the KGB by emphasizing his firm commitment to Gorbachev and to perestroika, although later he was to be one of the key plotters against Gorbachev. But, with a very firm ally in Shevardnadze as Foreign Minister and with his rapid promotion of Aleksandr Yakovlev to a senior secretaryship of the Central Committee (supervising international affairs from 1988), Gorbachev pursued a foreign policy in which the priority of ending the Cold War was not allowed to become hostage to the sectional interests of the military or the security apparatus. From a very different perspective, Kryuchkov emphasizes how Gorbachev kept foreign policy under his personal supervision and, especially from 1989 onward, shut out of the policymaking process those who, from Kryuchkov's standpoint, were "firmly committed to defending . . . the fundamental interests of our state." The former KGB chief was acutely conscious of being bypassed, as was much of the military establishment. In Kryuchkov's words: "First of all, our collective leadership had for all intents and purposes already ceased to exist in 1989, when instead of having the basic issues discussed and decisions made in the Politburo, as was done previously, they were settled by a narrow group of individuals, such as Gorbachev, Shevardnadze, [Vadim] Medvedev, and occasionally two or three other people would chime in."[44]

A limited number of key appointments could make a far greater impact in foreign policy than in, to take the most notable contrast, economic policy. The institutional structures were crucially different in these two areas of policy. The multiplicity of participants in the economic policymaking process, including dozens of ministries and (until late 1988) economic departments of the Central Committee running into double figures, meant that the same control over economic policy could not have been achieved even if Gorbachev had had a clear idea of precisely what kind of economic reform he wanted (beyond a general disposition to make concessions to the market). Had appointments to the Chairmanship of the Council of Ministers and of Gosplan (the State Planning Committee) been better than they were, there would still have been ample scope for authority leakage and the watering-down of policy in the implementation stage of the policy process.[45] Hundreds of thousands of party and government regional officials, factory managers, and farm chairmen would have left their imprint on the eventual outcome. In contrast, Gorbachev himself was the implementer of much of the new foreign policy in his face-to-face discussions with Western leaders. Furthermore, by appointing the like-minded Shevardnadze to be Foreign Minister and by putting the International Department under the supervision of Yakovlev, Gorbachev ensured that new thinking would prevail in the foreign policy sphere.

Agency

In turning from structures to agency, and the crucial difference made by Gorbachev, the main link between them lies precisely in the General Secretary's power of appointment and the character of Gorbachev's actual foreign policy appointments. When Gorbachev appointed Shevardnadze, Yakovlev, and Chernyaev, he knew very well their critical views and general political dispositions. The same was true of his February 1988 appointment of Georgiy Shakhnazarov as his aide on East European questions (as well as on reform of the political system). Dobrynin was much less of a radical reformer than the others, but a pragmatic Ministry of Foreign Affairs professional who, after his exceptionally long stint as Soviet Ambassador to the United States, knew the corridors of power of Washington better than those of Moscow. Putting him in charge of the International Department of the Central Committee signaled, on the one hand, that Third World revolutionary movements would henceforth have a low priority and emphasized, on the other, the collaborative but subordinate status of the Department in relation to the Ministry, where Shevardnadze's closeness to

Gorbachev meant a confirmation of the institutional preeminence of the Foreign Ministry in the foreign policy process as well as in the conduct of state-to-state relations. This is confirmed by Dobrynin who, in his memoirs, is highly critical of both the style and the content of Gorbachev's foreign policy and of Shevardnadze's implementation of it. Dobrynin writes:

> Initially the agendas for all the meetings Gorbachev had scheduled with foreign leaders, especially the Americans and whether in Moscow or abroad, were minutely discussed by the Politburo. Gromyko had usually presented the foreign ministry's discussion papers, drafts of documents to be signed and other paraphernalia of such international meetings. But when Shevardnadze became foreign minister, fewer papers were presented or discussed. Gorbachev clearly strove to avoid Politburo guidelines and directives and sought a free hand in dealing with foreign heads of state. Ultimately, with Shevardnadze's help, Gorbachev reached his goal. In fact if not in form, he single-handedly devised the foreign policy of the country and implemented it as well.[46]

From the earliest months of his General Secretaryship, Gorbachev had in view more far-reaching change in foreign as well as domestic policy than a majority in the party apparatus, the military, or the KGB were ready to contemplate. While there was a lowest common denominator agreement that it was time to get the economy moving again, there was no consensus on the nature of economic reform required,[47] on the need for political reform, or on how far the Soviet Union should go in order to achieve a genuine reduction in international tension. There is some truth in Peter Shearman's statement that "the idea for reform did not originate with Gorbachev," but only in the sense that a significant minority of intellectuals within the Communist Party had been developing heterodox, and even reformist, ideas over a period of years.[48] Those party intellectuals were, however, powerless to implement any of their innovative notions until they found a leader, manifested in Gorbachev, who was truly convinced that "we can't go on living like this."[49] As Robert D. English, noting the political and intellectual interdependence of this relationship, aptly puts it: "the new thinking was ready, and its proponents eager, by the late 1970s. However, bitterly opposed by powerful reactionary interests, it stood no chance of influencing policy except through a reformist leader. But Mikhail Gorbachev, a bold and ambitious leader in his own right, grew equally dependent—intellectually and politically—on the new thinkers."[50] There is a body of opinion that holds that Yakovlev was the "unsung hero" of the end of the Cold War rather than Gorbachev who, it has even been claimed, did not intend to end it. One curious argument put forward to support that contention is that Gorbachev did not until fairly late in the day accept the unification of Germany and at no time wished to see the disintegration of the Soviet Union.[51] What this viewpoint overlooks is that Yakovlev was able to spend the most important political years of his life as a leading and notably reformist member of the Soviet top leadership team entirely because of the support and patronage of Gorbachev. Yakovlev himself, despite the fact that he became estranged from Gorbachev in the 1990s,[52] is under no illusions that an alternative General Secretary to Gorbachev in 1985 would have pursued a remotely similar policy. He has said: "With the exception of Gorbachev, all the members of the party-state leadership at that time leaned toward non-democratic methods. . . . They wanted to crush anyone whose political or philosophical views went beyond the boundaries of Marxism."[53]

Gorbachev, Yakovlev, Shevardnadze, Vadim Medvedev, Chernyaev, Shakhnazarov, and even Dobrynin were far more open-minded people than their predecessors. They were devoid of xenophobia and ready to modify ideological belief when it was clearly at odds with reality. Gorbachev was chosen by a Politburo that had little option but to endorse him and did so without realizing that he was a serious reformer by disposition. And Gorbachev himself did not know then that he would, within a few years, move beyond a desire to reform the system to a realization that nothing short of systemic transformation was needed. But the other six people were chosen, knowingly, *by* Gorbachev, for the very reason that he wanted to make a fresh start in foreign policy.

In emphasizing Gorbachev's decisive role in the transformation of the Soviet political system and of Soviet foreign policy, I do not discount many other factors making for change. Neither Gorbachev nor anyone else could have pursued the same policies in the immediate aftermath of Stalin's death. Soviet society had changed greatly in the meantime. It was better educated, better (although, apart from a fairly small minority, not well) informed about the outside world, and far less atomized. There was also the push of growing political and social problems as well as the pull of a society in which it was increasingly anomalous that even millions of educated professionals should not be trusted to form an independent political judgement.

Russia's hard-line foreign and defense policy had been such that it was still ascribed superpower status in 1985, but the Gromyko years were hardly ones of diplomatic triumph. When Gorbachev came to power, relations were bad with the United States, China, and Japan and not much better with Western Europe. In Eastern Europe the leaders were, for the most part, highly responsive to, and dependent upon, their Soviet counterparts, but the populations were more hostile to Moscow than were the peoples of Western Europe. At home, infant mortality rates had been getting worse, alcoholism and drunkenness were major concerns, and Russian males were dying younger. The rate of economic growth was in long-term decline from the mid-1950s through to the stagnation of the early 1980s. The technological gap between the Soviet Union and the West—and, indeed, between the Soviet Union and the newly industrializing countries of Asia—had been widening, not narrowing, in spite of lots of bombastic talk in Russia over the previous twenty years about the "scientific and technological revolution."

These worrying political, social, and economic indicators were certainly a stimulus to Gorbachev, and to those of his colleagues who could see further than the end of their noses, to try to reform the Soviet system and to end the Cold War, which, apart from its obvious dangers, led to a bloated military-industrial complex and underinvestment in the civilian sector of the Soviet economy. But it is quite wrong to imagine that the Soviet system was on the verge of collapse in 1985. The Soviet Union was losing the "struggle between the two systems" that it traditionally claimed it was winning. But it could surely have muddled through or muddled down into the twenty-first century by selling energy resources and other raw materials and by dealing severely, whenever necessary, with any signs of restiveness on the part of the intelligentsia. In that context it is salutary to note that Russian production at the end of the 1990s was little more than half of what it was in the late Soviet period and the country was still getting by largely on the basis of selling raw materials and receiving foreign loans. Moreover, most of the social trends that were causing concern by 1985 got worse in the first post-Soviet decade. Alcoholism is at a higher level today than in the Communist period, and the life expectancy for men in Russia has declined still further to an average of 59 (in 1999)—very low for an industrialized country. Failure, both social and economic, is not of itself a guarantee of transformative change. It has to be *perceived* as failure, and bold leadership is required to accept the risks involved in radical reform.

Most of the Soviet leadership at the time when Gorbachev became General Secretary of the Central Committee of the Communist Party believed that any change other than tinkering reform was dangerous. If we ignore the *long-term* dangers of continued oppressive rule and economic failure (which could not be sustained forever), it is incontrovertible that, in one important sense, they were right. Seriously liberalizing reform, not to speak of the measures of democratization that Gorbachev pushed through the Nineteenth Party Conference in 1988, *were* a threat not only to the Communist system but also to the very existence of the Soviet state. The Soviet system was, of course, both inefficient and corrupt. But in 1985 it was faced by slow decline rather than terminal collapse. Authoritarian, corrupt regimes are not in immediate danger of disintegration just because they are authoritarian and corrupt. The former dictator of Zaire, Sese Seke Mobutu, was overthrown only in 1997 when he was already gravely ill. He ruled, stealing from his people and oppressing them, for 32 years. It took a war, launched by the world's one remaining superpower in 2003, to remove Saddam Hussein from power. Internal opponents had been dispatched ruthlessly by Saddam and his henchmen. Yet the Soviet system had far more sophisticated and complex defenses against internal opposition than any Third World authoritarian regime. All attempts to change it from below—including that of the dissident movement (whose activities had been reduced to a trickle by the mid-1980s)—had ended in political failure, no matter how worthy they were morally.[54] If the Soviet elite had maintained the unity in defense of the fundamentals of the system that they had long displayed, it is highly likely that there would still today be a Soviet system and a Cold War. It was the choice of Gorbachev as General Secretary that paved the way for the ending of elite consensus, even if his own election superficially exemplified it.

It took extremely skilful political maneuvering for Gorbachev to get the Soviet leadership to adopt policies that went against the conditioned reflexes of a majority of the Politburo and the interests of the military-industrial complex. Gorbachev, after he became party leader, headed the minority reformist wing of the Politburo as well as chairing that body as a whole. He succeeded, notwithstanding tactical retreats from time to time, in getting a majority of its members to back policies they disliked. Oleg Shenin, a member of the Politburo (and Secretary of the Central Committee) only from July 1990, is one of the few who, in the midst of condemning Gorbachev's apostasy, has touched upon the behavior of those the General Secretary outwitted. At the June 1999 Cold War Conference in Moscow, Shenin said: "You can talk about the absence of a political will, even about the cowardice of those who understood that Gorbachev was leading the country in the wrong direction, but couldn't counteract him."[55]

Gorbachev's Aims and Achievements

What were Gorbachev's intentions when he became Soviet leader? They can be summarized briefly. He wanted to reform the Soviet system, not dismantle it. He wished to make its economy more dynamic, introducing some market elements, but without turning it into a fully fledged market system. He wanted more openness and tolerance but did not yet have in mind movement to pluralist democracy. In foreign policy, as is clear from many memoirs and interviews with participants in the foreign policy–making process, his aims were more far-reaching. He wanted to pull Soviet troops out of Afghanistan after negotiating as early as possible an end to the conflict there. He intended to make plain to East European leaders that there would be no more Soviet military interventions to keep them in office; it was up to them to satisfy the aspirations of their peoples. He wanted to end the Cold War *both* because he wished to divert resources from the wasteful arms race to the civilian sector of the Soviet economy *and* because he believed that high tension in East-West relations increased the chances of Cold War turning into hot war, if only by miscalculation or accident.

The new concepts that Gorbachev embraced were no less important than the appointments he made. The two are, of course, interconnected, for the new foreign policy team was encouraged to come up with fresh ideas and to convey to scholars in the policy-oriented institutes that they were now free not only to think the previously almost unthinkable but also to communicate their ideas to Gorbachev (sometimes directly, more usually by way of Yakovlev or Chernyaev) and, before long, to publish them.[56] By October 1986 Gorbachev had espoused a dramatic change in Soviet doctrine whereby "all-human values" had a superior authority to "class values" and universal interests had to take precedence over class or other sectional interests.[57] This amounted to a radical departure from Leninism, even though Gorbachev would find an obscure quotation from Lenin to attempt to justify it and though he continued to hold Lenin in misplaced esteem.[58]

There are many candidates for the most important causes of the end of the Cold War. They are discussed in greater detail elsewhere in this volume. The longer the time perspective, the more candidates come into view. Clearly the dismantling of Communist systems was intimately linked to the ending of the Cold War. There are those who argue that the election of a Polish Pope in 1978 was "the beginning of the end of Communism" or, alternatively, that this accolade should be accorded to the emergence of Solidarity in Poland in 1980. These events may well have been the beginning of the end of Communism in Poland, but even *there* a Communist system did not give way to pluralist democracy until well into the Gorbachev era. Solidarity may have been much admired, but, as a movement, it was not copied anywhere in Eastern Europe, and in Poland itself it could lead only an underground existence from the imposition of martial law in December 1981 until 1988–89.[59] One might, with even more justice, say that Khrushchev's "secret speech" in 1956 was the beginning of the end of Communism, for its repercussions were felt in every Communist Party, including the Soviet one but especially strongly in East-Central Europe. Khrushchev shattered the myth of the Communist Party's infallibility and the reality of its unity. One could go still further back and say that since Stalin's dictatorial regime produced a distorted economy and massive repression, in time it would be rejected. Moreover, the whole edifice was based on Lenin's false premises that, inter alia, saw no place for legitimate political conflict. The Cold War had to end sometime, just as hot wars eventually do, but none of the above suppositions are of any help in showing why it came to an end between 1985 and 1990 and, more specifically, in 1988–89.

Gorbachev and Reagan

Slightly more plausible as the major cause of the Cold War's ending, and a highly popular view in many American and even some Russian circles, is that the hard-line policy of President Ronald Reagan was an immediate cause of the transformation in Soviet policy that brought the Cold War to an end. In particular, it is argued that Reagan's Strategic Defense Initiative (SDI) was a "trigger" for this.[60] There is a fragment of truth in the latter statement, but it is not the fragment that most of its advocates have grasped. It was not so much the hard-line policies of Reagan's first term that ended the Cold War, but his willingness to enter into serious negotiations and treat the Soviet leader more as a partner than an enemy (the Reagan of 1985–88) that played a crucial part in bringing the Cold War to a relatively peaceful conclusion. That Reagan did this was partly a result of his own abhorrence of nuclear weapons and partly a consequence of his being persuaded that Gorbachev was a different kind of Soviet leader from his predecessors, one with whom you could do business. That view was famously put to him, first of all, by Margaret Thatcher, who could scarcely be thought to be "soft on Communism," and was amply reinforced by George Shultz and Jack Matlock from within his own entourage. Shultz, as noted earlier, established an excellent working relationship with both Gorbachev and Shevardnadze, and Matlock was an exceptionally well-informed American Ambassador to Moscow between 1987 and 1991.[61]

When Matlock arrived in Moscow to take up his ambassadorial post, he already took the view (by no means universally shared back in Washington) that Gorbachev was sincere about political reform. He also believed that if the Soviet leader was serious as well as sincere, he would have to tackle reform of the Communist Party itself—and then he would meet resistance. If it were to begin to look as if reform could no longer be controlled, Matlock's assessment of "the most likely outcome" was "a decision by Gorbachev to reverse course before things got out of hand."[62] While Gorbachev did, on occasion, make tactical retreats (most notably, and in many respects mistakenly, in the winter of 1990–91) he did not, in fact, ever reverse course. On the contrary, he was prepared to live with the consequences of his strategic choices.

Given Gorbachev's desire to improve East-West relations dramatically for the better, and his willingness radically to reassess the Soviet Union's relationship with Eastern Europe, there is a sense in which any American President should have been able to have a productive relationship with him. Former President Carter can certainly count himself unfortunate that he had to contend with the Brezhnev-Gromyko-Ustinov triumvirate rather than with Gorbachev and Shevardnadze. Yet, it must be acknowledged that any Democratic President would have found himself under fierce attack in Washington if he had expressed even the cautious view of Jack Matlock that a General Secretary of the Central Committee of the Communist Party was sincere in his desire to bring about political reform in the Soviet Union. The opposition to arms control agreements from

Washington hard-liners that even Reagan encountered would have been far more threatening for a Democratic President and, perhaps, even for a Republican who did not have Reagan's long-standing and unquestionable anti-Communist credentials.

In that sense, Reagan was an interlocutor who made ending the Cold War easier than it might otherwise have been. Moreover, in spite of all their differences, there is a sense in which Gorbachev and Reagan were similar in not being mere pragmatists, still less cynical pragmatists. Rather, "those two men were very idealistic. . . . They both believed in something. They were not just men who could change their sails and go any way the wind blows," observed Aleksandr Bessmertnykh, the former Soviet Foreign Minister, who, before he succeeded Shevardnadze in that post, was a leading member of the support team at numerous summit talks.[63] Or as George Shultz has put it: "Now, as far as the U.S.-Soviet relationship is concerned, I think that [Reagan's] characteristics were important . . . when Reagan said, 'Yeah, I think this man is different,' . . . that was an expression of this internal confidence, as I see it, and willingness to stand against people all around him if he felt this was the right course."[64] The "Reagan factor" contributed, then, to the end of the Cold War, but was much less decisive than the role of the Soviet leader. The immediate causes of the end of the Cold War were the coming to power of Gorbachev, his selection of a new foreign policy team with different values and orientations than their predecessors, his willingness to liberalize the Soviet system and then to embark on its democratization, his rejection of the ideological underpinnings of the Cold War and espousal of a conceptual revolution in the Soviet Union, and, above all, his decision that force would no longer be used in Eastern Europe to uphold Communist regimes loyal to Moscow.

Soviet Domestic Change Decisive

That is not, however, to deny that in an important sense the end of the Cold War was a victory for the West. Over the long run Western systems had proved their superiority politically—in terms of levels of freedom, accountability, and rights of citizens—as compared with Communist regimes. Their economic superiority had long been clear, but by the 1980s was increasingly evident. The countries of Western Europe and North America enjoyed not only greater economic efficiency but higher levels of economic welfare than the Communist states. There was, though, nothing very new about that. What was new—and of decisive importance—was a reform-minded General Secretary, open to innovative and critical ideas, given the fact that in the hierarchical Soviet system no bold reformist initiative could get off the ground without the endorsement of the very highest echelons of the Communist Party.

A series of crucial decisions that changed the Soviet domestic political context as well as foreign policy underpinned the policy of bringing the Cold War to an end. In January 1987 Gorbachev first put political reform explicitly on the party agenda and, still more crucially, in the summer of 1988 at the Nineteenth Party Conference he persuaded the party to endorse, against the better judgement of many of its officials, the pluralization of the political system through the decision to move to contested elections for a new legislature. In foreign policy, Gorbachev had from the outset intended to remove Soviet troops from Afghanistan, but the public announcement of this, when it came, was a landmark decision. Even more fundamental was the policy first enunciated at the Nineteenth Conference of support of the rights of states to decide for themselves the nature of their political and economic system. The latter point attracted more attention when it was repeated in Gorbachev's United Nations speech in December of that year, although even then most of the press missed the most crucial passages because, as George Shultz later remarked, "it was captivated by the 'hard news' of Soviet troop withdrawals from Eastern Europe."[65]

The contested elections of 1989 and the debates at the First Congress of People's Deputies (the new legislature) in the spring and early summer of that year further liberalized and pluralized the Soviet political system. If up to the end of 1988 what had occurred was a "revolution from above"—or, more precisely, a struggle over the direction and intensity of reform within the higher echelons of the Communist Party—open political contestation and debate in the mass media were given a huge stimulus by the 1989 elections and the live broadcasting of the parliamentary proceedings that followed. These changes *radicalized the society* and brought new actors on to the political stage, including the leaders of national (and, in a number of cases, separatist) movements. All of these internal changes had implications for Soviet foreign policy, but the Cold War had ended more than two years before the Soviet Union itself ceased to exist.

To sum up, it was a combination of new Soviet leadership and fresh ideas that was decisive in eliminating the reasons for a Cold War by the end of the 1980s. Many of the ideas had been lying around, but no one in authority had dared pick them up until Gorbachev succeeded Chernenko. The new thinkers themselves, however, became radicalized during the perestroika years as self-censorship became unnecessary, as they interacted with each other and (increasingly freely) with their Western counterparts, and as it became clear that those now in charge of Soviet foreign policy positively welcomed fresh thinking. Gorbachev was able to change the balance of forces (first of influence, then of power) within the Soviet system, even though he was himself always at risk of being overthrown. As Andrei Grachev has pertinently observed: "People seldom ask how many coups d'état Gorbachev managed to avoid in six and a half years of reform."[66] Had Gorbachev been ousted earlier, much of his domestic and foreign policy would have been put into reverse. In terms of material capabilities, the Soviet Union was, of course, far worse off than its Western rivals (and the gap was widening), but that—as has already been noted—has not prevented far poorer countries than Russia and the Soviet Union from sustaining highly authoritarian regimes and antagonistic relations with much of the outside world. In general, leadership, ideas, and changing *perceptions* of interests in the Soviet Union, following Gorbachev's coming to power in March 1985, rather than interests or material capabilities in a more "objective" sense, played the most decisive part in the ending of the Cold War.

Notes

1. Knell Goldmann, "International Relations: An Overview" in Robert E. Goodin and Hans-Dieter Klingemann, *A New Handbook of Political Science* (Oxford and New York: Oxford University Press, 1996), p. 408.
2. John Lewis Gaddis, "International Relations and the End of the Cold War," *International Security* 17 (3) Winter 1992–93, p. 18.
3. Speculation by Richard Pipes that such considerations governed the choice of Gorbachev are not borne out by study of the memoir literature or the transcript of the Politburo meeting that proposed Gorbachev's nomination to the Central Committee. See Pipes, "Misinterpreting the Cold War: The Hardliners Had it Right," *Foreign Affairs* 74 (1) (January-February 1995), pp. 154–60; and (for a report of the Politburo meeting that proposed Gorbachev as party leader), *Istochnik* 0/1 (1993), pp. 68–75.
4. They included Georgiy Arbatov, Oleg Bogomolov, Aleksandr Bovin, Fedor Burlatsky, Lev Delyusin, Gennadiy Gerasimov, Georgiy Shakhnazarov, and Nikolay Shishlin.
5. Angus Roxburgh, *The Second Russian Revolution* (London: BBC Books, 1991), p. 17.
6. Bogolyubov was expelled from the Communist Party during the Gorbachev era.
7. Interview with Arkadiy Volsky—tape in Russian and East European Centre Library of St. Antony's College, Oxford, and transcript in *The Second Russian Revolution Transcripts* in the British Library of Political and Economic Science, London School of Economics.
8. Mikhail Gorbachev, *Memoirs* (London: Transworld, 1996), p. 156.
9. Ibid., p. 124.
10. Ibid., p. 125.
11. Brezhnev himself took that decision in March 1982, although the plenary session of the Central Committee that formally elected Andropov a Secretary of the Central Committee did not take place until May of that year (Gorbachev, *Memoirs*, p. 126).
12. Andrey Grachev, *Gorbachev* (Moscow: Vagrius, 2001), p. 84.
13. Ibid., p. 86.
14. Archie Brown, *The Gorbachev Factor* (Oxford: Oxford University Press, 1996), pp. 82–83.
15. See M. S. Gorbachev, *Zhivoe tvorchestva naroda* (Moscow: Politizdat, 1984). The speech was republished in M. S. Gorbachev, *Izbrannye rechi i stat'i* (Moscow: Politizdat, 1987), 2, pp. 75–108. For further discussion of that speech, see Archie Brown, "Mikhail Gorbachev: New Man in the Kremlin," *Problems of Communism* XXXIV (3) (May-June 1985), pp. 1–23; and Brown, *The Gorbachev Factor*, pp. 78–81 and 121–22.
16. Gorbachev, *Zhivoe tvorchestvo naroda*, p. 11.
17. Yanaev, speaking at the Moscow Cold War Conference organized by the Mershon Institute of Ohio State University and the Institute of General History of the Russian Academy of Sciences, June 1999, in which I, along with the other contributors to this volume, took part (from my own notes of Yanaev's remarks).

18. Jerry F. Hough, *Democratization and Revolution in the USSR, 1985–1991* (Washington, D.C.: Brookings Institution, 1997), pp. 73–79.

19. See Archie Brown, "Transnational Influences in the Transition from Communism," *Post-Soviet Affairs* 16 (2) (2000), pp. 177–200; and Brown, "Mikhail Gorbachev: Systemic Transformer," in Martin Westlake (ed.), *Leaders of Transition* (Basingstoke: Macmillan, 2000), pp. 1–26.

20. I have in mind institutional structures—primarily Soviet institutions, but also international institutions such as the Warsaw Pact and NATO. I am not concerned with what is generally called structural theory in International Relations, much of it devoted to already somewhat outdated arguments about the relative stability of bipolar and multipolar international systems. For Gaddis's critical discussion of that body of literature, see "International Relations Theory and the End of the Cold War," op.cit pp. 29–38.

21. Some Russian nationalists and many Communist hard-liners still bitterly resent the way Eastern Europe was so readily allowed to go its own way. Responding to their views, Gorbachev has written: "Critics at home have also charged that we lost our allies in Eastern Europe, that we surrendered those countries without compensation. But to whom did we surrender them? To their own people. The nations of Eastern Europe, in the course of a free expression of the will of the people, chose their own path of development based on their national needs. The system that existed in Eastern and Central Europe was condemned by history, as was the system in our own country." Some of those critics to whom Gorbachev is responding believe that the threat of force, and evidence of the political will to unleash it, would have been sufficient to preserve the Communist order in Eastern Europe. They may well (as I have suggested above) be right in that assessment, though Gorbachev came to embrace, in the course of his General Secretaryship, the larger truth that those systems were not worth preserving. See Mikhail Gorbachev, *On My Country and the World* (New York: Columbia University Press, 2000), p. 206.

22. More precisely, the Politburo unanimously voted on March 11 to recommend to the Central Committee that Gorbachev be the next General Secretary. The formal election (also unanimous) was by the Central Committee of the CPSU.

23. With the creation of an executive presidency, into which Gorbachev was voted by the Congress of People's Deputies of the USSR in March 1990, the Politburo's direct responsibility for state policy was weakened and the position of the all-union legislature as the body to which he was constitutionally responsible strengthened. By that time, though Gorbachev was less constrained by the institutions of the Communist Party, the pluralization of Soviet politics had introduced other pressures and constraints, which are discussed below.

24. See G. A. Arbatov, *Zatyanuvsheesya vyzdorovlenie (1953–1985 gg.): Svidetel'stvo sovremennika* (Moscow: Mezhdunarodnye otnosheniya, 1991), p. 229; Eduard Shevardnadze, *The Future Belongs to Freedom* (London: Sinclair-Stevenson, 1991), p. 26; and A. S. Chernyaev, *Moya zhizn' i moe vremya* (Moscow: Mezhdunarodnye otnosheniya, 1995), pp. 399–401.

25. William J. Tompson, *Khrushchev: A Political Life* (Oxford: Macmillan, London, in association with St. Antony's College, 1995), p. 271.

26. The Politburo was officially known at that time as the Presidium of the Central Committee.

27. Tompson, *Khrushchev* op.cit., op. 270–71.

28. See Brown, *The Gorbachev Factor*, esp. ch. 8, pp. 252–305; and Rogers Brubaker, *Nationalism Reframed: Nationhood and National Consciousness in the New Europe* (Cambridge: Cambridge University Press, 1996), esp. ch. 2, pp. 23–54.

29. If settlement of the issue of the Kuriles—or the "Northern Territories," as they are known in Japan—were to be the criterion for the end of the Cold War, then it is not over yet, for those islands are still part of the Russian Federation.

30. George P. Shultz, *Turmoil and Triumph: My Years as Secretary of State* (New York: Scribner's, 1993), p. 1131.

31. A case could be made for dating the end of the Cold War to the reunification of Germany in 1990. It is a view taken by Philip Zelikow and Condoleeza Rice, *Germany Unified and Europe Transformed: A Study in Statecraft* (Cambridge, MA: Harvard University Press, 1995). But, as Zelikow and Rice are not alone in noting, the unification of Germany did not divide political actors on straight East-West lines. Margaret Thatcher and François Mitterrand were far from enthusiastic about German unification. Their opposition to it came out more clearly in private than in public, for they trusted that the Soviet Union would block it for them and thus avoid the embarrassment of public disagreement among Western leaders on a major foreign policy issue. In that connection, I recall a meeting in which I was invited to take part at 10 Downing Street on December 14, 1984, the eve of Gorbachev's first visit to Britain, specifically to brief the Prime Minister on Gorbachev's background, views, and political prospects. I can no longer remember why at that particular time (since it was still rather a remote contingency) I mentioned, *inter alia,* that Gorbachev was against German reunification, but I remember very clearly Margaret Thatcher's instant response: "And so are we!" Her foreign policy adviser rather boldly interjected: "That's not what you said in Bonn, Prime Minister," to which she replied: "Oh, you've *got* to say that in Bonn!" (meaning pay lip service to German unification).

32. Pavel Palazchenko, *My Years with Gorbachev and Shevardnadze: The Memoir of a Soviet Interpreter* (University Park: Pennsylvania State University Press, 1997), p. 81.

33. V. I. Vorotnikov, *A bylo eto tak . . . Iz dnevnika chlena Politbyuro TsK KPSS* (Moscow: Sovet veteranov knigoizdaniya, 1995), p. 461.

34. M. S. Gorbachev, *Gody trudnykh resheniy* (Moscow: Al'fa-Print, 1993), p. 24.

35. See A. S. Chernyaev, *Shest' let s Gorbachevym: Po dnevnikovym zapisyam* (Moscow: Kul'-tura, 1993), pp. 75–76; and Andrei S. Grachev, *Final Days: The Inside Story of the Collapse of the Soviet Union* (Boulder, CO: Westview Press, 1995), pp. 74–75.

36. K. N. Brutents, *Tridtsat' let na staroy ploshadi* (Moscow: Mezhdunarodnye otnosheniya, 1998), pp. 157–58.

37. Gorbachev, *Memoirs,* p. 457.

38. Fred I. Greenstein and William C. Wohlforth (eds), *Retrospective on the End of the Cold War: Report of a Conference Sponsored by the John Foster Dulles Program for the Study of Leadership in International Affairs* (Center of International Studies Monograph Series, No. 6, Princeton University, 1994), p. 30.

39. That distinction is elaborated in Brown, *The Gorbachev Factor,* pp. 97–111.

40. Gorbachev, *Memoirs,* pp. 180–81.

41. Anatoly Dobrynin, *In Confidence: Moscow's Ambassador to America's Six Cold War Presidents (1962–1986)* (New York: Random House, 1995), p. 626.

42. Dmitriy Yazov, transcript of tapes of Moscow Cold War Conference, June 1999.

43. Vladimir Kryuchkov, ibid.

44. Ibid.

45. See Stephen Whitefield, *Industrial Power and the Soviet State* (Oxford: Clarendon Press, 1993).

46. Dobrynin, *In Confidence,* pp. 622–23. That the Politburo was increasingly bypassed in major foreign policy issues was confirmed by the participants in the June 1999 Moscow seminar on the Cold War—a majority of whom were, admittedly, major opponents of Gorbachev, including Oleg Baklanov, Valeriy Boldin, Vladimir Kryuchkov, Oleg Shenin, Gennadiy Yanaev, and Dmitriy Yazov. See also V. M. Falin, *Bez skidok na obstoyatel'stva: politicheskie vospominaniya* (Moscow: Respublika, 1999), pp. 433, 447, and 452–53.

47. Gorbachev has noted the divisions on economic policy in the Soviet Politburo at that time. Some of the members, Gorbachev relates, believed that the answers to the country's problems lay in Andropov-style restoration of "order"; others, including Chairman of the

Council of Ministers Ryzhkov, emphasized scientific and technological progress. Only Vadim Medvedev and Aleksandr Yakovlev (and the latter not a full member of the Politburo until 1987) advocated transformative change. See Gorbachev, *Memoirs,* p. 218.

48. Peter Shearman, "Gorbachev and the End of the Cold War," *Millennium: Journal of International Studies* 26 (1) 1997, pp. 125–35.

49. Gorbachev's well-known words to Raisa Maksimovna Gorbacheva on the eve of his election to the General Secretaryship. See, for example, Raisa Gorbacheva, *Ya Nadeyus'* (Moscow: Kniga, 1991), p. 13.

50. Robert D. English, *Russia and the Idea of the West: Gorbachev, Intellectuals, and the End of the Cold War* (New York: Columbia University Press, 2000), p. 195.

51. Shearman "Gorbachev and the End of the Cold War," p. 134.

52. Yakovlev was, however, among the invited guests who attended Gorbachev's seventieth birthday celebration in Moscow on March 2, 2001.

53. Aleksandr Yakovlev, cited by English, *Russia and the Idea of the West,* p. 191.

54. Asked in a BBC interview of March 11, 1997, whether radical change and an end to the Cold War would have come about without Gorbachev, Aleksandr Yakovlev replied: "No, it would have been impossible without him. It would never have been done without him, the Secretary General. . . . I think that the totalitarian regime could have been demolished only through the totalitarian Party. There was no other way. No dissident movement would have been helpful here. It is ridiculous." (Transcript of that interview in my possession, courtesy of the BBC.)

55. Oleg Shenin, Transcripts of Moscow Cold War Conference, June 1999.

56. I have discussed some of these points in greater detail in *The Gorbachev Factor,* op. cit., especially chapters 4 and 7. See also English, *Russia and the Idea of the West,* esp. ch. 6, "The New Thinking Comes to Power."

57. *Literaturnaya gazeta,* November 5, 1986, p. 2. In their book, *The Wars of Eduard Shevardnadze* (London: Hurst, 1997), Carolyn McGiffert Ekedahl and Melvin A. Goodman overestimate Shevardnadze's role in the formulation and especially the conceptualization of foreign policy. Thus, they suggest (pp. 44 and 65) that Shevardnadze was "out in front of Gorbachev" by speaking about "common human values" in *October 1989*—three years after Gorbachev had first broken that particular taboo and after he had elaborated on it on numerous occasions in between.

58. Moreover, Lenin was not actually putting forward the idea Gorbachev attributed to him. See Stephen Shenfield, *The Nuclear Dilemma: Explorations in Soviet Ideology* (London: Routledge, for the Royal Institute of International Affairs, 1987), pp. 45–46; and Brown, *The Gorbachev Factor,* pp. 222–23.

59. For a fuller elaboration of some of these points, see Archie Brown, "Transnational Influences in the Transition from Communism," *Post-Soviet Affairs,* op. cit.

60. See, for example, Martin Malia, *The Soviet Tragedy: A History of Socialism in Russia, 1917–1991* (New York: The Free Press, 1994), pp. 414–15; and Richard Pipes, "Misinterpreting the Cold War," pp. 154–60.

61. During the earlier Gorbachev and Reagan years, Matlock was on the staff of the National Security Council in Washington.

62. Draft of talk by Jack F. Matlock, Jr., "The Last Years of Soviet Power: The View from Embassy Moscow," Princeton, October 28, 1997 (with acknowledgements to Jack Matlock for kindly providing me with a copy of this paper).

63. Greenstein and Wohlforth (eds), *Retrospective on the End of the Cold War,* p. 27.

64. Ibid., p. 26.

65. As cited by Pavel Palazchenko, *My Years with Gorbachev and Shevardnadze,* p. 370.

66. Andrei Grachev, *Final Days: The Inside Story of the Collapse of the Soviet Union* (Boulder, CO: Westview, 1995), p. 101.

Chapter 3

Regional Conflicts as Turning Points

The Soviet and American Withdrawal
from Afghanistan, Angola, and Nicaragua

Richard K. Herrmann

Introduction

Conflicts in the Third World were an important part of the Cold War. Although Moscow and Washington were involved in many regional conflicts, three took on special importance near the end of the Cold War: (1) the civil war in Angola; (2) the anti-Somoza revolution and subsequent Sandinista takeover in Nicaragua; and (3) the coup d'etat and revolution imposed from above in Afghanistan that led to the Soviet invasion and occupation.

In this chapter, we examine the Soviet and American withdrawal from these three conflicts as turning points in the end of the Cold War. The chapter begins with a discussion of why withdrawal from these regional conflicts should be seen as a turning point and what sort of turning point. It then includes a brief history of Soviet and American policy in each case. The later part of the chapter deals with the question of why these changes occurred.

Part 1: Regional Conflicts as Turning Points

Finding a way to end Soviet-American competition in regional conflicts was a necessary step toward the end of the Cold War. It did not represent irreversible material change but made change in other areas easier. Conservatives in America saw Moscow's involvement in these conflicts as a litmus test of Gorbachev's intentions. Secretary of State James Baker identified these conflicts as the criti-cal proving ground for Soviet new thinking.[1] He gave regional conflicts the pri-ority in Soviet-American relations that had traditionally been reserved for arms control.[2] Regional conflicts became the leading edge in the relationship both be-cause of the domestic importance they played in conservative Republican circles (Baker had to make progress in these political issues if progress was to be achieved elsewhere) and because the bureaucratic obstacles to innovation in pol-icy in these areas, while serious, were not nearly as substantial as the institu-tionalized bureaucratic interests connected to arms control. Baker argued that these conflicts involved interests and commitments that were important enough to signal meaningful change, but, at the same time, sufficiently removed from vital security matters that compromise would not put national security at risk for either superpower. They also would not evoke such fierce bureaucratic in-fighting in Moscow or Washington that progress would be stifled for sure.

Afghanistan was an issue Gorbachev had to deal with for both domestic and international reasons. The occupation of Afghanistan had crippled Soviet for-eign policy, and getting free of this albatross was essential for Gorbachev, whether he wanted to compete aggressively against the United States or seek a rapprochement with it. If he wanted to persuade China to balance with Moscow against Washington, Gorbachev had to get out of Afghanistan. To join forces with anti-U. S. sentiment in the Arab and Moslem world and to improve Soviet relations with Western Europe, he had to do the same thing. At the same time, if Gorbachev could couple a Soviet pullback with an American exit from the Afghan conflict as well, then he could answer his conservative critics at home who pointed to Washington's "neoglobalism" as a reason that it was too danger-ous to pursue domestic reform.

Regional conflicts as theaters of hot confrontation were both causes of the Cold War and partly the consequences of the superpower competition. Regional conflicts typically had indigenous roots unrelated to either superpower, but once a conflict began, the superpowers read important strategic consequences into it. Often the material interests at stake in a specific conflict were marginal, but the symbolic importance of success as an indicator of will and resolve were taken to be almost vital.[3] At the height of the Cold War almost any regional conflict could be pictured in East-West terms in Moscow and Washington. Leaders of both superpowers more often than not knew rather little about the complicated regional scene and array of local actors, and organized their thinking in bipolar ideological terms: whether regional actors were democrats or communists in substantive terms, was less important than whether they were deemed pro-American or pro-Soviet.

The importance of the symbolic meaning attributed to these conflicts com-pared to their material impact on intrinsic strategic interests is seen most clearly when we recognize that at the point of Soviet and American withdrawal in two of the three cases considered here, the conflict was far from settled. In both Afghanistan and Angola, fighting continued with horrendously bloody episodes well after the Soviets and Americans decided to leave. In Nicaragua, the subsequent course was more peaceful but still difficult. And beyond these conflicts there were many others, some erupting as the Cold War waned. Wars in both the Persian Gulf and former Yugoslavia had been favorite scenarios around which people during the Cold War forecast the outbreak of World War III. When these wars occurred in 1990–91, prevailing leaders in neither Washington nor Moscow saw them as East-West contests. This reflects the change in the strategic relationship that by then had occurred, but it also highlights the role reconceptualizing regional conflicts played as the Cold War ended. Had the United States and the Soviet Union not changed their ideas about the meaning of regional conflicts, they may well have read the Cold War into the host of ongoing regional conflicts and found plenty of fuel to keep the Cold War alive.

Before discussing what lessons leaders in the superpowers learned and why they decided to reduce their competition in regional conflicts, it is necessary to outline briefly the course of events that unfolded in these contests.

Part 2: The Turning Point in Afghanistan, Angola, and Nicaragua

All three conflicts discussed here entered a violent phase in the 1970s that lasted throughout the 1980s. Angola's civil war erupted in 1975 on the heels of the Portugese decision to grant independence to its colony.[4] Three major Angolan groups sought control. To advance their causes they sought support from the outside world, finding aid in Moscow, Havana, Washington, and Beijing.

In Afghanistan, an April 1978 coup d'etat overthrew the traditional monarchy and began a revolution from above that provoked fierce resistance.[5] The revolutionary regime sought support from Moscow. The resistance turned to Pakistan and the United States. By December 1979, the Soviet Union had a substantial investment in the revolutionary regime but little to show for it. The revolutionary leadership was out of Moscow's control and pursuing radical change that could not be sustained. The Soviet Union invaded in December 1979, put a new revolutionary leader in power, and announced that it would not allow the United States and Pakistan to take advantage of the instability on its southern periphery.[6] In retaliation, Washington imposed economic sanctions on the Soviet Union, accelerated the development of forces that could rapidly be deployed to the Middle East, and gave arms to the Afghan mujahedeen.[7]

At the same time political forces in Nicaragua were threatening to destabilize Washington's long-time ally Anastasio Somoza. In the late spring of 1979, Somoza faced imminent defeat.[8] Although Washington considered intervening, President Carter decided otherwise.[9] On June 19, the Sandinistas took power.

In all three cases the main engine of change came from domestic forces. Local players sought support from the superpowers which gave it largely to forestall the geopolitical gains they thought the other superpower would accrue from the regional development. The competitive interference continued until 1988, when Soviet-American agreements to disengage from these contests began to take shape. The superpowers' exit took time, proceeding in stages through the end of 1991. It is important to note some of the specific milestones in each case.

Afghanistan

Change came first in Afghanistan. In April 1985 Mikhail Gorbachev initiated an internal review of Moscow's Afghan policy.[10] Although he continued a tough rhetorical policy and offensive battlefield operations, by spring 1986 the combat role of Soviet troops declined as Moscow shifted more of the fighting to Afghan units. In July 1986, Gorbachev announced that Moscow would initiate a partial withdrawal from Afghanistan, including six Soviet regiments. He also pressed the regime in Kabul to consider new ways to co-opt and compromise with the opposition.[11] When Afghan leader Babrak Kamal refused to follow this course, the head of the KGB, Vladimir Kryuchkov, visited Kabul and in May 1986 Kamal was replaced by Najib.[12] In January 1987 Najib announced a plan for national reconciliation and included an announcement of a cease fire, a call for a coalition government, amnesty for detainees, and a linkage between Soviet withdrawal and an end to "international interference."

During this period, the Reagan Administration increased U.S. support for the mujahadeen. In 1980, the CIA spent $30 million providing weapons to the Afghan resistance.[13] This program increased to $50 million in 1981 and continued at roughly this level until 1984, when the United States allocated $120 million to the program and doubled this to $250 million in 1985. The supplies nearly doubled again to $470 million in 1986 and rose to $630 million in 1987.[14] In February 1986, the United States decided to provide Stinger anti-aircraft missiles. These missiles were used on the battlefield beginning in September 1986 and were delivered in substantial number to the mujahadeen in mid-1987.[15]

In April 1988 Gorbachev traveled to Kabul to insure that Najib would sign the UN-mediated Geneva Accords. These accords, signed by Washington and Moscow on April 14, 1988, called for the complete withdrawal of Soviet troops by February 15, 1989, and outlined a cutoff in arms supply by both sides. Gorbachev insisted at the December 1987 summit in Washington that U.S. aid to the mujahedeen cease with the signing of the accords. The Reagan Administration did not accept this idea and in a side letter to the accord said it would continue to provide arms.[16] This resulted in both Moscow and Washington continuing to provide military assistance to the warring parties in Afghanistan. An agreement to halt deliveries from both sides was not achieved until September 1991 and the cutoff did not begin until January 1992. At that time, Najib was still in power. His regime collapsed in April 1992. An Afghan interim government fought to take power in 1992 but never secured stable control. The country's civil war continued.[17]

Angola

Only eight months after the Geneva Accords were signed, an important accord was agreed to regarding Angola. The Brazzaville Protocol, signed by South Africa, Cuba, and Angola in December 1988, codified South Africa's agreement to grant Namibia independence by November 1, 1989, and Cuba's agreement to withdraw its forces from Angola over 27 months.[18] Both the United States and the Soviet Union continued to provide military assistance to competing forces in Angola, and, as in Afghanistan, continued this policy into 1991. On May 31, 1991, the primary warring groups in Angola, the forces of the MPLA-led government and the forces of UNITA's opposition, agreed to the Bicesse Peace Accords, which called for a cease-fire.[19] It included an attachment spelling out fundamental principles, which included UNITA's recognition of the MPLA as the government until elections could be held. It also included an additional protocol spelling out the rules for elections to be held between September 1 and November 30, 1992. The May 1991 accords also called for the end of Soviet and American military supply.

By the time the Bicesse Accords were signed, Angolans had been at war for more than 15 years. Fighting had begun between the MPLA, UNITA, and the FNLA in March 1975. Before the year was out, Cuban advisors were assisting the MPLA, covert U.S. military assistance was flowing to the FNLA, and South Africa was intervening with forces from the South.[20]

In 1983, with United Nations Security Council prodding, South Africa and Angola agreed to the Lusaka Accords, agreeing that South African forces would withdraw from Angola in return for Angola's constraint of the South West Africa People's Organization (SWAPO) in Namibia. By this time, negotiators had also hit on a formula that linked South African withdrawal from Namibia with Cuban withdrawal from Angola, but as mentioned above, achieving agreement on this took until December 1988.

In the meantime there was a lot of fighting. The Reagan administration succeeded in July 1985 in repealing the Clark Amendment, which had barred U.S. military assistance since December 1975. Jonas Savimbi, the leader of UNITA, arrived in Washington in January 1986.[21] By summer, the United States had delivered $15 million in military assistance—including Stinger anti-aircraft missiles to UNITA. It delivered another $15 million in 1987 and by 1991 had delivered $250 million total.[22] During this time fighting escalated on the ground in Angola. The MPLA launched a major offensive on UNITA strongholds in July 1985, drawing in response the largest South African intervention since 1975. In August 1987 the MPLA attacked again, this time with Soviet General Konstantin Shagnovitch helping to coordinate the battle plan and Soviet advisors as well as Cuban troops taking part.[23] Again, UNITA was rescued by South African intervention, but this time South Africa went on the offensive, driving MPLA forces back and laying siege to Cuita Cuanavale.

If South Africa hoped for a quick and decisive victory, it did not get it. The battle raged on and eventually MPLA forces supplied with advanced Soviet aircraft and backed by Cuban pilots and a Cuban expeditionary force compelled a South African retreat. The Cuban force marched to the Angolan-Namibian border and threatened South African troops still pulling back as well as South African forces in Namibia. In August 1988, South Africa agreed to allow the implementation of UN Resolution 435 calling for the independence of Namibia. In return it demanded the withdrawal of Cuban forces from Angola. This is what was accomplished in the Brazzaville Protocol signed in December 1988. The war between UNITA and MPLA would continue, as would U. S. and Soviet military deliveries.

In June 1989 at Gbadolite, Angolan president Jose Eduardo dos Santos agreed to a cease- fire with Jonas Savimbi. It did not hold and fierce fighting continued. With substantial U.S. and Soviet encouragement, however, talks between the MPLA and UNITA continued in Portugal and after six rounds and almost another year the Bicesse Accords were agreed upon in May 1991 setting up an election plan. Elections were held the last two days of September 1992. The MPLA won 54 percent of the vote, UNITA had 34 percent. Dos Santos won 49.6 percent of the votes for president compared to 40.7 percent for Savimbi. The called-for second round of elections, to see which presidential candidate could win 50 percent or more of the vote, never took place. Savimbi and UNITA rejected the electoral results and the country returned to full-scale civil war.[24] Although the United States and the Soviet Union were out of the conflict, between October 1992 and late 1994 another 300,000 Angolans lost their lives.[25]

Nicaragua

After the 1979 revolution in Nicaragua, the United States pledged nonaggression and the Sandinista government pledged to limit their military buildup and not to assist the guerillas in El Salvador. The Carter administration suspended aid to Nicaragua, alleging that the Sandinista government was sending supplies to El Salvadorian rebels. It used the possibility of resuming aid as a lever in talks with Nicaragua. When the Reagan administration took office in 1981, U.S. policy moved in a decidedly tougher direction. The aid program was terminated in April 1981 and in November the NSC issued Directive 17, providing secret funding for an anti-Sandinista force with $19 million committed to establish a 500-man force.[26] The Contras, as they came to be known, began to carry out attacks in Nicaragua in March 1982.

Reversing the communist success in Nicaragua was a centerpiece of the conservative ideology in far-right Republican circles.[27] President Reagan in his first two years in office gave more speeches on Central America and the communist threat there, than on any other foreign policy issue. Despite the President's efforts, he could not persuade a majority in Congress to follow his lead on Central American policy. Consequently, funding remained limited and operations remained covert. In January and February 1984 this involved mining the harbors of Nicaragua, an action critics saw as an act of war and a clear violation of international law, made more serious because it was done directly by the CIA and not the Contras. The Reagan administration could not defuse the Congressional criticism of this policy and faced substantial pressure to engage in some sort of dialogue with the Sandinistas. In May 1984, Secretary of State George Shultz went to Nicaragua to pursue such a dialogue.

In October 1984, Congress passed and Reagan later signed into law (he evidently assumed a veto would be overridden), an amendment offered by Rep. Edward Boland baring further funds for the Contras. Faced with this Congressional ban on military aid, the Reagan administration in January 1985 suspended its participation in the talks with the Sandinistas, arguing that nothing good could come from them without the military lever.[28]

Despite the President's articulation of what came to be known as the Reagan Doctrine, most of Congress was still not buying his picture of events in Central America or his call for escalating military activity.[29] Unable to win approval for the use of force, the administration on May 1, 1985, imposed an embargo on Nicaragua. Sandinista leader Daniel Ortega responded by going to Moscow, a visit followed by increasing Soviet military deliveries to Managua. By the summer of the following year (June 25, 1986), the Soviet escalation gave Reagan the argument he needed to persuade Congress to approve $100 million for the support of the Contras, 75 percent of which could be in military supplies. By this time, however, Costa Rica, Honduras, Guatemala, El Salvador, and Nicaragua had signed the Esquipulas Declaration in May 1986 committing themselves to a regional peace arrangement and voicing their opposition to military escalation.

Throughout 1987 Costa Rican President Oscar Arias pursued a diplomatic course that culminated in August in the presidents of Costa Rica, Honduras,

Guatemala, El Salvador, and Nicaragua signing Esquipulas II. This agreement called for a cutoff in both U.S. aid to the Contras and Soviet aid to Nicaragua. It also called for free elections in Nicaragua. The Soviet Union encouraged Nicaragua to accept this agreement and welcomed it. George Shultz felt the agreement had been heavily influenced by a bipartisan U. S. proposal sent to Esquipulas and that it provided a reasonable diplomatic avenue.[30] The Assistant Secretary of State for Latin America, Elliot Abrams, disagreed, as did other more conservative voices at the NSC. The conservative voices won the day inside the administration and the United States did not endorse the agreement. In November 1987, Speaker of the House Jim Wright met with Daniel Ortega and suggested that Congress would move forward with the peace plan despite the administration's position. Wright had no authority to negotiate in this way and could not deliver U. S. policy in the end, but his action reflected the weakness of the Reagan administration on this issue at home. The Congress cut off further military assistance to the Contras.

Secretary of State Baker negotiated the Nicaraguan issue on two fronts. He began at home trying to construct a bipartisan agreement. This involved moving away from the right-wing's interest in providing arms to the Contras and enlisting liberal support for the insistence that the Sandinistas agree to free elections as called for in Esquipulas II.[31] On Baker's first trip to Moscow in May 1989 he put the Central American issue up front, telling Soviet Foreign Minister Shevardnadze and General Secretary Gorbachev that settlement in Nicaragua was a test case of the practical implications of the professed "new thinking" in Moscow.[32]

The issue was not resolved by the time Gorbachev and President Bush met at Malta in December 1989, where Baker described it as the biggest obstacle to improved U.S.-Soviet relations. Although the Bush administration, at this point, was encouraging a coalition of opposition forces to participate in the elections, it refused to negotiate with the Sandinistas. The elections were held February 26, 1990. To the great surprise of conservatives in Washington, they were mostly free and fair and Violeta de Chamorro and the opposition coalition won 55.2 percent of the votes. The Sandinista won 40.8 percent.[33]

Reviewing the course of events in Afghanistan, Angola, and Nicaragua makes clear that Cold War competition prevailed from the mid-1970s through 1986. While there were signs of change in 1986 and 1987, the Geneva Accords calling for the withdrawal of Soviet forces from Afghanistan was not signed until April 1988, and the Brazzaville Protocol establishing a timetable for South African and Cuban withdrawal from Angola was not signed until that December. Soviet and American military supplies continued to flow into Afghanistan and Angola through most of 1991. In Latin America, U.S. military supply to the Contras wound down after Esquipulas II was signed by Latin American presidents in August 1987. This was not, however, part of an agreement with the Soviet Union but rather a result of Congressional opposition. Soviet military supply to Nicaragua ended in 1989. Clearly, between 1986 and 1991 the Soviet Union and the United States ended their competition in these regional affairs even if they did not end the regional conflicts. Why they changed course is, of course, the question we are most interested in.

Part 3: Why Did the Soviet Union and the United States Make the Turn?

As with the other turning points, in these regional conflicts a case can be made for the importance of power, ideas, domestic politics, and leadership. We take these up one at a time.

Power

Interpretations relying on power emphasize two mechanisms: (a) direct costs and (b) indirect costs. We look at these sequentially.

Direct costs. The strictest version of the direct costs argument would posit that one side or the other won on the battlefield and left the loser little choice but to retreat. None of the conflicts, however, turned out this way. In Afghanistan, neither the mujahedeen nor the Soviet-backed PDPA won on the ground. The Geneva Accords led to the Soviet exit but not to the end of fighting, which escalated in the winter. In Angola, the MPLA had some success in August 1987, but were not successful in conquering UNITA headquarters in Mavinga and then barely kept Cuito Cuanavale out of the hands of South Africa. Cuban escalation only led to a new stalemate. The Contras also were not successful militarily. For Americans who construct the period as one of Soviet withdrawal in defeat, it is important to keep in mind that in Afghanistan and Angola, 1991 ended with the former Soviet client in power; the same was true in Namibia.

A looser version of the direct costs argument could emphasize costs that eventually "broke the bank." For instance, the Soviet economy might have been so weak that Moscow had to retreat. Despite the intuitive appeal of this to Americans, the argument faces several empirical problems. First, neither the Soviet Union nor the United States was investing large amounts of money in these conflicts as a percentage of their overall defense budgets. They also devoted small percentages of their armed forces or material supplies. Leaders in Moscow may have come to see the price paid in these conflicts as too high, making a political judgment about their relative worth, but certainly had the material capability available to do more.

Second, if either superpower was compelled to exit because of the costs, it is odd that neither side cut off arms supplies and realized savings until after the Cold War was over. In the Afghan case, Moscow reduced the cost in terms of Russian lives but increased the provision of supplies.[34] The arms pipeline from Moscow to Kabul stayed open until early 1992 and was closed by a decision of President Yeltsin of the Russian Federation, which succeeded the Soviet Union.

Neither Moscow nor Washington realized short-term savings in Angola. Cuban troops began to leave after the Brazzaville Accords were signed in December 1988. Soviet advisors stayed and Soviet assistance continued.[35] U.S. support for UNITA went on as well.

In Nicaragua, supplies from the Soviet Union continued to flow well into 1989, and when they were cut off the savings were small.[36] The Reagan and Bush administrations were constrained not by financial scarcity but domestic opposition.

A third interpretation might point to carrots and sticks. Secretary of State Shultz argues, for example, that the delivery of U.S. weapons to the Contras compelled the Sandinistas to accept elections.[37] Maybe the Reagan Doctrine of challenging the Soviets in regional conflicts persuaded both Moscow and its regional clients to make political concessions. Unfortunately, claims like Shultz's rest fundamentally on the counterfactual claim that without this aid concessions would not have been made and critics can argue in an equally counterfactual way that the military supply prolonged the fighting and delayed an agreement that could have been reached earlier.[38]

In considering whether the delivery of assistance accelerated or delayed a political settlement, it is useful to consider both the involvement of the superpowers and the actions of the regional parties. Superpower deliveries of arms followed a tit-for-tat pattern. As U.S. aid increased to the Afghan mujahedeen, so did Soviet supply to the PDPA.[39] American arms for UNITA were met with Cuban and Soviet escalation, and until 1989, U.S. aid for the Contras was followed by more Soviet deliveries to the Sandinistas.[40] The delivery of weapons became a stumbling block in negotiations in all three cases, with Moscow and Washington refusing to halt arms supplies until late 1991.

Important leaders on both sides did not see the delivery of arms as a bargaining chip but as a means to a decisive victory. For example, Secretary Shultz argues that a negotiated outcome should have been pursued after the signing of Esquipulas II in August 1987, but was not, because right-wing ideologues in the Reagan administration saw aid to the Contras not as a bargaining lever but as an end in itself.[41] Given the support for settlement among the regional states and the Sandinista agreement in Esquipulas to hold elections, it is possible that the Reagan administration's refusal to endorse Esquipulas II, partly because it would mean a cutoff in aid to the Contras, delayed settlement. Selig Harrison makes a parallel argument about settlement in Afghanistan, arguing that because officials in the Reagan administration wanted to make the Soviet Union "bleed" in Afghanistan, a settlement was delayed.[42]

In all three conflicts, regional parties to the conflict sought unilateral victory. Had they been able to achieve victory it is unlikely they would have accepted the compromises they eventually did. The offsetting provision of military assistance from the superpowers thus contributed to the battlefield stalemate, and, in turn, to the search for diplomatic alternatives.

Over time the PDPA, the MPLA, and UNITA all moved toward some sort of national reconciliation plan that included a role for the opposition. In the early and mid-1980s this amounted to little more than co-optation. As Gorbachev announced his new thinking and as the Reagan Doctrine began to arm anti-communist insurgents more fully (1986–1988), these plans for reconciliation became more substantive. This might reflect PDPA, MPLA, and Sandinista judgments that because of the U.S. military assistance, compromise was necessary. It also might be the result of their judgment that Soviet support was waning because of Gorbachev's new agenda and if they agreed to these political and electoral processes they would win, thus legitimating their status. In both Afghanistan and Angola, Moscow's ally stayed in office after the international agreement was signed. The MPLA won the elections, and the PDPA was still holding its own when Yeltsin ended assistance in January 1992. The Sandinistas ran a competitive election and did not lose to the Contras. That the elections were held only in 1990, and not before, gives credence to the argument that military pressure did not force them to take this step. After all, Congress had forbid military assistance to the Contras for most of the 1980s and cut it off entirely after Esquipulas II was signed in August 1987. Even if U.S. arms delivered to the Contras played a role in Sandinista decisions to accept Esquipulas II, that the Sandinistas kept on this election course in 1988 and 1989 could not have been due to American supply of weapons to the Contras. There was almost no chance Reagan or Bush could get Congressional approval for additional arms after 1987. The elections were not held until February 1990. It is likely that change in Soviet policy and pressure from regional states had as much influence on Sandinista decision making regarding the course of events after Esquipulas II as U.S. military pressure did.

In the Afghan case, the American supply of weapons to the Mujahedeen did not cause the PDPA to compromise on domestic matters. It stayed in power and made few concessions to the Pakistani-encouraged and U.S.-backed Afghan Interim Government (AIG). Neither side agreed to a process of transition. Vladimir Kyuchkov, former head of the KGB, reports that he favored withdrawing Soviet troops because he expected that the PDPA would be able to stay in power without the delegitimating presence of foreign troops.[43] He was right in the short run.

It is in the Angolan case that the relationship between military assistance and political compromise at the regional level appears most likely. Between 1986 and 1988 both the MPLA and South Africa went for a knockout blow. In both instances, the parties failed and provoked instead major escalation by the other party. The MPLA's offensives led to South African counterattack, which in turn led to Cuban and Soviet escalation. Battlefield stalemate brought South Africa and Cuba to agreement at Brazzaville and battlefield stalemate preceded the MPLA-UNITA agreement in the Bicesse Peace Accords of May 1991. The Bicesse Accords, however, were a product of Soviet and American insistence that their own allies compromise as much as they were a product of the superpower determination to deliver more weapons. By the time these talks even started, Eastern Europe had already been liberated and the Cold War was over.

Indirect costs. Another way to explain the turning point represented by these regional conflicts is to focus on the indirect costs or the opportunities that had to be put aside because of them. For instance, Mikhail Gorbachev's new thinking in foreign affairs might be understood as a rationalization for Moscow's pulling back from regional conflicts to turn to domestic priorities. Of course, as already noted, Soviet deliveries did not decline but to the contrary increased in Afghanistan and held steady in the other two cases, and Moscow did not pull out of these conflicts until the Cold War was over in 1992.[44] This should not obscure the fact, however, that after 1988 Gorbachev granted lower priority to these conflicts.

A second version of indirect costs moves from a purely financial to a political conception of costs. This may reflect Gorbachev's judgment that Moscow paid too high a price globally for its involvement in these regional conflicts, alienating China, upsetting Third World countries, and making it easier for the United States to mobilize the rest of the world against the Soviet Union. Perhaps Gorbachev had no choice but to pull back to escape strategic isolation. Clearly, the United States had better relations with China, Europe, Japan, and the emerging new industrial countries in Southeast Asia. This, of course, had been the case throughout the Cold War, with the exception of relations with China. Even though this was not a new situation, perhaps the cumulative effect crossed a threshold Moscow could no longer tolerate.

It is, of course, very difficult to evaluate threshold arguments that rely on "breaking points" unless we can establish the threshold independent of the change in behavior. In the case of regional conflicts, the problem is compounded because pulling out could affect Soviet political leverage and status in world opinion in different ways: withdrawal could be seen as a sign of weakness and lack of trustworthiness or as a sincere effort to facilitate peace. In the Angolan and Nicaraguan cases, the Soviet Union was on the same side as most of the rest of the world.[45] The MPLA was accepted as a member of the Organization of African Unity and the United Nations. UNITA's dependence on South Africa alienated most of black Africa and much of Europe and Asia. The Sandinistas, likewise, enjoyed international support. Public opinion in Latin America and Europe was opposed to "U.S. imperialism." To the frustration of the Reagan administration, few U.S. allies followed its lead on Nicaragua.

Afghanistan was clearly another story. In this case, Moscow paid a price in Europe and the Islamic World as well as in Asia. Gorbachev's change of course here probably did have the intent of getting free of Moscow's diplomatic albatross. As Gorbachev moved to take Soviet troops out of Afghanistan, he also moved to take the "China Card" away from the United States, to seek new ties with Iran and to exploit anti-U.S. sentiment in the Moslem world, and to accelerate Soviet–West European relations regardless of how Soviet-American relations proceeded. It is possible, even likely, that between 1986 and 1988 Gorbachev was pursuing policies designed to strengthen Moscow's competitive position vis-á-vis Washington. That is certainly consistent with the effect of his decisions in these regional conflicts. Given that he did not realize financial savings in these cases, it seems unlikely Moscow was simply turning inward and surrendering foreign policy to domestic priorities. Rather, it appears Moscow was preparing to compete with Washington if necessary while beginning to search for a way to probe the possibilities of a detente.

The discussion of priorities and leverage depends heavily on ideas. It is ideas about national interests and ideas about foreign threats and opportunities that establish national priorities. And in diplomacy, leverage, which is an idea about power, is often as important, or more so, than an objective counting of material assets. At this point, arguments that rely on power blend into those that emphasize ideas. It is to those interpretations that we turn next.

Ideas

The importance of political actors as proactive agents lies at the core of interpretations attributing change in superpower relations to changing ideas. These arguments recognize that capabilities establish parameters but conclude that the range of choice available is substantial and leaders are not compelled to adopt a single predictable course. Identifying three ideas about regional conflicts is necessary before considering if change in these played a role in ending the Cold War.

These ideas were (1) that regional conflicts in the Third World were strategically important and had consequences for the core East-West confrontation; (2) that the involvement of the superpower adversary was central to, if not the main cause of, regional conflicts; and (3) that military intervention to stop the other superpower's interference and help a regional client was likely to be successful.

The logic behind the U.S.'s containment strategy was that if the United States denied the regime in Moscow success around the world, then it would eventually undermine the Communist Party's claim that it represented the worldwide vanguard, and leaders in Moscow would then need to deliver to the Soviet people a higher quality of life at home.[46] The perceived need to counter communist advances transformed otherwise relatively insignificant conflicts into major tests of will and resolve.[47] For instance, the intrinsic material importance of Nicaragua, Afghanistan, or Angola were marginal, but the symbolic importance of these conflicts due to the global ideational construction of the Cold War was seen as vital by conservative Americans.

In Moscow, the initial importance of Third World conflicts was based on the idea that unless socialism spread beyond the Soviet Union, the socialist experience would be isolated and vulnerable. While discussions in Moscow about regional conflicts were colored with ideological labels, the core logic typically followed a geopolitical pattern of interests rather than ideology.[48] Anti-communists, such as the leaders in Iraq, could be described as progressive and worthy of support if they were anti-American. Pro-American forces, on the other hand, no matter their ideological agenda, were described as reactionary and opposed.

In the United States, "regionalists" and "globalists" debated the causes of Third World conflicts. Globalists saw the conflict in East-West terms, identifying pro-American and pro-Soviet forces and arguing that the outcome had important implications for the superpower balance. Typically, globalists saw the pro-American forces as more democratic than the pro-Soviet forces. Regionalists, in contrast, saw the labeling of local actors with these ideological terms superficial at best and questioned whether the outcome of the regional conflict made any concrete difference to Washington's or Moscow's power. They argued that inclinations to attach symbolic importance to poorly understood conflicts only made these conflicts more deadly and difficult to manage.

Related to the idea that regional conflicts had significant strategic importance was the belief that interference by the rival superpower was central to their initiation. Globalists accused the Soviets of stimulating or stoking conflict while regionalists argued that globalists not only misread local actors but also exaggerated the role Moscow played. The inclination to blame Moscow for developments contrary to American interests at times produced arguments that the KGB was secretly manipulating indigenous players. Meantime, in Moscow, U.S. imperialism and the CIA were blamed for most regional setbacks. If national liberation forces (read pro-Soviet or at least anti-U.S. forces) were in power, then Soviet voices insisted that any resistance to them was orchestrated in Washington. This was the standard Soviet line on Afghanistan and Nicaragua.

Because leaders of both superpowers saw regional conflicts in East-West terms, a third set of ideas was popular during the Cold War: the effectiveness of intervention. If the unrest was caused and stoked by the other superpower, then, if this interference could be stopped, the conflict could be managed. The logic led to a two-part strategy: (1) deploy military forces or provide military assistance to counter the opponent's supply, and (2) deliver economic assistance to win popular support for the local groups aligned with your country.

The ideas that regional conflicts were strategically important, caused by the other superpower, and dealt with effectively by military and economic intervention all changed as the Cold War ended. Tracing when they changed and how this affected policy sheds light on the causal importance these cognitive changes had on ending the Cold War. The change in these ideas came first in the United States. The Vietnam War had a substantial impact on Cold War thinking in America.[49] In the 1970s prominent Democrats like President Carter came to doubt all three main ideas about regional conflicts.[50] The revolution in Iran and the Soviet invasion of Afghanistan, along with Ronald Reagan's victory, however, brought back to office people who believed in all three Cold War ideas. This was especially true in the early Reagan years, when Secretary of State Alexander Haig and Ambassador to the UN Jeanne Kirkpatrick led the foreign policy team.

When George Shultz in 1982 replaced Haig, he empowered a less ideological view that supported negotiation in Southern African and Nicaragua but faced substantial opposition from members of the National Security Council. In 1986, the embarrassment surrounding the Iran-Contra scandal (the revelations that members of the NSC had sold arms to Iran and used the proceeds to supply the Contras) weakened the NSC. It also strengthened more moderate voices, like Schultz's. By the time James Baker became Secretary of State in 1989, the ideas guiding policy toward regional conflicts had changed substantially. Rather than tests of will and resolve, Baker saw regional conflicts as of peripheral strategic importance, although still carrying large domestic political significance. He concluded, therefore, that they were good places to test the concrete implications of Gorbachev's new thinking.[51]

On the Soviet side, ideas also changed in the 1980s. In the later 1970s, Soviet leaders welcomed a series of regional developments that were read as American loses, and when the revolution in Afghanistan spun out of control, Brezhnev ordered the invasion, evoking all three stereotypical ideas: (1) the conflict in Afghanistan was vital to Soviet security, and instability there invited U.S. mischief; (2) the instability was caused by U.S. and Pakistani subversion; and (3) military intervention to stop the foreign infiltration coupled with humanitarian assistance would secure the new Afghan regime and allow it to win over public support.[52] The logic made sense at that time to many Soviet leaders, including some who would later become prominent reformers.[53] Regional experts, however, were not consulted and report that they never shared these beliefs.[54] At the same time, academics writing about regional conflicts were introducing into the

expert literature in the Soviet Union ideas similar to those advanced by regionalists in the United States. They questioned the sensibility of applying standard
East versus West ideological labels to Third World movements and criticized the
need to fit these complex phenomena into predetermined scripts.[55]

As the war in Afghanistan dragged on, the ideas of the regionalists made their
way into the higher levels of Soviet decision making. Gorbachev, for example,
ordered a review of Afghan policy early in his tenure that brought some of these
ideas into focus.[56] Vladimir Kryuchkov, former head of the KGB, reports that
Gorbachev initially escalated the military effort but concluded fairly quickly
that this would not be successful and then began moving Soviet troops out of
combat roles and eventually out of the country.[57] By 1986 it was clear that Gorbachev recognized that the Afghan opposition had an important domestic base
and that domestic Afghan reconciliation and not just an end to U.S. and Pakistani interference was necessary. Gorbachev's government pressed Babrak
Kamal, the revolutionary Afghan leader, to search for a broader base and supported his replacement with Najib when he was not forthcoming. Having already shown that he was not wed to traditional ideas about the utility of military
force nor impressed by descriptions of the local scene that featured bipolar labels, in 1988 Gorbachev signaled that he also was not persuaded that protect-
ing Soviet control in Afghanistan was vital to Soviet security.[58] He, for instance,
ordered the withdrawal of Soviet troops and signed the Geneva Accords even
though America refused to stop the supply of arms to the mujahedeen, and Gorbachev continued to describe U.S. intentions in traditional Cold War terms. As
his description of U.S. neoglobalism and Washington's imperial ambition were
familiar, it is possible what had changed most were his ideas about the regional
scene.

In 1979 fear of an American comeback in the area in retaliation for the U.S.
loss in Iran may have contributed to Brezhnev's decision to intervene in Afghanistan.[59] By 1986 it seemed very unlikely Washington would be able to do
this. The Reagan administration's covert overtures to Iran had backfired, infuri-
ated Washington's Arab allies, and precipitated a U.S. tilt to Iraq. Islamic Iran
had demonstrated an independent posture, as had some of the Islamic groups in
Afghanistan. If Gorbachev accepted this construction of the scene, then he may
have concluded that it made sense to pull Soviet troops out of Afghanistan regardless of U.S. intentions. Regional factors constrained Washington's ability to
threaten Moscow from this direction.

In all three of the regional conflicts, U.S. and Soviet arms supplies were not
ended until late 1991 or even the beginning of 1992, when many people would
say the Cold War was already over. It is thus possible that the change in ideas
about regional conflicts was as much a product of the end of the Cold War as
its cause. As the bilateral contest relaxed, the importance attached to peripheral

commitments declined. Of course, this shift in perceptions and priorities provoked domestic debate and may have been motivated by domestic political considerations.

Domestic Politics

It is possible that leaders changed course on regional conflicts mostly to enhance their domestic support. For instance, involvement in these conflicts might have been a diversionary adventure intended to whip up nationalist sentiment at home and to win public support for the leader. Likewise, change in a leader's behavior may not reflect new ideas about a regional conflict, but simply be their attempt to use the conflict to outmaneuver their domestic competitors. In the three cases considered here, this sort of argument is not very persuasive.

Leaders rarely have only one reason for the decisions they make, and certainly gaining and retaining domestic power is an important consideration in most decisions. Reagan, for instance, spoke about regional conflicts as he sought office, pointing to them as indicators of declining American prestige and poor leadership by Carter. Yet even if pointing to these conflicts in the 1980 election won votes for Reagan, his policies toward Nicaragua and Angola won little public acclaim. There was no public outcry for intervention. To the contrary, the Reagan administration had to fight continually to win Congressional approval for U.S. action and typically lost in the cases of Nicaragua and Angola. Right-wing conservatives certainly favored Reagan's policies in these conflicts, but the president probably enjoyed their support regardless. Reagan and later Bush, rather than winning votes with their regional policies, were constrained by Congressional opposition. Bush and Baker, for instance, pointed to overwhelming Congressional opposition to explain why they would not send arms to the Contras.

Mikhail Gorbachev faced domestic constraints as well, and may have been motivated by domestic political considerations to pull back from regional conflicts.[60] The war in Afghanistan was unpopular, as were Soviet commitments elsewhere in the Third World. Public opinion, however, was not a major factor in securing domestic power for Gorbachev. Maintaining the elite coalition necessary to pursue domestic reform was the essential ingredient. Certainly, pulling back from these regional conflicts would please reform-minded elites, but these people were in Gorbachev's camp anyway and many of them owed their position and bureaucratic authority to Gorbachev. Changing course in regional conflicts would not save the Soviet Union much money, especially since it kept supplying arms and thus was not freeing up resources with which to pursue domestic reform.

Withdrawal had the potential to upset traditional communist leaders in the CPSU, the KGB, and the Red Army and to give them ammunition to use against Gorbachev. Gorbachev could win these traditional elites over not by compromising on regional conflicts but by defending Soviet credibility and sticking by local allies. Reportedly, there were important voices in the Kremlin that opposed leaving.[61] Even though top leaders in the KGB said they were confident that Najib's regime would survive without Soviet troops, the Army's leadership was not so certain.[62] And the Soviet officers in Afghanistan had to deal daily with their Afghan counterparts, who were not happy to see Soviet forces leave and who blamed Moscow for deserting them.

Although neither Reagan nor Gorbachev could ignore opponents in their systems, they both nevertheless enjoyed substantial latitude in policy making, Reagan due to his public popularity and Gorbachev due to this administrative role. Both leaders had power over key personnel appointments and injected into the bureaucratic establishment people who shared their ideological perspective. In this way, Gorbachev, Reagan, and later Bush as individual leaders became key elements in this turning point.

Leadership

Gorbachev initially used the office of General Secretary to staff the CPSU's International Department with people skeptical about the strategic value of regional conflicts and who knew the price Moscow paid in Washington for involvement in them. He then shifted authority to the International Department and away from the Foreign Ministry. In 1988 Gorbachev assumed the state presidency, while continuing as party leader. He then shifted foreign policy matters increasingly into the hands of the Foreign Ministry, which was thoroughly under the influence of the reformist Foreign Minister Eduard Shevardnadze.

Because both Gorbachev and Reagan were able to affect the ideas prevailing in their governmental bureaucracies through key personnel appoints, their importance to the story seems clear. Whether another leader would have empowered the same people or at least the same ideas is more controversial, but a good case can be made for the unique importance of Gorbachev. As Brown argued in his previous chapter, there were no other reform-minded leaders in competition for the office of Secretary General.

Interpretations that place emphasis on Reagan's individual role, typically assume that if a liberal had been president instead of Reagan, Moscow would not have compromised and/or that if a liberal president had made the deals Reagan and Bush did, they could not have persuaded the majority of Americans to follow them. In other words, just as "only Nixon" could open relations with communist China, only a conservative with Regan's hard-line credentials could convince the country to accept compromise outcomes. The first argument assumes that U.S. power compelled Soviet retreat, and we have already discussed the problems with that argument. The second argument revolves around an evaluation of the American political scene that requires further consideration.

In the 1970s President Carter tried to move away from all three of the traditional ideas that transformed regional conflicts into Cold War contests. In the end he was not successful. His failure can be attributed to a number of factors, one of which might be that he was not sufficiently conservative and therefore unable to instill confidence in the public. Carter was able of course to lead the country out of Cold War interpretations of most regional conflicts until the Iranian hostage crisis and Moscow's invasion of Afghanistan. If the Iranian revolution had not occurred and Moscow had not invaded Afghanistan, then Carter might have been able to continue to persuade the country to change traditional ideas about regional conflicts.

It may seem too farfetched a counterfactual to remove the Iranian revolution and the Afghan crisis from the story. The key question, however, is whether a liberal president could have persuaded the country to abandon the Cold War. To answer this question we need to take into account what was happening in the world outside the United States. Carter faced a difficult external environment, as did Reagan until Gorbachev took power. With the arrival of Mikhail Gorbachev things began to crack loose, starting with his decision to withdraw forces from Afghanistan. Had President Carter interacted with Gorbachev and been able to point to the Soviet abandonment of Eastern Europe and to the reunification of Germany, he also might have been able to persuade the public that the Cold War was ending. It is worth noting in this regard that two of the three conflicts studied here continued for the next decade and others erupted in the former Yugoslavia, while in the United States a liberal President was in office, who unlike Carter had no military experience and came from the liberal, not conservative, wing of the Democratic party. In this context, nonetheless, there was not a return to the Cold War, these regional conflicts were not seen in bipolar terms, and the American public did not call for action or intervention.

There is no way to prove that the Soviet Union would have behaved the same way in these regional conflicts if a liberal had been in the White House. However, it is important to keep three points in mind. (1) Even though the Sovietologists at CIA expected Najib's regime in Afghanistan to collapse with the Soviet withdrawal, the KGB did not. The view that Najib might survive was shared by Jon Glassman, the senior U.S. foreign service officer in Kabul. Soviet military deliveries increased just to be sure. (2) In Angola the MPLA enjoyed steady Cuban and Soviet support and won the election and stayed in power. (3) In Nicaragua, the U.S. Congress had cut off arms to the Contras, which did not win the elections when they were held. Given this record, it is not clear why

Moscow would have behaved radically different in any of these cases with a liberal in the White House.

Perhaps if Shultz and later the Bush and Baker team had not replaced the far-right Republican leaders of the early Reagan years, then hard-liners in Moscow would have continued to demand escalation in these conflicts, but this is not an entirely persuasive argument either. The far-right in the United States preserved the open CIA pipelines to the AIG and UNITA well into 1991. At the same time, Gorbachev was pulling back from Eastern Europe. If traditional voices in Moscow could not save the Warsaw Pact, it is hard to see why they would be able to make the case for peripheral allies. Clearly, in Moscow ideas about the basic nature of the Cold War conflict were changing and the leadership of Mikhail Gorbachev was central.

Part 4: Conclusions

Power, ideas, domestic politics, and leaders all are parts of the story of this turning point. These causes are difficult in many ways to separate from one another. Ideas, for instance, need to be connected to leaders who have influence. Leaders constrained by domestic opponents cannot translate their ideas into policy. Power, of course, is associated partly with the policies leaders enact. In the regional conflicts discussed here, power did not compel change. There were no unilateral victories. Rather than compelling change, power in these conflicts produced stalemate. In this way, the provision of arms by the superpowers narrowed the options of the other side. They could not win by military force. This still left the parties with an array of options, ranging from persistence and hopes of winning by attrition to compromise and agreement. Power provided bargaining leverage but also provoked counterescalation. Without new ideas about the conflicts and the Cold War in general, it is unlikely the superpowers would have withdrawn simply because of the costs.

Ideas are critical to regional conflicts because so much of the strategic importance of these conflicts is constructed and dependent on ideas about the Cold War. These peripheral conflicts were important not because of the material value intrinsic to them but because of the symbolic and instrumental importance leaders attached to them. They were important because the Cold War was understood to be a global contest. The bipolar lens imposed a construction of the regional scene that transformed it into a theater of major global contest. As ideas about the global nature of the contest changed, the importance of the region disappeared. As ideas about the local scene became more complex and broke the constructed association with the East versus West global storyline, the importance attached to the region also declined rapidly.

Because the strategic importance of regional conflicts is constructed and not intrinsic to the region and because the image of these conflicts among many leaders in Moscow and Washington were so simplified and poorly connected to facts on the ground, it seems that ideas had an unusually important role in explaining this turning point. The early agreements that might be associated with battlefield stalemate did not lead to superpower withdrawal. Once the central Cold War was over, the importance of these conflicts collapsed for both superpowers. The regional conflicts continued in Afghanistan and Angola and in new places as well but without competitive interference from Moscow or Washington.

By the end of 1991 regional conflicts were still raging, but the strategic significance of these conflicts had changed dramatically. Few leaders in either Washington or Moscow saw these conflicts as central to national security. Few leaders on either side analyzed these conflicts in simple dichotomous terms as pitting "good guys" against "bad guys," and most leaders doubted that military intervention would lead to stable political solutions. The Cold War mindset had changed dramatically, and with this change the construction of the ongoing and new regional conflicts was transformed. Unfortunately, although the superpowers ended their Cold War, they did not resolve the regional conflicts, leaving the local combatants still deeply divided and heavily armed.

Notes

1. James A. Baker III, with Thomas M. DeFrank, *The Politics of Diplomacy: Revolution, War and Peace, 1989–1992* (New York: G. P. Putnam's Sons, 1995), pp. 71–74.
2. Interview with Dennis Ross, October 1999.
3. On symbolic nature of regional conflicts see Robert Jervis, *The Meaning of the Nuclear Revolution: Statecraft and the Prospects of Armageddon* (Ithaca, NY: Cornell University Press, 1989), pp. 174–225, and *Dominoes and Bandwagons: Strategic Beliefs and Great Power Competition in the Eurasian Rimland,* eds. Robert Jervis and Jack Snyder (New York: Oxford University Press, 1991).
4. John Marcum, *The Angolan Revolution, Volume 2: Exile Politics and Guerilla Warfare, 1962–1976* (Cambridge, MA: MIT Press, 1978).
5. See Barnett R. Rubin, *The Fragmentation of Afghanistan: State Formation & Collapse in the International System* (New Haven, CT: Yale University Press, 1995), pp. 111–21.
6. See Raymond Garthoff, *Detente and Confrontation: American-Soviet Relations from Nixon to Reagan* (Washington, D.C., 1985), pp. 887–965. Also see Andrew Bennett, *Condemned to Repetition? The Rise, Fall, and Reprise of Soviet-Russian Interventionism, 1973–1996* (Cambridge, MA: MIT Press, 1999).
7. See Charles Kupchan, *The Persian Gulf and the West: The Dilemmas of Security* (Boston: Allen & Unwin, 1987), pp. 68–125. Zbigniew Brzezinski, *Power and Principle: Memoirs of the National Security Advisor 1977–1981* (New York: Farrar, Straus, Giroux, 1983), pp. 426–69.
8. Martha Cottam, *Images and Intervention: U.S. Policies in Latin America* (Pittsburgh: University of Pittsburgh Press, 1994), p. 89–101.
9. Robert Pastor, *Whirpool: U.S. Foreign Policy toward Latin America and the Caribbean* (Princeton, NJ: Princeton University Press, 1992), pp. 42–64.

10. Anatolii Chernyaev reports that Gorbachev persuaded the Politburo to that withdrawal from Afghanistan as early as October 17, 1985. See Bennett op. cit., p. 289 citing Chernyaev, *Shest' Let s Gorbachevym, po dnevnikovym zapisyam* (Moscow: Kultura, 1993), pp. 57–58.

11. Diego Cordovez and Selig Harrison, *Out of Afghanistan: The Inside Story of the Soviet Withdrawal* op. cit., pp. 201–09. Also see Riaz M. Khan, *Untying the Afghan Knot: Negotiating Soviet Withdrawal* (Durham, NC: Duke University Press, 1991), pp. 65–66.

12. Najibullah, "Consolidating the Revolution," *Pravda,* May 16, 1986, p. 5 (*FBIS-SOV–86–098),* pp. D1–2.

13. Cordovez and Harrison, *Out of Afghanistan,* pp. 53–4.

14. Cordovez and Harrison, *Out of Afghanistan,* p. 157.

15. Cordovez and Harrison, *Out of Afghanistan,* pp. 198–201.

16. See George Shultz, *Turmoil and Triumph: My Years as Secretary of State* (New York: Charles Scribner's Sons, 1993), pp. 1086–94.

17. Rubin, *The Fragmentation of Afghanistan,* pp. 247–80.

18. See W. Martin James III, *A Political History of the Civil War in Angola 1974–1990* (New Brunswick, NJ: Transaction Publishers, 1992), p. 240.

19. See Margaret Joan Anstee. *Orphan of the Cold War: The Inside Story of the Collapse of the Angolan Peace Process, 1992–93.* (New York: St. Martin's Press, 1996).

20. Garthoff, *Detente and Confrontation,* op. cit., 502–37.

21. Schultz, *Turmoil and Triumph,* op. cit., p. 1120.

22. Michael McFaul, "Rethinking the Reagan Doctrine," *International Security* 14 (3) (Winter 1989–90), pp. 99–135, pp. 106–07.

23. McFaul "Rethinking the Reagan Doctrine," op. cit., p. 123 and James III, W. Martin, *A Political History of the Civil War in Angola 1974–1990,* op. cit., p. 246.

24. Anstee, Margaret Joan, *Orphan of the Cold War,* op. cit.

25. Human Rights Watch, *Angola Unravels: The Rise and Fall of the Lusaka Peace Process* (New York: Human Rights Watch, 1999).

26. Pastor, Robert, *Whirlpool* op. cit., pp. 65–82.

27. See Alexander M. Haig, *Caveat: Realism, Reagan and Foreign Policy* (New York: Macmillan, 1984) and Constantine C. Menges, *Inside the National Security Council: The True Story of the Making and Unmaking of Reagan's Foreign Policy* (New York: Simon and Schuster, 1988).

28. See Shultz, *Turmoil and Triumph,* op. cit., pp. 426–27.

29. Ronald Reagan, "The State of the Union, Address Delivered before a Joint Session of the Congress," February 6, 1985, *Presidential Documents,* 21 (February 11, 1985), p. 145.

30. Shultz, *Turmoil and Triumph,* op. cit., pp. 958–59.

31. Baker III, with DeFrank, *The Politics of Diplomacy, 1989–1992* pp. 53–58.

32. Baker III, with DeFrank, *The Politics of Diplomacy, 1989–1992,* op. cit., p. 59.

33. Gary Prevost. " The FSLN in Opposition." In Vanessa Castro and Gary Prevost (eds.), *The 1990 Elections in Nicaragua and Their Aftermath.* (Lanham, MD: Rowman and Littlefield publishers, 1992), pp. 48–179.

34. Soviet deliveries to Afghanistan between 1986 and 1989 increased by 262 percent compared to deliveries made between 1982 and 1985. Richard Grimmett, *Trends in Conventional Arms Transfers to the Third World by Major Supplier, 1982–1989* (Washington, DC: Congressional Research Service, June 19, 1990), p. 60. Also see Bennett, *Condemned to Repetition,* op. cit., pp. 285.

35. Deputy Foreign Minister Anatolii Adamishin arrived in Luanda in March 1988 and reportedly told MPLA leaders that Moscow was tired of the costs and wanted the conflict to end. See James III, *A Political History of the Civil War in Angola,* p. 227.

36. Between 1985 and 1989 the flow of Soviet military supply to Nicaragua increased. In 1984 it was $350 million, in 1985 $280 million, in 1986 $600 million, in 1987 $500

million, and in 1988 $525 million. Jan S. Adams, *A Foreign Policy in Transition: Moscow's Retreat from Central America and the Caribbean, 1985–1992* (Durham, NC: Duke University Press, 1992), p. 111.

37. Shultz, *Turmoil and Triumph,* op. cit., p. 960.
38. Cordovez and Harrison, *Out of Afghanistan,* pp. 198–201.
39. Cordovez and Harrison, *Out of Afghanistan,* pp. 198–200, 247–52. First Deputy USSR Foreign Minister Vadim Perfilyev announced Moscow's readiness to counter American military aid by sending MIG 29 and other highly advanced weapons to Afghanistan. TASS, June 7, 1989 *(FBIS-SOV–89–109),* p. 12.
40. U.S. Arms Control and Disarmament Agency, *World Military Expenditures and Arms Transfers, 1989* (Washington, DC: U.S. Government Printing Office, October 1990), p. 101.
41. Shultz, *Turmoil and Triumph,* op. cit., p. 961.
42. Cordovez and Harrison, *Out of Afghanistan,* pp. 187–200.
43. Interview with Vladimir Kyuchkov, Moscow 1999.
44. For a flavor of the Soviet thinking on continued support, see CPSU CC Politburo Decision of January 24, 1989, with attached Report of January 23, 1989, in *Cold War International History Project Bulletin* 8–9 (Winter 1996/1997), pp. 181–84.
45. For evidence that Soviet leaders understood this point about their policy, see Anatolii Chernyaev, "Ideas for Gorbachev's Speech," December 17, 1987, in *Understanding the Cold War: Reagan/Gorbachev Years,* A Briefing Book for Oral History Conference, Brown University, May 7–10, 1998.
46. John Gaddis, *Strategies of Containment: A Critical Appraisal of Postwar American National Security Policy* (Oxford: Oxford University Press, 1982).
47. See Robert Jervis, The Meaning of the Nuclear Revolution: Statecraft and the Prospects of Armageddon (Ithaca, NY: Cornell University Press, 1989), pp. 174–225 and Robert Jervis, "Domino Beliefs and Strategic Behavior," in Jervis and Snyder (eds.), *Dominoes and Bandwagons,* pp. 20–50.
48. For a review of the thinking that led to the Soviet involvement in Angola, see Odd Arne Westad, "Moscow and the Angolan Crisis, 1974–1976: A New Pattern of Intervention," in *Cold War International History Project Bulletin,* 8–9 (Winter 1996/1997), pp. 21–32.
49. Ole Holsti and James Rosenau, *American Leadership in World Affairs: Vietnam and the Breakdown of Consensus* (Boston: Allen and Unwin, 1984).
50. See President James Carter, "A Foreign Policy Based on America's Essential Character (address made at the commencement exercises of Notre Dame University, South Bend, Ind., May 22, 1977), *Department of State Bulletin* (June 13, 1977), pp. 621–25. Also see Jerel Rosati, *The Carter Administration's Quest for Global Community: Beliefs and Their Impact on Behavior* (Columbia: University of South Carolina Press, 1991).
51. Baker III, with DeFrank, *The Politics of Diplomacy,* pp. 71–74.
52. See David Welch and Odd Arne Westad (eds.), *The Intervention in Afghanistan and the Fall of Detente,* Nobel Symposium 95, September 17–20, 1995 (Oslo: The Norwegian Nobel Institute, 1996). Also see Richard Herrmann, "The Empirical Challenge of the Cognitive Revolution: A Strategy for Drawing Inferences About Perceptions," *International Studies Quarterly* 32 (1988), pp. 175–203.
53. See, for instance, A. Bovin, "Afghanistan: A Difficult Decade," *Izvestiya,* Dec. 23, 1988, 5 *(FBIS-SOV–88–247),* pp. 24–26.
54. Yu. V. Gankovskiy, "A Lesson Worth Learning. War in Afghanistan Through a Historian's Eyes," *Izvestiya,* May 5, 1989, 5 *(FBIS-SOV–89–089).*
55. For a review of these developments, see Jerry Hough, *The Struggle for the Third World: Soviet Debates and American Options* (Washington, DC: Brookings Institution, 1986).
56. Gorbachev reported in late 1986 that a basic course to leave Afghanistan had been set in mid-1985. See CPSU CC Politburo transcript (excerpt), November 13, 1986, in *Cold War International History Project Bulletin,* 8–9 (Winter 1996/1997), pp. 178–81.

57. Bennett, *Condemned to Repetition?* op. cit., p. 262.

58. See Sarah Mendelson, *Changing Course: Ideas, Politics, and the Soviet Withdrawal from Afghanistan* (Princeton, NJ: Princeton University Press, 1998). Also see Bennett, *Condemned to Repetition?* op. cit., pp. 247–94.

59. For insight into Soviet thinking at the time of the intervention, see "The Soviet Union and Afghanistan, 1978–1989: Documents from the Russian and East German Archives," *Cold War International History Project Bulletin* 8–9 (Winter 1996/1997), pp. 133–78. Also see Welch and Westad, *The Intervention in Afghanistan and the Fall of Detente.*

60. For a strong argument that domestic politics played a key role, see Mendelson, *Changing Course*

61. Yazov, Dmitri, Statement at International Oral History Conference, "The Crash of the Bipolar World: The Soviet Factor" (1988–1991), Moscow, June 21–22. Transcript Tape 6, p. 34–35 and Tape 7, p. 1.

62. Vladimir Kryuchkov, Statement at International Oral History Conference, "The Crash of the Bipolar World: The Soviet Factor" (1988–1991), Moscow, June 21–22. Transcript Tape 6, page 28.

Chapter 4

Turning Points in Arms Control

Matthew Evangelista

Introduction

A main cause of the Cold War was a Western perception of a Soviet military threat at the end of World War II. Concerns were initially focused on areas contingent to the Soviet Union, particularly in Europe, where the Red Army had defeated the forces of Nazi Germany and occupied the territories of neighboring countries in Eastern Europe. Later, following the first test of a Soviet atomic bomb in 1949, the threat of a Soviet nuclear attack against the United States and its allies began to loom large in Western fears. Symmetrically, a key factor in ending the Cold War was the Soviet effort, launched by Mikhail Gorbachev, to reduce such fears of Soviet military aggression. The effort consisted of new initiatives in the realm of arms control and unilateral reductions of Soviet military capability. Some of these actions constituted significant turning points because they represented major departures from past practice and policies that would be difficult to reverse.

This chapter focuses on four key turning points that contributed to the end of the Cold War and the U.S.-Soviet arms race: (1) the Soviet unilateral moratorium on nuclear tests, initiated in 1985, and the subsequent provisions for on-site seismic monitoring by foreign scientists; (2) the Treaty on Intermediate-Range Nuclear Forces (INF) of 1987, with its removal of entire categories of nuclear weapons from Europe and intrusive measures of verification; (3) the unilateral reduction and restructuring of Soviet conventional forces, announced by Gorbachev in December 1988, and the concomitant pledge to allow political "freedom of choice" for the member countries of the Soviet bloc; and (4) the substantial reduction in U.S. and Soviet strategic nuclear forces represented by the 1991 START Treaty, and carried out despite the challenge posed by the U.S. Strategic Defense Initiative.

In examining these four turning points, I find that the material factors—particularly military and economic—associated with realist theories provide a general context for understanding what happened. To understand the sources and nature of Soviet policy initiatives, however, we must look to the ideas promoted by Soviet reformers and their transnational allies and the general worldviews and values of Soviet leaders. The Soviet initiatives should be understood in their domestic political context, but, perhaps surprisingly, domestic politics per se does not appear to have played a major role in shaping the policies that helped end the Cold War. This is not because there was a general consensus in the Soviet leadership on the nature of the foreign policy predicament and how to deal with it, as some have argued.[1] Archival documents, memoirs, and interviews reveal a wide range of perceptions of the situation and proposals for dealing with it. The Soviet domestic political *structure,* however—particularly the centralization of authority in the top leader of the Communist Party—favored the perceptions and proposals of Gorbachev and his reformist allies over those of their opponents. Understanding the sources of the reformers' views helps us understand why the Cold War ended when and as it did.

To check the plausibility of an account that emphasizes the perceptions, ideas, and policy proposals of Gorbachev and his allies, I suggest counterfactual thought experiments, with comparison of the present cases to similar ones during different leadership periods and considerations of changes in timing and substance to the initiatives that Gorbachev actually put forward. Such an exercise provides a better understanding of the interaction between individual leaders, the ideas promoted by various policy entrepreneurs, and the domestic political context.

The Unilateral Test Moratorium and On-Site Monitoring

In July 1985, the Soviet Union announced a unilateral halt of its testing of nuclear weapons to begin on August 6. The initiative represented nothing particularly new in Soviet policy, and the propagandistic element of starting the moratorium on the fortieth anniversary of the U.S. atomic bombing of Hiroshima was well within the standard Soviet diplomatic repertoire. Yet this initiative marked the beginning of a turning point. The Soviet unilateral test moratorium continued for 19 months without U.S. reciprocation, making the point (especially to Soviet domestic critics) that it was not necessary for the USSR to keep pace with the United States in every dimension of their security competition.

By deliberately deciding not to match the United States in its nuclear test program, Gorbachev was challenging the sacrosanct concept of "parity." For many in the Soviet armed forces, maintenance of parity with the United States was already a second- or third-best policy. Traditionally they would have preferred the pursuit of military superiority or what they called "equal security"—that is, matching not only U.S. capabilities but also those of China and U.S. allies in NATO.[2] Gorbachev's declaration that the Soviet Union no longer needed even to maintain parity with the United States did not go unchallenged. As Oleg Baklanov, the Central Committee secretary in charge of the military-industrial sector, recalled in an interview,

> On our own initiative, on a quarterly basis or more frequently, we asked Gorbachev to meet us so that we could express our views with regard to all elements of this unjustified unilateral action, whatever it's called—disarmament, surrender, or retreat from parity. What could we get in exchange for parity? We could only lose. Without receiving anything we yielded our positions one after another. We told Gorbachev about all this, but he would just answer, "Why are you looking at the West through a gun port? Take off your blinders!"[3]

Even when Gorbachev, under pressure from representatives of the armed forces and nuclear-weapons industry, ended the moratorium, he did not allow resumption of Soviet nuclear testing at anything like the previous rate. Gorbachev clearly hoped that the test moratorium would contribute to ending the nuclear arms race. When U.S. resistance thwarted that goal, he still sought to use the initiative to set a precedent. The Soviet Union would not match every U.S. step in the arms race.

More important than setting a precedent for the new policy idea of "reasonable security" (a less demanding standard than either parity or equal security), the test ban provided an opportunity for the first on-site monitoring of a Soviet arms control initiative. The proposal to install seismic monitoring equipment on Soviet soil to verify the moratorium arose from informal discussions among U.S. and Soviet scientists during 1985. The U.S. side of the project was run by a nongovernmental organization called the Natural Resources Defense Council. Soviet participation was brokered by Evgenii Velikhov, a Vice President of the USSR Academy of Sciences and an informal adviser to Gorbachev. In approving measures for on-site verification, Gorbachev bypassed the Foreign Ministry. Many observers, including former Soviet officials, tend not to recognize this precedent-setting quality of the test moratorium.[4]

The NRDC project did not fully resolve the internal Soviet debate on the merits of on-site verification. On a related issue, Gorbachev faced opposition from Marshal Sergei Akhromeev, chief of the general staff, to the provisions of the Stockholm agreement of September 1986 that allowed for challenge inspections and overflight of Soviet territory to verify compliance with the

confidence-building measures of that accord. The intrusive verification provisions of the subsequent INF Treaty engendered even more concern within
the Soviet security community. But by allowing NRDC involvement in seismic verification, Gorbachev had made the point that secrecy was more harm-
ful to Soviet security than transparency and he had backed it up by allowing
foreigners access to sensitive Soviet sites to set up their monitoring equipment. The precedent was important for the success of his subsequent arms
control initiatives.

Explaining the Moratorium

Realist accounts of the test moratorium could take a number of forms. The most
plausible version would point to the impetus for the initiative provided by the
Strategic Defense Initiative (SDI), a program to develop a U.S. antiballistic missile system, announced by President Ronald Reagan in March 1983. Clearly the
Soviet side sought to forestall development of U.S. strategic defenses by securing a bilateral moratorium on nuclear tests. The SDI program at that point en-
visioned nuclear-pumped lasers shooting Soviet missiles out of the sky. Despite
the antinuclear tenor of Reagan's remarks about the program, its success would
depend on extensive testing and use of nuclear explosions. A bilateral halt would
provide a setback to the SDI program, which would be worth whatever degra-
dation of Soviet nuclear technology would be entailed.

A less plausible explanation, compatible with some variants of realism, would
view the Soviet initiative as a response to U.S. "negotiation from strength"—one
of Ronald Reagan's favorite slogans, and a longstanding U.S. approach to arms
control dating back at least to the Eisenhower administration. In fact, however,
it is difficult to argue that the United States was pursuing a policy of negotiation from strength that in turn induced Soviet restraint in the form of a test
moratorium. On the contrary, the United States had withdrawn from negotiations with the USSR on a comprehensive test ban in 1982, and rejected the idea
of a complete halt to testing as anything but a very long-term goal. The United
States was not negotiating from strength, because it was not negotiating at all.
The Soviet initiative put the U.S. government in an awkward position because
it thrust the comprehensive test ban back onto the arms control agenda.

The decision to launch the unilateral moratorium did not apparently involve
much domestic political debate—not least because diplomats and military leaders viewed it, at least at first, mainly as a propaganda gesture. The fact that the
Soviet side extended the moratorium several times beyond the original period,
even in the face of U.S. refusal to go along, did elicit complaints within the military and nuclear-weapons communities, and even among some foreign policy
traditionalists, such as first deputy foreign minister Georgii Kornienko.[5] But do-

mestic politics did not play a prominent role in this initiative. Allowing foreigners to set up seismic monitoring equipment near the Soviet nuclear test ranges was a more controversial decision, but one taken within such a small group that it does not make much sense to speak of domestic politics as an important influence on the decision.

What if Gorbachev had not pursued the unilateral moratorium? The initiative served as an important focal point for Western peace movements and for Soviet reformers alike. In its absence perhaps some other initiative would have played the same role and not much else would have changed. On the other hand, the test moratorium exhibited features that made it an especially valuable opening wedge of Gorbachev's disarmament offensive—particularly in dealing with potential domestic opposition to his broader security reforms. A halt in testing would not in the near term affect the Soviet Union's core security, so criticism from the armed forces could be deflected for some time. The technical aspects of nuclear testing and monitoring a test ban invited participation by reform-minded scientists and their Western counterparts—an important Gorbachev constituency. Without their success in influencing Soviet policy on the test ban the scientists might not have been emboldened to pursue more ambitious security-policy reforms, including ones that more obviously challenged the prerogatives of the military authorities.

Finally, the acceptance of on-site inspections of arms control treaties might have been harder to achieve, without the precedent of the NRDC project. If Gorbachev could make the case that on-site monitoring by foreign specialists served Soviet interests even in the case of a unilateral initiative, it would be that much easier to advocate such measures for a bilateral treaty that imposed restraints on both sides. The negotiation of measures of verification for the subsequent nuclear-arms treaties would have been rendered much more difficult in the absence of foreign monitoring of the test moratorium.

The Treaty on Intermediate-Range Nuclear Forces

The Treaty on Intermediate-Range Nuclear Forces (INF), signed in Washington in December 1987, was a key turning point in arms control for two reasons. First, it entailed a highly disproportionate reduction in Soviet missiles—something that Soviet leaders before Gorbachev would never countenance, given their agreement with the military-industrial leadership on the need to maintain "parity" with the United States and "equal security" with all the other Soviet adversaries. Second, the Soviet side essentially accepted the U.S. "zero option" position, requiring outright destruction of all of the missiles of a certain class, including current-generation models, such as the SS–20. The treaty provided for extensive, intrusive verification provisions, including observation of the actual destruction of the weapons. Thus the INF Treaty easily meets the "difficult-to-undo" criterion for a turning point.

Explaining the INF Treaty

At first blush, the INF Treaty constitutes a strong case for material factors and a negotiation-from-strength argument. Although the Soviet leaders had for years favored negotiations on intermediate forces as a follow-on and complement to the strategic-arms treaties, they had been reluctant to make more than token gestures of restraint (in limiting deployment of SS–20 missiles, for example) to signal their interest. Only following the NATO deployment of new U.S. Pershing II and cruise missiles in the autumn of 1983 did the Soviet side negotiate seriously. So goes the standard story. It usually includes some reference to the confidence that Soviet leaders held in Moscow-directed European peace movements to block the deployment of the U.S. missiles. When peace activists failed to stop the deployment, Moscow saw no choice but to capitulate to U.S. terms.

Evidence from the archives, memoirs, and oral history is not as extensive as one would like on the question of Soviet views and motivations regarding the INF debate. There is enough, however, to cast doubt on the standard story. Of particular interest is a declassified transcript of a Politburo meeting held on May 31, 1983.[6] The meeting was intended to determine the appropriate reaction to the planned deployment of new U.S. cruise and Pershing missiles in Europe later that year. The scheduled deployment of the missiles was months away, and European peace activists were regularly organizing mass demonstrations against them. Nevertheless, every member of the Politburo who participated in the discussion voiced a firm conviction that the missiles would be deployed despite the protests. This fact undermines arguments, common at the time and since, that the Soviet side was counting on the peace movement to prevent the deployment and only got serious about arms control once the weapons were in place.

It is true that the Politburo in the early 1980s had trouble advancing arms control proposals that could lead to an agreement. But the problem lay mainly in a failure of imagination and excessive caution, not in any sense of optimism that the Reagan buildup could be halted without Soviet concessions. Even when they assumed the U.S. missile deployment as a fait accompli, for example, the Soviet leaders could hardly think of anything worth changing in their approach to arms control. General Secretary Iurii Andropov, chairing the session, asked early on whether there was a point in even continuing any arms negotiations with the United States after the deployment. (In the event, the Soviets broke off all negotiations for over a year.) Foreign Minister Andrei Gromyko thought that it would not be useful to continue them in the current form. "It's necessary to introduce something fresher," he ventured. But the best he could come up with was a proposal to unite the talks on intermediate-range nuclear forces (including Pershing II, cruise, and Soviet SS–20 missiles) with the talks on strategic nuclear weapons ("and tactical nuclear weapons," added Andropov). Gromyko offered no changes in the Soviet negotiating position, let alone unilateral reductions of the sort that Gorbachev would later carry out.[7]

Defense Minister Dmitrii Ustinov flatly declared that "everything that we are doing in relation to defense we should continue doing. All of the missiles that we've planned should be delivered, all of the airplanes put in those places where we've designated." So much for a conciliatory response to "peace through strength." Ustinov did, however, make a suggestion for arms control. The exchange that followed between Ustinov and Gromyko indicates just how out of touch some of the leaders responsible for Soviet security policy were. Ustinov started by suggesting that the Soviet Union propose that both sides reduce their missiles by 50 percent.

> *Gromyko:* "Reduce what?" *Ustinov:* "We could reduce all the missiles." *Gromyko:* "We have proposed that." *Ustinov:* "Yes, proposed, but we have to make the proposal again."

That was the extent of the discussion on arms control.[8]

Not a great deal had changed in the realm of material factors (economic conditions or the military balance) between 1983, when the U.S. missiles were deployed, and 1986, when Moscow made a series of concessions culminating in acceptance of the zero option: cancellation of the new U.S. missile deployment in return for destruction of all existing Soviet intermediate forces. The main difference was a change in the top Soviet leadership—with Gorbachev as General Secretary and his close ally Eduard Shevardnadze replacing Andrei Gromyko as Foreign Minister.

A realist perspective might argue that Gorbachev and Shevardnadze had better information about the state of the Soviet economy or the degree of U.S. resolve than their predecessors possessed, and that this clearer recognition of material forces informed their policy decisions. Some realists have also argued that as skeptics of the Gorbachev concessions came to understand better the true economic situation, they came to accept that there was no alternative to the Gorbachev policy. The first part of the claim seems plausible, that some Soviet officials would have better information than others. N. S. Leonov, a high official in the KGB during the Gorbachev years, suggested, for example, that "the people from the Military Industrial Complex or its representatives didn't take economics into account at all. They thought that our resources were unlimited. As if they had not been informed as to the country's real situation." But even with more accurate information, Leonov continued to oppose the conciliatory line favored by Gorbachev and Shevardnadze: "We did not favor the Military Industrial Complex or the military leaders who favored preserving our entire arsenal of weapons and demonstrated an uncompromising position on all issues. But we never shared the views of the foreign ministry."[9]

Certainly Gorbachev and his allies were less sanguine than the Brezhnev-era leaders about the impact of military spending and a confrontational foreign policy on Soviet economic well-being. But that was more a question of values than of information. Compared to the previous leadership cohort, Gorbachev and his allies simply held a different view of the world and the USSR's role in it, and a different set of priorities for Soviet domestic development.[10] This is essentially what distinguished Gorbachev and the reformers from the hard-line skeptics—not a difference in information, but in values and priorities.

Consider, for example the views of Oleg Baklanov, the Central Committee secretary in charge of the military-industrial sector. Despite Leonov's claims, Baklanov was someone in a position to know the true dimensions of Soviet military spending and capabilities, even if he remained complacent about their effects on Soviet society and international standing. When asked in 1999 to "comment on the point of view according to which in the mid-80s the Soviet Union exceeded all reasonable limits on military spending," he replied, "that's completely untrue. That's a propaganda maneuver on the part of those who brought about our ruin." Baklanov's response is consistent with the position he took publicly at the time, for example, in November 1990 at an international conference in Moscow on conversion of the military industry to civilian production, when he presented figures on the Soviet military burden far lower than those of the civilian economists in attendance.[11]

Baklanov's views on military spending reflected his views on parity. When he was asked directly about the situation in the late 1980s, "In your opinion, should defense spending have been cut?" he replied as follows: "I would answer your question by saying that if the Americans cut defense spending, then we also had to make cuts." His interviewer pointed out that "the United States didn't make cuts." "Therefore," responded Baklanov, "we also shouldn't have made cuts. Everything should be identical."[12]

Given their disagreements with the interpretation of the situation and the values espoused by Gorbachev and his reformist colleagues, it is not surprising that Soviet hard-liners would also object to the policies associated with the "new thinking." Serious differences arose in the negotiation of the INF Treaty, in particular. Some of Shevardnadze's colleagues in the Foreign Ministry and the Central Committee's International Department charged him with unprofessionalism. Valentin Falin, a senior specialist on Germany and former Soviet ambassador to the Federal Republic, accused Shevardnadze of representing the "Capitulationist Line" in arms control negotiations and of exceeding his mandate.[13] The "veterans" of Soviet foreign policy reserve their harshest criticism for Shevardnadze's agreement to give up the SS–23 "Oka" missile, even though, according to Soviet specifications, it did not even fall within the range provisions of the treaty.[14] As Baklanov complained, "in 1987, for no reason at all, Gorbachev gave away a missile with a range of five hundred kilometers."[15] Marshal Sergei Akhromeev felt so betrayed by Gorbachev and Shevardnadze on the SS–23 issue that he nearly resigned his post as chief of the general staff.[16]

In the context of the new thinkers' vision of a united, nuclear-free "common European home," the question of which side, Soviet or American, achieved a temporary advantage in the petty wrangling over medium-range missiles seems trivial. The Cold War did not, however, end with the mutual dissolution of military blocs, as Shevardnadze and Gorbachev expected, but with the Eastern expansion of a still nuclear-capable NATO alliance—contrary to what Soviet officials took to be firm Western commitments not to enlarge the alliance and to forswear the further deployment of nuclear weapons.[17] Thus, even years after the end of the Cold War, the veteran opponents of the Gorbachev-Shevarndadze concessions remain bitter.

In retrospect, a number of former Soviet officials believe that the INF controversy could have been resolved much earlier with far fewer Soviet concessions, if the Soviet leadership under Leonid Brezhnev had shown a little more imagination and flexibility. Falin, for example, presents considerable evidence concerning the efforts that then West German Chancellor Helmut Schmidt made to persuade Brezhnev to show some restraint in deployment of the SS–20 missiles in the late 1970s.[18] Falin, Kornienko, and others believe that some minor concessions on Brezhnev's part might have undermined NATO support for the "counterdeployment" of Pershing and cruise missiles.[19] Such counterfactual reasoning produces a plausible alternative history,[20] but one that would not have constituted a turning point of any significance. It would have simply represented a return to the prior situation of a (somewhat less) heavily nuclear-armed Europe rather than a dramatic removal of an entire class of nuclear weapons from the continent.

We see, then, by comparing the actual history to the counterfactual one, that the nature of the top Soviet leadership, along with its ideas and worldview, were crucial for transforming the INF controversy into a turning point that contributed significantly to ending the Cold War. An INF Treaty codifying the status quo or status quo ante of the late 1970s would not have represented an important turning point.

Clearly it is unrealistic for the realists to assert that a consensus emerged among the Soviet leadership on how to respond to U.S. pressure, as more officials came to understand the true nature of the constraints facing the USSR. Even among the Soviet hard-liners, there were disagreements about the importance of particular military programs and how much to insist on retaining them. Falin, Kornienko, and like-minded colleagues sharply criticized the unilateral Soviet concessions that led to the INF Treaty, for example. But Oleg Baklanov, an even more prominent hawk and former head of the strategic missile–building ministry, had a different perspective on the INF controversy. As he recalled more than a decade later, "from the point of view of our strategic military position and our scientific and technological capabilities, you could say that the deployment of SS–20 missiles was not absolutely critical. Likewise, the later deployment of Pershing–II missiles on the part of the United States was not absolutely critical. It was really a matter of 'an eye for an eye.'" In Baklanov's view, "we should not have deployed SS–20 missiles in Europe after all. Our actions gave the Americans an excuse to escalate the situation."[21]

Yet despite Baklanov's judgment that neither the SS–20 nor the Pershing–II deployments were necessary, he opposed the INF Treaty because of its challenge to the principle of parity. He especially objected to the early Gorbachev-Shevardnadze concession that left the British and French nuclear forces out of the terms of the proposed treaty. "Suddenly the negotiators say that we aren't taking into consideration France and England," complained Baklanov. Contrary to widely held interpretations of Soviet policy making at the time, conservatives such as Baklanov did sometimes express their opposition openly. "When passions started flaring, and I made categorical objections and wouldn't sign the proper documents or would sign them with reservations, this caused a great hullabaloo. . . . However, I stuck to the point of view that the nuclear forces of France and Great Britain ought not be left out of parity considerations."[22]

Dmitrii Iazov, the Soviet Defense Minister, also harbored serious doubts about the INF Treaty. As he later complained to an interviewer, "we destroyed almost an entire army of missiles, in all over a thousand medium- and shorter-range missiles, that is, much more than the Americans did."[23]

How, then, did Gorbachev and Shevardnadze implement their policy over the objections of hawkish skeptics? In Iazov's case, he claims that it was a matter of bad timing: "I became minister of defense in 1987. So I played hardly any role at all. The process was already mature. Everything was prepared for the signing of the Intermediate Forces Treaty in December of 1987. I was appointed only in May of that year. But I couldn't just walk in and say: 'Stop! Let's turn back the clock!' I needed to get up to speed."[24]

Baklanov proposes a more general explanation, consistent with other accounts of Gorbachev's approach. In the domain of arms control, Gorbachev chose Lev Zaikov, a respected veteran of the military-industrial sector, to represent and placate the skeptics, and then made sure that reformist allies would overwhelm Zaikov's potential opposition.

In general, on this question Gorbachev acted in "Gorbachev style." He set up a Politburo commission, put Zaikov at the helm as padding, and did what he needed to do through Zaikov. In addition to Zaikov, Shevardnadze, the chief instigator of the senseless disarmament, formed part of the commission together with his negotiators. It was disgraceful that the talks with the Americans were led not by specialists, but by "negotiators," according to the terminology of the time. You see, they knew the language, the situation, and among them were even representatives at the deputy minister level who led the talks with the Americans. But the heads of defense ministries and specialists from institutes, leading academicians, were, in essence, kept away from the negotiation process.

Iazov, too, points to the importance of the Zaikov commission. When an interviewer asked, "Did you personally suggest to Gorbachev alternative solutions?" Iazov responded that "before approaching Gorbachev on this question, I had to get by Zaikov's commission." When the interviewer persisted, he elicited from Iazov a picture of the structure of domestic politics that inhibited opposition to the General Secretary's initiatives:

> *Interviewer:* But you could have gone straight to him, bypassing the commission.
> *Iazov:* That's what I did. In response to my information about the commission's decision, Gorbachev said: "Act in accordance with this decision." More often Zaikov would take the whole commission to Gorbachev and say: "Look, they're opposed." Gorbachev would become upset: "Why are you opposed? What do you want, nose to nose, bayonet to bayonet?"
> *Interviewer:* He meant you and Baklanov?
> *Iazov:* Yes. He said: "What are you? You have to look ahead!"
> *Interviewer:* And did you ask, in which direction?
> *Iazov:* At that time Gorbachev was general secretary.
> *Interviewer:* Did he use his authority to apply pressure?
> *Iazov:* It's not that he used his authority to apply pressure, but we had to use certain tact with him.

Leonov, the KGB official, reported a similar evaluation of Gorbachev's use of the Zaikov commission and the General Secretary's collusion with Foreign Minister Shevardnadze. The Foreign Minister, recalled Leonov, "very often ended discussions on the commission by saying things like: 'We did not reach an agreement. I will report to Gorbachev and we'll see what he says.' And after that the question was settled in typical Gorbachev style. Any system of checks, any fight lost all meaning. If you raised an objection, you were heard out, but afterward the completely opposite decision was made."[25]

Gorbachev deployed a number of such techniques for keeping his domestic opposition off balance, in both internal and foreign policy. In that respect it would not be correct to suggest that domestic politics played no role in the key turning points that ended the Cold War. Yet Soviet policies were not by and large the result of compromises and log-rolling between competing domestic political coalitions in the sense that we typically think of "domestic politics" as an explanation for policy outcomes. Most of the time Gorbachev manipulated the situation to get his way.[26] Thus, in the case of the INF Treaty, although there were persistent domestic differences on the understanding of the situation and the appropriate policy responses—contrary to realist interpretations—domestic politics per se did not play a major role in this case. Despite opposition, the top leadership of reformers grouped around Gorbachev managed to promote their new ideas of how to deal with the old problem of the nuclear arms race.

Unilateral Conventional-Force Reductions

Perhaps the key turning point in the realm of arms control—and, indeed, a major turning point for the end of the Cold War as a whole—came with Gorbachev's speech to the United Nations in December 1988. In it he announced a dramatic unilateral reduction in Soviet conventional forces and equipment and a commitment to allow political "freedom of choice" for the Soviet Union's allies in Eastern Europe. This initiative marked the end of the Cold War in Europe, as it rendered Soviet forces incapable of either a standing-start invasion of the West or a major intervention to maintain control of the "fraternal" allies of Eastern Europe. Even diehard skeptics of past Soviet "peace offensives" recognized that Gorbachev's plan represented a significant reduction in Soviet military capability, even if they did not fully grasp the implications for the Soviet alliance system.

Explaining the December 1988 Initiative

There is much to puzzle over when considering competing explanations for Gorbachev's initiative. Conventional forces were an expensive drain on the Soviet military budget and reducing them would serve obvious material ends. On the other hand, the demobilized troops and officers entering the labor force would put a strain on a reforming economy that was supposed to be shedding excess labor in favor of market efficiency. The role of a U.S. policy of negotiation from strength seems doubtful in this case. In conventional forces the West always credited the Soviet side with superiority in most major indices of military strength—particularly personnel, tanks and other armored vehicles, and artillery.

The West did arguably pose a challenge in one respect: the threat of a longer-term competition in advanced military technology. But here the Soviet security-policy elite was divided over the degree and nature of the threat, with some leading figures expressing considerable complacency about relative Soviet military-technical prowess. In any case, no prominent military leader sought to meet the challenge by counseling major unilateral reductions of the sort that Gorbachev announced in December 1988.[27] By the same token, Gorbachev and the other supporters of the unilateral reductions were not driven by the desire for a temporary "breathing space," in order to prepare to triumph in some future high-tech arms race. For them, reducing military tensions in Europe served another goal—the promotion of a new system of common security under which East-West political and economic relations would flourish.

Two key aspects of the December 1988 announcement reveal origins associated mainly with the realm of ideas. The first is Gorbachev's emphasis on the restructuring of conventional forces to emphasize their defensive orientation and reduce their offensive potential. The second is the commitment to political "freedom of choice" for the Warsaw Pact allies in East-Central Europe. The two issues are clearly linked, as Moscow had always imposed limits to the freedom of choice of its allies primarily through the threat or use of offensive military force.

The role of ideas in generating the December 1988 announcement suggests that Gorbachev's initiative was not simply the capitulation of a declining power to the demands of its stronger adversary. The ideas behind "nonoffensive defense" were not endorsed by the United States or NATO. They were never part of the West's negotiating position on conventional forces, and indeed NATO itself had during the 1980s increasingly adopted a more offensive posture known under the rubrics AirLand (*sic*) Battle and Follow-On Forces Attack.[28] Nonoffensive defense was promoted mainly by the peace movement and peace research networks in Western Europe and their influence on the formulation of Soviet policy on conventional forces is apparent from a wide range of evidence.[29]

Nor was the idea of "freedom of choice" for Eastern Europe, although congenial to Western values, a main goal of NATO. The major European powers and the United States all seemed willing to grant the Soviet Union its sphere of influence while accepting the military reductions. So where did Gorbachev's ideological embrace of freedom of choice come from? The main sources appear to be: (1) his affinity for West European–style social democracy and Eurocommunism and their commitment to a democratic, parliamentary route to socialism; (2) his liberal advisers' longstanding contacts with reformers in Eastern Europe; and (3) his consequent (misplaced) confidence in reform communism as a model for Eastern Europe.[30]

In retrospect, the ideas and ideological underpinnings of Gorbachev's December 1988 speech seem somewhat naïve. His expectations—of a new European security regime made up of friendly reform-communist allies and NATO members who would transform their military alliance into a political club—

were quickly dashed. East European citizens overthrew their communist governments, reformist or otherwise, and NATO expanded eastward and fought a war against Serbia on Russia's doorstep and despite Moscow's protestations. Russia itself seemed hardly welcome as a member of the European community of states. If the outcome at this point seems compatible with theories of long-term geopolitical shifts in the balance of power, that should not obscure the key role that ideas and politics played in bringing about the peaceful Soviet withdrawal from Europe.

The political process by which Gorbachev's December 1988 initiative came about reflects a pattern that began with Gorbachev's announcement of the unilateral nuclear test moratorium, continued with his January 1986 speech proposing the total elimination of nuclear weapons by the year 2000, and was evident in the story of the INF Treaty: potential opponents were simply excluded from decision making. N. S. Leonov spoke of the reaction within the KGB to Gorbachev's January 1986 initiative:

we were shocked in 1986 by the sudden proposal to achieve a nuclear-free world by the year 2000. Neither the military nor we were asked about it. We immediately started calling our colleagues in the army. "Is this from your department? Was this proposal made on your initiative?" Their response was, "No, we don't know anything either. It wasn't our proposal." So the proposal was born in Staraia Ploshchad' [Old Square], the quarters that serve the general secretary of the Central Committee of the Soviet Union.[31]

Leonov lodged a similar complaint about the speech to the United Nations: "Announcements such as those on the non-use of force for preserving the socialist order in Eastern European countries or on reducing the armed forces by five hundred thousand people were usually made bilaterally under the seal of secrecy. They were not made publicly. But Gorbachev in his typical manner made this pronouncement at the U.N. It created an explosion!" His interviewer suggested that "for you and your colleagues this speech was unexpected." "Absolutely unexpected."[32]

The high command of the armed forces was also brought into the discussion at a very late stage. In the summer of 1987 Marshal Akhromeev and the new Defense Minister, Dmitrii Iazov sent Gorbachev a report outlining their views on Soviet policy toward Eastern Europe and European security. They included a request that he "examine along with the military the aggravation of the situation and the problems that had arisen." Gorbachev read the report and examined the situation, writes Akhromeev, "but without us, and, as I understood, that was no accident." Gorbachev's style was to address "the most significant military-political problems with the military step by step, without straining relations with them, where that was possible," but basically keeping them in the dark about his overall views. "Not once in my memory," wrote Akhromeev, "did M. S. Gorbachev thoroughly discuss with the military leadership the military-political situation in Europe and perspectives on its development during 1986–1988." Only "in relation to concrete decisions already taken did the military introduce proposals concerning the armed forces."[33]

Akhromeev suggests that Gorbachev knew what kind of reaction he would receive from the military if he forthrightly discussed his proposals for reductions, retrenchment, and restructuring. Gorbachev's policy would have been revealed as a radical break with "the entire understanding by the military leadership of the essence of the country's defense capability in Europe." Withdrawal from Eastern Europe meant giving up "that which had been won at a cost of enormous amounts of blood and millions of lives."[34] In an interview conducted four years after the marshal's death, his wife Tamara Vasil'evna summarized the sources of her husband's resistance to Gorbachev's reforms: "Sergei Fedorovich [Akhromeev] understood that Gorbachev's policy would lead to the breakup of the Warsaw Pact, the whole system of security in Europe. He considered his participation in the creation [of that system] his life's work. . . . Having left the General Staff, he couldn't work as Gorbachev's adviser for very long. He wrote several letters of resignation." At that point, Marshal Akhromeev ceased to influence the Soviet leader's views on European security. "Gorbachev was listening to other people."[35]

Of course Gorbachev needed the general staff to implement his proposed restructuring and reductions. As Akhromeev later explained, the military's proposals came only in response "to concrete decisions already taken" by Gorbachev and his allies.[36] Specifically, on November 9, 1988, the Soviet defense council, chaired by Gorbachev, instructed the defense ministry to work out a plan for the withdrawal of Soviet troops from Eastern Europe.[37] Thus the military's participation in planning the reductions came long after the foreign ministry and various transnational organizations had persuaded Gorbachev of the merits of a large-scale unilateral withdrawal, combined with a shift to a clearly defensive posture. Finally, armed with foreign ministry proposals and the general staff's implementation plan, Gorbachev was ready to seek formal approval from his fellow political leaders to launch his unilateral initiative, virtually at the last minute. Anatolii Dobrynin, former Soviet ambassador to the United States, captures well the flavor of the decision process: "Before going to the UN General Assembly in New York in 1988," he recalled, "Gorbachev urgently pushed through the Politburo a bold unilateral reduction of our armed forces by half a million men." Dobrynin's account is consistent with the recollections of Leonov, Iazov, Akhromeev, and others: "Gorbachev clearly strove to avoid Politburo guidelines and directives and sought a free hand in dealing with foreign heads of state. Ultimately, with Shevardnadze's help, Gorbachev reached his goal. In fact if not in form, he single-handedly devised the foreign policy of the country and implemented it as well."[38]

START and the SDI Connection

The Reagan administration's Strategic Defense Initiative (SDI) was a proposal for a space-based system of anti-missile defenses, dubbed "Star Wars" by its critics. Reagan's supporters view SDI as the linchpin in a strategy to end the Cold War and many of them—most notably National Security Adviser Robert McFarlane— explicitly credit the program with bringing down the Soviet Union.[39] An alternative interpretation would portray Star Wars as a major stumbling block on the road to improving U.S.-Soviet relations, an ill-considered program that threatened to undermine Mikhail Gorbachev's efforts to demilitarize Soviet society and international relations. This was certainly Gorbachev's own view, echoed by a range of Soviet participants in the SDI debates: from younger academic researchers (*institutchiki*) such as Aleksei Arbatov and Andrei Kokoshin to older foreign policy professionals such as Georgii Kornienko and Aleksandr Iakovlev, to the dissident physicist and human rights activist Andrei Sakharov.[40]

Undoubtedly Gorbachev and his allies viewed SDI as, at best, a hindrance to their reformist efforts overall. In the realm of arms control, SDI directly threatened the goal of nuclear disarmament. By the traditional logic of nuclear deterrence, the Soviet Union needed to maintain a force of nuclear weapons adequate to absorb a U.S. nuclear attack and still be able to threaten retaliation. The deployment by the United States of a defensive "shield," however rudimentary, would increase the requirements for Soviet offensive nuclear forces.

Reducing Soviet nuclear forces in the face of the SDI challenge was virtually unthinkable. Yet Gorbachev managed to negotiate a strategic arms reduction treaty (START I) with the United States while essentially finessing the Star Wars issue. His accomplishment marks a key turning point in the Cold War endgame because it removed SDI as a stumbling block to internal and external demilitarization and achieved the first significant reductions in the arsenals of strategic nuclear weapons of Russia and the United States.

Explaining the Role of Star Wars

How did he do it? Proponents of the negotiation-from-strength position would hold that Gorbachev was simply responding to a tough bargaining position on the part of the United States. Given the poor state of the Soviet economy, Gorbachev could afford neither to match SDI nor to maintain the expensive nuclear arsenal necessary to defeat it. His only alternative was to agree to nuclear reductions and hope that the United States would never use its Star Wars shield in combination with its offensive nuclear sword.

Undoubtedly Gorbachev did not relish the prospect of spending billions of rubles competing with the United States to build strategic defenses, especially given his commitment to improving the consumer economy. Playing up the Star Wars threat to Soviet economic reform had its drawbacks, however, because some leading officials refused to accept the argument. Gorbachev's Defense Minister, Dmitrii Iazov, for example, railed against the U.S. attempt "to attain military superiority over the USSR" and use "SDI to exhaust it economically." But, argued Iazov, such efforts were doomed to failure: "Only a blind person does not see that our possibilities to support a strong defense and simultaneously resolve social and other tasks have repeatedly grown."[41] Gorbachev feared that the Defense Ministry's willingness to spend money in a race for strategic defenses would undermine his program of domestic reforms.

Baklanov expressed a confidence in Soviet capabilities similar to Iazov's:

> I always told Gorbachev and the other leaders that the United States couldn't do any more than we could in space. And I explained why. By creating parity, we had amassed a potential industrial power that could resolve any technical issues. There is another aspect to this problem: we had spent tremendous amounts of money and created a powerful Military Industrial Complex, so it would simply have been foolish not to use it, both for the benefit of defense and for developing new technologies as a whole. You can't stop progress; the future would lie in conquering space and developing space technologies.[42]

Other top officials, such as Vladimir Kriuchkov, head of the KGB, were also rather sanguine about SDI. Speaking of his fellow intelligence agents, he told an interviewer in 1999, that "in the late '80s we were firmly convinced that there was no need to hurry in creating our own SDI, and that the United States wasn't going to build a global SDI system, because it realized such a measure was unsound." Moreover, he argued that "Gorbachev in general agreed with the evaluations of the KGB."[43]

Not all Soviet military officials favored development of strategic defenses in response to the U.S. program. Many of them had long since embraced the logic that underpinned the 1972 treaty limiting anti-ballistic missile (ABM) systems: it was cheaper "at the margin" to build offensive weapons to overwhelm a defense than it was to build a reliable ABM system. In fact, the most cost-effective countermeasure to the proposed American strategic defense system was the existing force of Soviet intercontinental ballistic missiles with multiple warheads. The argument that the Soviet Union needed to reduce its nuclear forces for economic reasons is false. The cheapest, most effective way for the USSR to beat

Star Wars was to do nothing—neither build its own defenses, nor reduce its existing offensive weapons.

Gorbachev did not choose this cost-effective route to security, however. His commitment to nuclear disarmament is not easily explained by rationalist arguments based on material factors. It has roots in his student days at Moscow University, when in June 1955 he met Jawaharlal Nehru, the Prime Minister of India, and the first proponent of a comprehensive nuclear test ban.[44] It was reinforced by his contacts with prominent Western supporters of disarmament such as Olof Palme of Sweden and West Germany's Willy Brandt and Egon Bahr; by his association with transnational organizations of scientists and physicians whose membership included Gorbachev's own science adviser and the head Kremlin physician.[45] Thus, the transnational diffusion of ideas and the politics of transnational coalitions played a key role in Gorbachev's approach to nuclear disarmament and SDI.

The gist of the solution to Gorbachev's Star Wars problem was put forward at a conference in Moscow in April 1985, just a month after Gorbachev came into office. Jeremy Stone, president of the Federation of American Scientists, and a leading transnational disarmament activist since the 1960s, made the case to an audience of 40 scientists:

> You people are saying that if we go ahead with Star Wars, there can be no disarmament. I agree, but you should turn it around. You should see that if both sides go ahead with disarmament, there can be no Star Wars. Disarmament in and of itself might be the answer to Star Wars. With offensive reductions underway, there would be no political support for Star Wars [in the United States]. On the other hand, if there are no offensive reductions in prospect, there will be all the more support for Star Wars. You need political restraints, not further legal assurances concerning the ABM treaty.[46]

It was an ingenious suggestion—not surprising from the person who two decades earlier launched the seemingly quixotic but ultimately successful campaign to persuade the Soviet Union to forsake defenses against nuclear attack in favor of an ABM treaty. Stone and his U.S. colleagues worked with Velikhov, Sakharov, and other prominent Soviet scientists and officials to bring Gorbachev around to this position.

Thus, the major strategic nuclear disarmament agreement that contributed to the end of the Cold War was not a response to Star Wars, as Robert McFarlane and others would have it. It was a goal that Soviet reformers pursued despite Star Wars. Their successful achievement of the START treaty, which entailed deep reductions in both sides' arsenals, then undermined the SDI program to such an extent that the prospect of a U.S. "space shield" faded into irrelevance. In 1990, the U.S. Congress passed legislation cutting the SDI budget by a quarter from the previous year and reorienting research away from any programs that would promote early deployment of a strategic defense system. Even the Clinton administration's efforts, a decade later, to promote a limited National Missile Defense, did not envision anything like the grandiose Star Wars system of the Reagan years. And even if, as seems likely, the current U.S. pursuit of strategic defenses slows or halts progress in nuclear disarmament, we are unlikely to see a return to the high levels of strategic nuclear weapons that characterized the late Cold War. Mikhail Gorbachev's ability to overcome the obstacles posed by SDI to achieve substantial nuclear disarmament thus fits well the definition of a Cold War turning point: unprecedented, significant, and difficult to undo.

What if Gorbachev had not been able to ignore SDI in his pursuit of strategic reductions? Because nuclear weapons were such a potent symbol of the Cold War and East-West conflict, it might have been more difficult for Western leaders and publics to recognize the end of the Cold War without some substantial reductions in nuclear arsenals. Given the extent to which Gorbachev and his advisers came to see an important link between the nuclear arms race and the perception of a Soviet conventional threat to Europe, a stalemate in the nuclear talks might have hindered pursuit of reform of the army as well.

What if a major strategic arms agreement had come earlier, say at the summit meeting in Rejkyavik in October 1986? It was there that Gorbachev and Reagan came close to an agreement to eliminate all of the offensive nuclear missiles on both sides. Only Gorbachev's insistence that Reagan drop his Star Wars plans—and Reagan's refusal to do so—seemed to stand in the way. What if Reagan had agreed to give up Star Wars? After all, the threat of offensive missile attack, which it was intended to meet, would be eliminated. One could imagine that an agreement on such widescale nuclear disarmament as early as the end of 1986 would have accelerated the process of rapprochement and brought the Cold War to an end all the sooner.

Perhaps more likely, however, is the prospect that such a dramatic initiative would have galvanized opposition, within the United States, within the NATO alliance, and within the Soviet Union. As it was, the Rejkyavik summit and its near achievement of a nuclear-missile disarmament led to outspoken criticism within the Reagan administration, from close allies such as Margaret Thatcher, and among Soviet security officials. Paradoxically, a too-early achievement of success in nuclear disarmament might have derailed much of the subsequent movement toward ending the Cold War.

The Role of Arms Control in the End of the Cold War

If the perceived threat of Soviet military aggression contributed to the onset and perpetuation of the Cold War, Gorbachev's initiatives in arms control and unilateral military restraint surely helped end it. The importance of the changes in Soviet security policy has been somewhat obscured, however, by the dramatic political transformations that followed in their wake: the peaceful liberation of Eastern Europe from communist rule, the demise of Soviet communism, and the disintegration of the USSR itself.

Russia and the Soviet successor states are no longer considered a military threat to the West, even though their economic and political instability raise concerns about security. When the North Atlantic Treaty Organization expanded to include former members of the Warsaw Pact, it did not do so to thwart a Russian military invasion. Even as relations between the West and Russia worsened—not least as a consequence of NATO's expansion and its war against Serbia—the prospect for a revival of the Cold War and an East-West arms race remained out of the question. Gorbachev's security-policy initiatives buried the Soviet military threat, making the revival of a militarized Cold War unlikely for decades to come.

Of course in the most literal sense one cannot have a "Soviet threat" without a Soviet Union. In that respect we might be tempted to view both the end of the Soviet military threat and the end of the Cold War as consequences of the end of the Soviet Union. This interpretation does not do justice to the history of the late 1980s. Most observers recognized that the Cold War was over well before the end of the decade. In the context of security policy the "turning point of turning points" came in December 1988 when Gorbachev announced the unilateral withdrawal of the most offensively oriented Soviet troops and weapons from Eastern Europe and renounced the "Brezhnev Doctrine" of military intervention to prop up pro-Soviet regimes. The new Soviet approach emphasized political "freedom of choice" (what one Soviet official termed the "Sinatra Doctrine," after the line in the famous song, "I did it my way").

The absence of the Soviet military threat, if not fully obvious when the anticommunist demonstrations began in Eastern Europe in autumn 1989, became apparent as Soviet authorities stood by and allowed the peaceful overthrow of communist regimes. Without the ideological transformation that led to Gorbachev's renunciation of force, and his public decision to reconfigure the Soviet army to comply with the new policy, the demonstrations in Eastern Europe—if they took place at all—would likely have resulted in bloodshed. Violent repression of peaceful demonstrators would have easily revived the image of a Soviet military threat, even if Gorbachev's other initiatives in nuclear arms control had still gone forward.

Instead of the spill-over effect that peaceful overthrow of East European communism had on the constituent republics of the Soviet Union, we might have seen a dampening effect on separatist tendencies there. The breakup of the USSR might have been forestalled or carried forth with considerable violence.

In that case the disintegration of the Soviet Union, resisted militarily by Moscow-based Russian authorities, would hardly have contributed to the peaceful end of the Cold War. The East-West conflict would have continued or even been transformed into something more dangerous. It was Gorbachev's decision to transform Soviet security policy through arms control and unilateral initiatives that made the peaceful end of the Cold War possible.

The realists' focus on material factors is difficult to gainsay when the topic is arms races and arms control. Weapons and military forces are the instruments of power politics. They are expensive and dangerous. Yet political and military leaders rarely agree on the nature of an external threat or the proper means to counter it. In the case of the Soviet Union during the Gorbachev years, we have witnessed a wide range of views among policymakers about the degree to which the United States and NATO Europe should be seen as implacable enemies and about the wisdom of pursuing unilateral initiatives of restraint in order to win their trust. Many of the ideas came from transnational networks that brought together Soviet reformers with Western proponents of arms control, disarmament, and human rights. Through his control of the domestic agenda and relying upon the authority of his position as top communist leader in an extremely hierarchical system, Mikhail Gorbachev was able to implement, without substantial domestic opposition, the ideas that brought the Cold War to an end.

Notes

1. This is the argument in Randall L. Schweller and William C. Wohlforth, "Power Test: Evaluating Realism in Response to the End of the Cold War," *Security Studies* 9 (3) (Spring 2000), pp. 60–107.
2. For a review of these terms, see David Holloway, *The Soviet Union and the Arms Race* (New Haven, CT: Yale University Press, 1982), esp. chaps. 3–4.
3. Transcript of interview with O. D. Baklanov, conducted by O. I. Skvortsov, Moscow, 1999.
4. The background to the NRDC initiative is detailed in Matthew Evangelista, *Unarmed Forces: The Transnational Movement to End the Cold War* (Ithaca, NY: Cornell University Press, 1999), chap. 13.
5. S. F. Akhromeev and G. M. Kornienko, *Glazami marshala i diplomata* [Through the eyes of a marshal and a diplomat] (Moscow: Mezhdunarodnye otnosheniia, 1992), pp. 56, 95–96; hereafter, *Glazami.*
6. The transcript is located in F. 89, op. 42, d. 53, Russian State Archive of Contemporary History (Rossiiskii gosudarstvennyi arkhiv noveishei istorii), the former Central Committee archive, Moscow.
7. Ibid., p. 5.
8. Ibid., p. 7.
9. Transcript of interview with N. S. Leonov, conducted by O. I. Skvortsov, Moscow, April 21, 1999.
10. The most comprehensive discussion of the origins of the new thinking among Gorbachev and his advisers is Robert D. English, *Russia and the Idea of the West: Gorbachev, Intellectuals, and the End of the Cold War* (New York: Columbia University Press, 2000).

11. From my notes from the conference held in Moscow, November 12–15, 1990. For background on "big Oleg," see Roald Sagdeev, *The Making of a Soviet Scientist* (New York: John Wiley and Sons, 1994).

12. Skvortsov interview with Baklanov.

13. Valentin Falin, *Politische Erinnerungen* [Political memoirs] (Munich: Droemer Knaur, 1993), pp. 476–77; Mikhail Gorbachev, "Kak eto bylo: K 10-letiiu ob'edineniia Germanii" [How it was: towards the tenth anniversary of the unification of Germany], *Nezavisimaia gazeta,* July 9, 1999 (electronic version).

14. G. M. Kornienko, *Kholodnaia voina: svidetel' stvo ee uchastnikia* [The Cold War: testimony of a participant] (Moscow: Mezhdunarodnye otnosheniia, 1992), pp. 251–56.

15. Baklanov interview with Skvortsov.

16. Akhromeev and Kornienko, *Glazami,* p. 109.

17. Falin, *Politische Erinnerungen,* pp. 493–97.

18. Falin, *Politische Erinnerungen,* pp. 274–83.

19. On this point, see also Kornienko, *Kholodnaia voina,* chap. 10.

20. There still, however, would have been strong domestic U.S. pressures for deploying something. On U.S. motives for deploying nuclear weapons in Europe, see Matthew Evangelista, "Case Studies and Theories of the Arms Race," *Bulletin of Peace Proposals* 17 (2) (June 1986).

21. Baklanov interview with Skvortsov.

22. Baklanov interview with Skvortsov.

23. Transcript of interview of Dmitrii Iazov by O. I. Skvortsov, Moscow, March 11, 1999.

24. Skvortsov interview with Iazov.

25. Transcript of interview with N. S. Leonov, conducted by O. I. Skvortsov, Moscow, April 21, 1999.

26. Matthew Evangelista, "Norms, Heresthetics, and the End of the Cold War," *Journal of Cold War Studies* 3 (1) (Winter 2001).

27. Evangelista, *Unarmed Forces,* chaps. 9 and 14, esp. pp. 291–305.

28. For an overview and critique of these strategies, see Matthew Evangelista, "Offense or Defense: A Tale of Two Commissions," *World Policy Journal* 1 (1) (Fall 1983); on the Soviet strategy, see Richard Ned Lebow, "The Soviet Offensive in Europe: The Schlieffen Plan Revisited?" *International Security* 9 (4) (Spring 1985).

29. For an extensive discussion, see Evangelista, *Unarmed Forces,* chaps. 9 and 14.

30. On the influence of the social democratic model, see Jacques Lévesque, *The Enigma of 1989: The USSR and the Liberation of Eastern Europe* (Berkeley: University of California Press, 1997); on his advisers' East European contacts, see A. S. Cherniaev, *Moia zhizn' i moe vremia* [My life and my time] (Moscow: Mezhdunarodnye otnosheniia, 1995) and Georgii Shakhnazarov, *Tsena svobody: Reformatsiia Gorbacheva glazami ego pomoshchnika* [The Price of Freedom: Gorbachev's reformation through the eyes of his assistant] on Gorbachev's sympathy for Eurocommunism and the Italian Communist Party in particular, see Antonio Rubbi, *Incontri con Gorbaciov: I colloqui di Natta e Occhetto con il leader sovietico* [Meetings with Gorbachev: The discussions of Natta and Occhetto with the Soviet leader] (Rome: Editori Riuniti, 1990).

31. Leonov interview with Skvortsov.

32. Leonov interview with Skvortsov.

33. Akhromeev and Kornienko, *Glazami,* pp. 69–71.

34. Ibid.

35. Tamara Vasil'evna Akhromeeva, "Ia nikogda ne poveriu, chto on ukhodil na smert'" *Sovershenno sekretno,* no. 7 (1995), pp. 16–17.

36. Akhromeev and Kornienko, *Glazami,* p. 65; Falin, *Politische Erinnerungen,* pp. 488–89. Akhromeeva, "Ia nikogda ne poveriu," pp. 16–17.

37. Minutes of the Politburo meeting of December 27, 1988, located in Fond 89, op. 42, doc. 24, Rossiiskii gosudarstvennyi arkhiv noveishei istorii, and published in *Istochnik*, nos. 5–6, 1993, 130–47, at 143.

38. Anatoly Dobrynin, *In Confidence: Moscow's Ambassador to Six Cold War Presidents* (New York: Times Books, 1995), p. 626.

39. For a later reiteration of this view from its main proponent, see Robert C. McFarlane "Missile Defense, Then and Now," *New York Times,* May 4, 2000.

40. For the relevant quotations and citations, see Evangelista, *Unarmed Forces,* pp. 334–38.

41. D. T. Iazov, *Verny Otchizne* [True to the Fatherland] (Moscow: Voenizdat, 1988), p. 350.

42. Skvortsov interview with Baklanov.

43. Transcript of Vladimir Kriuchkov's interview by O. I. Skvortsov, Moscow, 1999.

44. M. S. Gorbachev, *Zhizn' i reformy* [Life and reforms] (Moscow: Novosti, 1995), vol. 1, p. 73.

45. Evidence for this argument is found in part IV of Evangelista, *Unarmed Forces.*

46. Quoted in Evangelista, *Unarmed Forces,* p. 333.

Chapter 5

The Emancipation of Eastern Europe

Jacques Lévesque

The end of the Cold War was the result of a complex and murky process of change in Soviet domestic and foreign policy. Up to 1989, many Soviet experts and Western leaders were still skeptical of the importance of the changes that were taking place in both realms of Soviet policy. Even those who were convinced that they were genuine and significant could not accurately measure their depth. In this respect, Soviet tolerance and even acceptance of the loss of power by the ruling Communist Parties of Eastern Europe in 1989 was a crucial turning point. It was the single most decisive indicator of the magnitude of the changes under way in the USSR.

Eastern Europe had always been the sphere in which Soviet foreign policy was most rigid and inflexible. The USSR had used direct armed force outside its borders only three times since the end of World War II—in Hungary, Czechoslovakia, and Afghanistan—and each time it was to keep a Communist Party in power. In addition to the two instances in which force was actually used in Eastern Europe, force was twice threatened against Poland, in 1956 and 1980. The idea of the irreversibility of socialism was one of the central tenets of Soviet ideology. It was not simply a matter of dogma: the pivotal claim of historical legitimacy for Soviet power within the USSR rested largely on the existence of other Communist regimes, of a World Socialist System, the core of which was in Eastern Europe. Therefore, Soviet acceptance of a change of regime in Eastern Europe was strong evidence that Gorbachev and his circle were seeking new sources of legitimacy and new foundations for Soviet power.

This became clearer of course at a later stage. The most immediately striking event was the actual radical change in Soviet behavior. Since the beginning of perestroika, many Western experts on the USSR and politicians had considered the repudiation of the Brezhnev Doctrine[1] as the litmus test for the credibility of Gorbachev's new foreign policy, which sought to end the Cold War. Gorbachev and Shevardnadze were regularly challenged by Western journalists to state explicitly that their comments about "the non-use of force in international relations" and "freedom of choice" meant the repudiation of the Brezhnev Doctrine. It was precisely to buttress the credibility of his foreign policy that Gorbachev gradually disclaimed the Brezhnev Doctrine, first very cautiously and indirectly, but with increasing clarity, at the beginning of 1989. When the reality check came a few months later, as Eastern European countries repudiated communism, the entire world held its breath. Soviet tolerance was the greatest surprise and the most decisive breakthrough in the events leading up to the end of the Cold War.

The fact that the USSR did not use force to stop the serial collapse of the Communist regimes of Eastern Europe, although its enormous power of coercion was still intact, was important and revealing in and of itself. But more remarkable is the fact that the USSR did not even threaten to use force; it did not make a single show of force to try to arrest or slow the events in Eastern Europe. This flies in the face of expectations based on realist and neorealist theories of international relations. Considered from the point of view of power relationships, if a state considers the use of force to be too costly, the least it can be expected to do to protect its interests is to impress opponents or would-be opponents with the forces at its disposal.

We now know that no use of force similar to the Soviet military action in Hungary in 1956 and Czechoslovakia in 1968 was ever contemplated by the top Soviet leadership under Gorbachev. Even those who took part in the putsch against Gorbachev in 1991 and who continue to malign his policies on all counts believe it would have been a mistake to use Soviet military power in Eastern Europe in 1989.[2]

But there was a wide range of possible uses of limited force, rather than a direct and massive use of Soviet military power. For instance, the Soviet leaders could have encouraged Communist leaders in Eastern Europe to issue threats or use local forces, which would have had much more modest consequences than direct Soviet action. Many East European leaders expected just such encouragement, but as shall be seen, they received quite the opposite.

It will be argued in this chapter that the general structure of material capabilities on both sides of the East-West relationship was a decisive factor in the changes in Soviet foreign policy, in which the new approaches and behavior toward Eastern Europe were a key component. However, the distribution of power did not in any way make necessary or even probable the kind of change that did in fact take place. Indeed, analysis based on material capabilities is totally misleading in explaining Soviet behavior and calculations in Eastern Europe. For instance, the dominance of realist theories has led many observers, including major East European actors, to believe that Gorbachev had decided to give up Eastern Europe, a costly and cumbersome burden, in favor of a strategic retrenchment on the USSR itself. As we shall see, this explanation is far off the mark.

It will be argued here that ideas—and more specifically the emergence at the top of the Soviet political system of a new vision of international processes and of Soviet interests in the world—provide the most useful key to making sense of Soviet behavior in Eastern Europe in 1989. But while ideas can account for the basic and ultimately decisive trends in Soviet expectations and behavior, they cannot explain all the actions or instances of inaction that had an important impact on the course of events. In many cases, we must look to Gorbachev's idiosyncrasies and leadership style, and to domestic pressures.

The Quest for a New International Order

The Soviet approach toward Eastern Europe in 1989 was part and parcel of a new vision of the world that took shape in the first three to four years of Gorbachev's rule. Soviet new ideas about international processes and the USSR's interests and role in those processes must be characterized as an ideology of transition with changing content and basic thrust. As a whole, this ideology reflected a shift from Marxism-Leninism toward social democracy, though this was not, as such, a conscious goal. It sought an entirely new form of socialism for the USSR and the future world order, a new "synthesis" of socialism and democracy based on "universal values." Soviet conceptions of the content of this new form of socialism were much more elusive than the conception of the new world order, which was to help bring the new socialism into being, and vice versa. Nevertheless, the "socialist idea" and its "renewal" had enormous driving power over Gorbachev.

The Soviet ideology of transition still bore the messianic imprint of Leninism. Gorbachev and his team were convinced that they had understood, if not discovered, the basic trends in an emerging new world order. In typically Leninist and voluntaristic fashion, they overestimated the USSR's ability to shape and channel the course of international events. That confidence was fed by Gorbachev's successes on the international stage: up to mid-1989, the USSR was able to hang onto the initiative in setting the agenda for world affairs.

In a nutshell, the Soviet program for international affairs was one of universal reconciliation stemming from the trend toward an increasingly "interdependent, interconnected and integrated" world, which called for "mutual security" through disarmament based on "reasonable sufficiency" and a renunciation of the use of force in international affairs.[3] A new international order was to be built on "the balance of interests," which would supersede the "balance of forces" and would be achieved through the strengthening of international organizations and gradual transfers of national sovereignty to the United Nations. This was far from empty rhetoric.[4] Nor was it disconnected from Soviet interests, for it revealed the way those interests were perceived.

Having fully realized the limits and the growing costs of Soviet military power, the Gorbachev administration sought to disengage the USSR from the arms race and from confrontation with the West. This is both true and trivial. What is more important for understanding the course of events is *the way* these goals were pursued and *the expected results* that made it possible to pursue them in the Soviet context. In order to be acceptable to the new Soviet leaders themselves, disarmament had to engage the United States, and disengagement from Third World conflicts had to strengthen the United Nations and multilateralism, not leave the field to the United States.

The series of unilateral concessions made by Moscow to bring about the INF Treaty was meant to irresistibly draw the United States into a process of disarmament and to impress world public opinion. This second purpose was nearly as important as the first. The new Soviet leadership sought to rely on building a broad, loose international coalition of political forces, governments, and intellectual movements and currents that would play a decisive role in bringing about a world order better suited to Soviet interests. By breaking with the tit-for-tat approach that had governed the arms race and making unilateral concessions while the USSR was still a superpower in military terms, Gorbachev did indeed make a big impression on world public opinion and put the United States on the defensive. He was convinced that he would recoup in political capital what he was giving up on the military side. In short, Gorbachev believed that he could win a new role of political and moral leadership in world affairs for the USSR through his new policies.

It might be tempting to sum up this Soviet vision of the world and of the USSR's role in it as merely a vast exercise in making a virtue of the necessities imposed on the Soviet Union by its predicament. This would, however, be a one-dimensional and reductionist conclusion. First, it should be noted that perceptions of interest are not given and do not arise on their own. The Soviet leaders' new perception of the USSR's interests influenced their reading of the international environment and trends, just as their view of the world influenced the redefinition of their interests and, above all, of the best way to pursue those interests. They ascribed great power to the role of ideas. Hence, they developed a very idealistic foreign policy and the conviction that voluntary renunciation of certain positions of power could be transformed into political capital, which would better serve Soviet influence and interests.

The Ideal European Subsystem

In the new Soviet perspective, the division of Europe was to be gradually overcome through a *controlled* rapprochement of its two parts, at three distinct but interrelated levels: military, economic, and societal. At the first two levels, the rapprochement was to be conducted through bloc-to-bloc negotiations between the Warsaw Pact and NATO military alliances and between the CMEA (Council for Mutual Economic Assistance) and the EEC economic blocs. The Warsaw Pact and NATO would not disappear but rather would be "de-antagonized" through disarmament and serve as an infrastructure for the construction of a new pan-European security system built on a strengthened and institutionalized CSCE (Conference for Security and Cooperation in Europe).[5]

The third level was obviously not a matter for negotiation. But Gorbachev's reformist advisers believed that a significant degree of democratization in the Soviet and East European societies was a crucial ingredient for overcoming the division of Europe and building a "Common European Home." At the same time, with the disappearance of global confrontation and the erosion of anti-communism, the democratic left in the West would make headway toward greater socialization of their own society, yielding a new, more convergent, and more integrated world.

Thus, despite the warnings from conservative members of the leadership, Gorbachev and his circle were deeply convinced that a reformed socialism was feasible and viable in Eastern Europe as well as in the USSR. Not only did they believe that the democratization of socialism was possible, but they even tried to persuade their Eastern European counterparts that this was the only way to prevent an eventual collapse.[6] As late as February 1989, the International Department of the CPSU Central Committee stated in a confidential report that "it is not appropriate to exaggerate the danger that one or another socialist state could simply switch to the capitalist road" because "the roots of socialism have penetrated too deeply."[7] The conviction that, if the Eastern European Communist Parties were bold enough to take the initiative of democratizing their regimes, they could keep control of the process, cannot be considered simply a miscalculation or an error in judgement. It was at the very core of Gorbachev's enterprise. If the reformist Soviet leaders were nearly deaf to the warnings from their conservatives, it was because they had staked their political future on these fundamental assumptions.

Discrepancies between Behavior and Ideas about Change in Eastern Europe

Given these ideas and expectations, a much more proactive Soviet policy to promote change and democratization across Eastern Europe could have been expected, at least in a measure comparable to what was happening in the USSR. Communist reformers in the more conservative regimes in the region expected and wished precisely that. But the signals they received from Moscow were not clear. To be sure, they received encouragement from Gorbachev's reformist entourage. But Gorbachev himself remained aloof.[8] He preached reform in general terms but carefully avoided giving communist reformers in Eastern Europe explicit and direct support in their bids for power. As a result, increased polarization was evident in Eastern Europe by mid-1989, with the Communist leadership in Poland and Hungary introducing far-reaching changes with support from Gorbachev, while any significant change was resisted by the majority in the other Warsaw Pact countries until the social upheaval of the last two months of 1989, which led to changes that went far beyond Soviet expectations.

To fully understand why Gorbachev pursued such an ambiguous course, we must turn to different types of explanations. First, it must be said that Eastern Europe was a low priority for Gorbachev's policy and was largely neglected. The reshaping of the East-West relationship, beginning with the United States, was the top priority and subordinated many other concerns. Some East European leaders complained about this neglect and some of Gorbachev's advisors called for greater attention to Eastern Europe and the development of a comprehensive policy.[9] But this was never done. Therefore it is more appropriate to speak of an approach or guidelines rather than of any elaborate Gorbachev policy on Eastern Europe.

Both during and after his tenure, Gorbachev and his advisers have explained his refusal to impose or directly press for a reformist course in recalcitrant Warsaw Pact countries by his observance of a strict principle of "non-interference." At a very early stage, Gorbachev made it clear to the East European leaders that times had changed and that the USSR would no longer impose its views on its partners.

But even if we grant the importance of principles in Gorbachev's case, there are other, more convincing explanations of his tolerance of conservative East European leaders. First, in the realm of domestic politics. Up to September 1988, when sweeping changes in the top Party leadership strengthened the position of reformers, Gorbachev's noninterference reflected a compromise based on the balance of forces in the leadership. During trips to Eastern Europe, Yegor Ligachev, the leading conservative member of the Politburo, reassured his counterparts by stating publicly that "each country can act independently" of the USSR.[10] In private discussions among Gorbachev's reformist advisors, some argued that it would be premature and risky "to open a new front in the battle" against Ligachev and his supporters by bullying the conservative East European leaders.[11] After the advance of perestroika in the summer of 1988 and the subsequent shake-up in the Soviet leadership, Gorbachev became less indulgent with conservative East European leaders. But he still brought only indirect pressure to bear. In his talks with them, he made parsimonious use of the immense authority he wielded, offering only "gentle" advice and vague warnings.

He insisted that "necessary changes must mature naturally."[12] He believed that a change in leadership imposed from outside could bring destabilization. To avoid this, the initiative for reform had to come from within, ideally from the top leadership of Eastern European countries. It must be said that "non-interference" was also a way for Gorbachev to avoid taking direct, personal responsibility if anything went wrong as a consequence of an imposed change.[13]

Reform and stability were at least partly contradictory objectives. Indeed, Gorbachev feared that destabilization or a major political crisis in Eastern Europe could have negative consequences or even jeopardize perestroïka at home, which obviously had higher priority. This returns us again to domestic politics.

Gorbachev's ambivalent approach to change in Eastern Europe is an example of idiosyncratic behavior that had a significant impact on the course of events with very negative consequences for the main goals of his policies. Counterfactual analysis is useful here to weigh the consequences of Gorbachev's reluctance to directly press for the replacement of conservative Communist leaders.

A credible scenario can be constructed for East Germany, which would have had crucial potential consequences for his policies. It is well known that until November 1989, all the groups in the democratic opposition in East Germany and all the opposition leaders were in favor of the continuation of East German statehood. Had Gorbachev pressed for Honecker to be replaced by a figure such as Hans Modrow (who was the preferred candidate of the Soviet reformers), and had Modrow made overtures to the democratic opposition, as his Polish and Hungarian counterparts did, with Gorbachev's blessing, the course of events would have been substantially different. The reunification of Germany would ultimately have been irresistible, but it would have occurred at a much slower pace and under very different conditions, without an insurrectional situation. East Germany could have been unified with West Germany, not absorbed. Had the process been delayed by only two years, Gorbachev would have been in a much better position to obtain some of his terms for German reunification, such as a nonimmediate inclusion of East Germany in NATO. The Warsaw Pact would have survived a little longer and the unification could have taken place within the framework of the new European security architecture, which Gorbachev's foreign policy sought to build in order to anchor his country in Europe not only in terms of security but also economically and politically.

Patterns of Expectation and Behavior toward Change in Poland and Hungary in 1989

In spite of Gorbachev's reluctance to directly press for change, the record shows that Soviet acceptance of profound changes in Eastern Europe was based on the conviction that the democratization of socialism was both desirable and feasible. Again, it was held to be desirable because it would help reshape the world order. The expectation of benefits from East-West reconciliation and the establishment of the rules and structures of a new world order were extremely high. Policies toward Eastern Europe were affected by the pursuit of those benefits and were clearly subordinated to their quest.

A few examples may be in order here. In a bid to make a political breakthrough, impress world public opinion, and give new impetus to arms control negotiations, Gorbachev announced a series of unilateral Soviet military reductions in his famous speech of December 7, 1988, before the General Assembly of the United Nations. The Red Army was to be reduced by 500,000 men. Of these, 10,000 were to be withdrawn from the three East European countries bordering on the West. Also, 5,000 Soviet tanks, half the Soviet total in those countries, were to be withdrawn. These decisions were made over the objections of the conservative Czechoslovak and East German leaders, who feared they could be interpreted as a sort of Soviet political disengagement (even if only a partial one) from Eastern Europe, and encourage opposition forces.

Of course, these measures and others announced by Gorbachev in the same speech were intended above all to enhance the credibility of the concepts of "non-offensive defense" and "reasonable sufficiency," which he contended were the guiding principles of Soviet defense policy, and advocated as arms control guidelines. It was also to enhance the credibility of the new Soviet foreign policy that he restated at the United Nations, the principle of "freedom of choice" (for a country to choose its sociopolitical system), which was his most recent step and formula in the process of dispelling the Brezhnev doctrine.[14]

Though it clearly was not their chief purpose, these measures and statements must be considered a form of indirect pressure on the conservative leaderships of Eastern Europe, which, for their own protection, wanted the preservation of the Brezhnev doctrine. Gorbachev was aware of their concerns, and his answer was that reform was the best way for them to secure internal support.

General W. Jaruzelski, the leader of Poland, was known at the time to be the East European leader in whom Gorbachev had the greatest trust. In early 1989, Jaruzelski became the first to introduce far-reaching changes in Eastern Europe. Gorbachev's clear support enabled him to defeat the conservative opposition within Poland's Communist Party (PUWP[15]) and push through the decision to open the Roundtable talks, which were meant to legalize Solidarity both as an independent trade union and as an opposition force.

For Gorbachev, the Polish Roundtable agreements reached at the beginning of April 1989 represented an ideal model for future developments in Eastern Europe and for the pursuit of his foreign policy. While keeping a majority of seats for the Communists and satellite parties, the agreements allowed Solidarity to enter Parliament and eventually to enter a coalition government. They introduced significant democratization measures but still guaranteed a dominant role for the PUWP, legitimized by the opposition's acceptance. Had the agreements held, the West would have felt compelled to encourage and support the process of change through economic assistance, since Solidarity itself was calling for such support. Not surprisingly, the official, pro-reform Soviet press reacted enthusiastically to the results of the Roundtable. *Izvestia,* for example, stated that the accords had "dealt a death blow to the myth that socialism cannot be reformed."[16]

The unreserved Soviet official support for the Roundtable process could be seen as another form of indirect pressure on the leadership of the conservative East European regimes to introduce reforms.[17] This writer asked General Jaruzelski whether this was part of Gorbachev's intention. He responded in the affirmative.

Soviet elation about the turn of events in Poland did not last long. Two months after their conclusion, the Roundtable agreements began to unravel when the Communists were unable to win their reserved seats in the first round of the parliamentary elections on June 4, 1989. Taking advantage of the Communists' suddenly glaring weakness, their satellite parties deserted them and refused to enter a coalition government unless it was also joined by Solidarity. Solidarity initially refused, raising the stakes. Poland entered a period of political uncertainty that lasted over two months.

Interestingly enough, it was during this period that Gorbachev went a step further in his repudiation the Brezhnev Doctrine (again, without using the term). In doing so, Gorbachev was defying the pointed advice the top Soviet leadership had earlier received from relatively reformist quarters. Indeed, the International Department of the CPSU Central Committee, which was an important part of the consensus against the use of force in Eastern Europe, nevertheless had recommended that the USSR "maintain a certain indeterminacy with respect to concrete actions we might take in response to a given upheaval." This indeterminacy was held to be necessary in order "not to encourage anti-socialist forces to put the bases of socialism to the test in any given country."[18] Nonetheless, in restating in July 1989 the principle of "freedom of choice," Gorbachev not only asserted its universal value, but for the first time explicitly applied it to "friend or ally" states.[19]

Again, it is important to stress the context in which this statement was made. It was part of an important speech Gorbachev delivered before the Council of Europe in Strasbourg, which was one of the highlights of a remarkably success-ful trip through Western Europe. His first stop had been Bonn, where he had received a triumphant welcome from the German people.[20] That visit also her-alded a new convergence of views with Chancellor Kohl on a series of political and economic questions, notably disarmament in Europe. At that time, Gor-bachev was near the acme of his international glory, and his plan for a gradual transformation of the European order could indeed appear, in the summer of 1989, as a realistic prospect. He knew that his tolerance of and even support for the changes under way in Poland and Hungary was an important factor in the success of his overall foreign policy, and his statement before the Council of Eu-rope was meant to sustain that success.

Quite certainly, in forcefully restating the "freedom of choice" principle, Gor-bachev did not mean to weaken Jaruzelski's bargaining power in Poland or to in-crease that of Solidarity. His intent was entirely different. He believed that Soviet acceptance of Solidarity as a legitimate political player in Poland could have a moderating effect on its behavior.

In the summer of 1989, developments were taking a very different turn in Hungary than in Poland. While negotiating with the opposition, Hungary's Communist Party (HSWP[21]) was openly preparing to officially transform itself into a social-democratic party in anticipation of the free elections it had agreed to hold in 1990. Things were thus going much farther than the Polish Round-table agreements. But the HSWP was in a much stronger political position than its Polish counterpart. Indeed, according to reliable polls taken in the summer of 1989, the Party was poised to garner close to 40 percent of the vote in a free election, with its closest rivals each receiving less than 20 percent. Therefore, it was expected that the Party would remain, at least for a few years to come, the pivotal force in Hungarian political life.[22] Moreover, the leading Communist re-former, Imre Pozsgay, was widely expected to win a free presidential election.

These developments were well ahead of what the Soviet leadership, including Gorbachev, was prepared to accept for the USSR. That is why they appeared as a crucial test of the limits of Soviet tolerance. But beneath the surface of stated positions, tortuous change was going on in Moscow. Though Gorbachev was still personally opposed to party pluralism and free competition between parties, the issue was being discussed among his political advisers.[23] In one scenario, the leadership of the CPSU would itself initiate a split in the Party and organize po-litical competition between its conservative and reformist wings. Party pluralism would then be circumscribed within the socialist framework. At the same time, the possibility of removing the constitutional provision concerning the Party's leading role was being discussed, although Gorbachev was still reluctant on this score.[24] Thus, it was the very core of the Leninist legacy that was beginning to erode in the USSR itself, though this was hardly perceptible at the time. This helps explain not only Soviet tolerance but also acceptance of the Hungarian process. For instance, *Pravda* described the Hungarian Party's goals in positive terms, as those of "a renovated party which seeks to become a force striving for a new synthesis of Communist and social-democratic values."[25]

The Elusive Limits of Soviet Tolerance

If the guaranteed political hegemony of the Communist parties in Eastern Europe was no longer the threshold of Soviet tolerance, were there any limits? First, it must be noted that the reformers' expectation that the Communist parties would retain if not a dominant then at least a major and crucial role was a significant factor in their readiness to cross that threshold.

Beyond that, the "safekeeping of socialism" seemed to be the limit. Most East European Communist reformers went through many efforts and contortions to stay within that murky limit.[26] Indeed, the meaning and content of "democratic socialism" was not at all clear. For Gorbachev and most of his reformist team, it was a matter of searching and experimentation. Gorbachev certainly saw himself more as a communist than as a social-democrat. However, as we have seen, social-democracy was now considered within the bounds of socialism, contrary to the entire communist tradition. Since 1988, socialism had become an increasingly elastic and eclectic concept. But it cannot be overemphasized that Gorbachev was not simply paying lip service to the "socialist idea" that he so often invoked. For him, it was a source of inspiration that was by no means devoid of meaning.[27]

Eclectic as it may have been, reformed socialism remained a crucial and operative vehicle of change and an essential motivation and justification for the risks Gorbachev was taking in both domestic and foreign policy.

The flexibility displayed by Gorbachev and other Soviet reformers concerning the Party's leading role and the content of socialism did not extend to all aspects of relations between the USSR and Eastern Europe. On the contrary: fearing that their permissiveness on these questions might lead to the erosion of the Warsaw Pact and the CMEA, they formulated very explicit demands that the two be kept intact. During his July 1989 visit to Budapest, Soviet Foreign Minister Shevardnadze asked the Hungarian leaders for a formal commitment that Hungary would honor its obligations to the alliance and not conclude any accords with Western "integrative institutions" without the USSR's prior agreement. The Soviet leaders had the European Community in mind as much as NATO.[28]

Clearly, it was not the defensive or military value of the Warsaw Pact that prompted the Soviet reformers' insistence that their allies remain members of the Pact; their entire foreign policy was built on the premise that there was no real military threat from the West. Rather, their insistence reflected the high priority they attached to their pan-European policy and to the political value of the Warsaw Pact. The Warsaw Pact institutionalized the USSR's place in Europe and was the main instrument of its European policy. It conferred upon the Soviet Union a certain parity with the United States in negotiations concerning Europe. In the future, the two largely demilitarized alliances were to be the foundations of the new European security architecture the Soviets were advocating. In the short term, they were concerned about separate agreements between Hungary or Poland and the European Community, leaving the USSR and others out in the cold.[29] They believed that the USSR and its allies could get much better terms by negotiating collectively, and that in this way the USSR could remain a major force in shaping the future of Europe.

The Stabilizing Role of the New East-West Relationship

The Soviet reformers' relatively high degree of confidence in a smooth and controlled process of change in Eastern Europe was directly related to their confidence in the mutual trust that was emerging in the USSR's relations with the United States and Western Europe. Their expectation was that because of that trust, the West would respect the USSR's basic security interests in Eastern Europe (beginning with the Warsaw Pact) and play a restraining role there. It must be said that in 1989 that expectation was by no means devoid of foundation—quite the contrary.[30]

In July 1989, George Bush paid an official visit to Poland and Hungary to show American interest in and support for the process of democratization. At the same time, in order to avoid complicating Gorbachev's position in Moscow and jeopardizing perestroika, he made a point of doing nothing to accelerate the course of events in Poland and Hungary.[31] He expressed concern on this score and even tried to slow the pace of change to some extent. According to accounts from members of his entourage, Bush found Solidarity leader Lech Walesa more unpredictable than Jaruzelski. Bush praised Jaruzelski in public and private, and announced before the Polish Parliament that he would ask Congress for a $100 million fund to assist Poland. General Jaruzelski wrote later that Bush's behavior during his visit to Poland played a crucial role in his tight reelection by both chambers of the new Polish Parliament a few days later, on July 16.[32]

In Hungary, Bush met with the leading communist reformers. Later, he met with leaders of the non-communist opposition. Irked by their impatience, he said in private after the meeting, "These people are not the right ones to lead this country. At least not right now."[33]

The Soviet reformist leaders had good reason to be satisfied with the results of Bush's visit. Commenting on the event, an *Izvestia* columnist had the presumption to boast that Bush "is essentially just approving the changes that Moscow has already approved or initiated in practice."[34]

This is not to say that Gorbachev and his reformist team were unaware of the serious risks attendant upon the process of change in Eastern Europe. But they were dealt with in the framework of their new approach and high expectations concerning world politics. This pattern of behavior would endure over the following months.

Poland Goes Over the "Limit"

It should be recalled that as late as September 1989, no one—whether in Moscow, Eastern Europe, or the West—foresaw the general collapse that was about to occur. But in August, events in Poland took a turn that had been entirely unexpected a few weeks earlier and nearly brought down the regime. The Communist Prime Minister designate had to give up his efforts to form a coalition government with the Solidarity-led opposition, and on August 20 Jaruzelski asked Tadeusz Mazowiecki, one of Lech Walesa's chief advisors, to form a new government. The Communists kept only four ministries. To be sure, they were four key ministries: the two "power ministries" of Defense and the Interior, plus Transportation (important for Warsaw Pact logistics) and Foreign Trade (crucial for the CMEA). The important Foreign Affairs portfolio was given to K. Skubichevski, an independent who had been a member of Jaruzelski's Consultative Council. Still, the Communists had lost not only their hegemony but even their dominant position in the system.

On August 22, before giving final approval to the Mazowiecki government's composition, Mieczyslaw Rakowski, who had replaced Jaruzelski as PUWP's leader, had a 40-minute telephone conversation with Gorbachev. This writer asked him whether his Soviet counterpart had issued any warning or expressed any reservations about the power-sharing agreement. "Not the least objection, nor the least reservation," was the answer.[35]

Even more interestingly from the standpoint of our argument here, Rakowski said that he proposed to go to Moscow to discuss the Polish situation and Gorbachev refused, saying that such a meeting would be inopportune under the circumstances because it could be interpreted as Soviet interference and opposition. This was quite typical of Gorbachev's approach. He believed the USSR needed to appear not only to be allowing the process but to be supporting it. The expectation was that this conduct would pay off. A few months earlier, Soviet reformist quarters had put the argument to the Soviet leadership that by going along with the process of change in Eastern Europe and developing good contacts with the "constructive opposition," the USSR would contribute to its "self-limitation."[36] In other words, it was believed that a sharp break with past conduct could redeem Soviet influence in Eastern Europe.

The benevolent Soviet attitude did seem to bear fruit, at least in the short run. On a trip to Moscow immediately after the formation of his government, Mazowiecki publicly stated again that Poland would honor its international obligations to the Warsaw Pact. Lech Walesa, though not a member of the government, had given the same assurances.

The concept of path dependency as presented by Herrmann and Lebow in this book, when applied to the outcome of perestroika, is very useful for understanding Gorbachev's apparently ready acceptance of a rather dramatic and unexpected shift in the balance of political power in Poland. Even if it was not welcome, this turn of events was a product of the whole thrust of perestroika and of the new Soviet foreign policy and had to be accepted as such. This single event was not enough to call into question the tremendous political and ideological investment that had been made in both domestic and foreign policy, particularly since, at this point, the hopes for beneficial outcomes were still running very high.

The fact that change had gone off the tracks in Poland did not prompt any shift in the Soviet course of conduct. On the contrary: Moscow began to show greater impatience with Honecker's resistance to change in East Germany. In September, the Hungarian government was given the green light to open its Western borders to a growing flow of East Germans wanting to emigrate.[37] It was understood in both Budapest and Moscow that this would be a serious blow to Honecker, though no one thought it would lead to the fall of the Berlin Wall two months later. In October, Gorbachev preached reform to the East German leaders as the way out of their troubles, and they removed Honecker very soon afterward.

Until the period following the fall of the Berlin Wall, the position of the Polish Communists was not desperate. They held the "power ministries." As Head of State, Jaruzelski was not only the Commander in Chief of the armed forces but also had the constitutional power to dismiss the government and declare a state of emergency. The Mazowiecki administration was a government under close watch. All of this, and also the fragile balance in Hungary, was called into question with the dramatic acceleration of events in Germany after the fall of the Berlin Wall. It might be said that all of Eastern Europe rushed through the breach in the Wall.

Actually, Gorbachev's East European dream did not unravel everywhere in the months that followed the fall of the Berlin Wall; it was realized in two member countries of the Warsaw Pact, Bulgaria and Romania. In Romania, reformist Communists—Gorbachevites, so to speak—took power under dramatic circumstances and were able to hold onto it in free elections. In Bulgaria, the pro-Gorbachev Communists who took power as the Berlin Wall was crumbling were also able to win an absolute majority in Parliament in free elections held several months later. Both countries' leaders shared Gorbachev's vision of a new European order and remained faithful to the Warsaw Pact to the end. Unfortunately for Gorbachev, however, they were the least important countries for the success of his European policy. The most crucial would have been East Germany.

The Fall of the Berlin Wall

The spectacular fall of the Berlin Wall brought Gorbachev's stature on the world stage to its acme. In the West it appeared to be a direct result of his policies. That it was, though the event was unexpected in Moscow and was not even the product of a clear decision by the East German leadership, as we were to learn later. It appeared as the most striking evidence of genuine Soviet willingness to transcend the division of Europe. To capitalize on this, Soviet officials even hinted to Western journalists that the move had been suggested to Honecker's successor by Gorbachev.[38] Publicly, Shevardnadze's spokesman elegantly declared: "These are changes in the right direction. We are evolving from a divided postwar Europe toward the common European home."[39]

Privately, however, Gorbachev and his reformist team were worried that they might be overtaken by the pace of events, though they did hope briefly that the East German government would be able to regain the initiative through its apparently bold move.

From that point on, they did in fact lose the initiative, which had been theirs on major international issues for the previous four years. The next spectacular move was made by Kohl on November 28, when he made public his 10-point plan for the unification of Germany in the relatively distant future, without notice even to his NATO allies. Gorbachev was furious, accusing Kohl of feeding instability.[40] The Soviets countered Kohl's plan with their own plan for "a contractual community" between the two German states, which reflected Gorbachev's vision of inter-German relations and was a microcosm of his pan-European project. He wanted a step-by-step rapprochement between the two German states through a process in which each East German and Soviet concession would be matched by West German and Western concessions on economic assistance, disarmament, and security arrangements. This was to lead slowly to a sort of confederation of the two German states. Similar plans had been recommended to the Soviet leadership for more than a year by Soviet "new thinkers."[41] But when Gorbachev did finally espouse them, events were already racing out of control.

It was at this point, with Communist power crumbling in Czechoslovakia as a direct result of the East German events, that the Bush-Gorbachev summit was held in Malta on December 3. After Malta, Gorbachev met with the other Warsaw Pact leaders to brief them on the summit results. Through confidential, diplomatic channels, the East German leaders had proposed holding the meeting in Berlin. In a note to Gorbachev, his chief advisor for Eastern Europe recommended him to decline the invitation, arguing that, given the events in Berlin, a Warsaw Pact summit there "would be seen as a type of show of force."[42] The meeting took place in Moscow.

The desire to avoid even such a muted display of force is quite extraordinary. The use of force in international affairs had become an operative ideological "taboo" and the assumed power of not using force had become a political instrument. It is perhaps even more remarkable that it was French President François Mitterrand who shortly after paid an official visit to East Germany, precisely to legitimize its existence as a sovereign state. Gorbachev did not.

It is facts such as these that lead those who see international relations uniquely as a game of power relationships to think that Gorbachev had decided to give up Eastern Europe, or to see him as a sheer incompetent[43] (which he certainly may have been in many respects).

A Crucial Role for Ideology

In his memoirs, Gorbachev recalls his last conversation with Romanian Communist leader Nicolae Ceausescu, at the meeting of Warsaw Pact leaders on December 4, following the Malta summit. He reports that he told Ceausescu that "the process we are living through at the moment had a clearly democratic character despite all its contradictions and the pain it was engendering. Due to this fact, *there was no reason to fear the collapse or the end of socialism.*"[44] Given the surprising character of the assertion, this writer asked Gorbachev, much later, if he really believed at that point that reformed socialism still had a chance in Eastern Europe or if he had said that only to appease Ceausescu. He answered: "At that moment, we believed that the guarantee of real freedom of choice and of real sovereignty in Central and East Europe would play in favor of socialism."[45]

One can see the degree of elasticity that reformed socialism had acquired at that point: everything that was good for freedom and democracy was deemed to be good for socialism! Quite clearly, at that stage, reformed socialism was much more a defensive than an offensive weapon. It was certainly ineffectual for convincing skeptics, not to mention Ceausescu, but it was crucial to Gorbachev as a way of rationalizing the unexpected turn of events. It helped him keep the bearings that had guided him up to that point. It was essential to enable him to continue along the path on which he had embarked. At the same time, it is obvious that he largely failed or refused to understand the magnitude and direction of the changes that were then taking place in Eastern Europe.

In spite of Gorbachev's wishes, the uncontrolled and rapid disintegration of not only the East German regime but of the East German state as well quickly placed reunification on the international agenda, sparking Western demands that the united Germany be a member of NATO. By the end of January 1990, Gorbachev had reconciled himself to the principle of reunification, but for months he and the Soviet leadership desperately resisted the inclusion of a united Germany in NATO. Once again, though, they made no threats.

It is no small wonder that the Soviets dug in their heels on this issue. It was clear that the inclusion of Germany in NATO would spell the end of the Warsaw Pact and shatter the entire Soviet policy for a new order in Europe. Gorbachev and Shevardnadze therefore insisted that progress toward the unification of Germany had to be synchronized with the establishment of a new pan-European security system that would supersede the two existing alliances. To no avail. It was not only the "socialist idea" that was fading away but also the USSR's place in Europe and world affairs.

While the international power structure is of limited usefulness for helping us understand the specifics of Gorbachev's policy toward Eastern Europe, it does a lot to explain the behavior of his counterparts both in the West and the East and the failure of his policies. An essential part of Gorbachev's political capital accrued from his refusal to resort to force. The value of that capital rested on outside observers' conviction that he had the option to use force and hence deserved credit and encouragement for not doing so. Another portion of his political capital was based on what he had to offer in concrete terms in the process of East-West rapprochement. The fall of the Berlin Wall was a crucial turning point on both these questions. In the weeks that followed, Gorbachev's counterparts became convinced that he would not or could no longer use force, and realized that what he had to offer was slipping out of his hands.

In Poland and Hungary, the same events convinced the opposition that the supposed limits of Soviet tolerance did not exist and that Soviet power had ebbed. This led to the withdrawal of many previous concessions made to Gorbachev and the disruption of the political equilibrium there.

In fact, it was not the real balance of power that changed in the months preceding the fall of the Berlin Wall; rather, Gorbachev's refusal to use force had become indisputable. His exclusion of that option was made clear by his consistent discouragement of any local use of force or show of force by East European Communists and, as has been seen, of any indirect show of force by the Soviet Union.

However, the precipitous unraveling of Soviet influence in Eastern Europe during the last month of 1989 and the first months of 1990, and the rapid deterioration in economic conditions in the Soviet Union, did lead to a real and decisive shift in the East-West balance of power. This, together with the general thrust of Gorbachev's foreign policy, made it easier for the United States and Kohl to hold firm and get their terms for German unification.

A Rare Case of Idealism in International Relations

Seldom in history has the policy of a great power continued to be guided, despite difficulties and reversals, by such an idealistic view of the world, one based on universal reconciliation, one in which the image of the enemy gradually blurs until it virtually disappears as an enemy.

Again, we should guard against the belief that the Soviet Union had no other options and that its policy was somehow the inevitable product of the structure of power in the world. The second chapter of this book shows convincingly and at length how the general situation of the USSR in the mid-1980s could have led to very different policy outcomes.

This is not, of course, to say that the policies pursued by the USSR under Gorbachev were entirely a matter of chance. If not a necessary outcome, they were certainly determined and impelled by the growing gap between the Soviet Union's economic performance and its foreign and defense commitments. The argument can be put in very simple and compelling terms: if the Soviet economy had been performing well (in comparative terms) and if the USSR had been catching up with the United States in the global competition for power, the ideas and policies of Gorbachev's team and the reformist think tanks could never have prevailed in a system based on the USSR's ideology and traditions. Gorbachev and all the members of his entourage explicitly recognize that their policies were a quest for a way out of the logjam in which the USSR was mired.

This must be taken in a broad sense. For example, we know that many Reagan supporters claim that his Third World and armament policies played a decisive role in bringing about the new thinking. While those policies did play a role, it was a limited and mixed one. They may have heightened the reformers' awareness of the deadlock in which the USSR was caught. But in 1986, for instance, when Gorbachev's concessions for an INF treaty were met by escalating U.S. demands, Reagan's policy fed traditional Soviet views of the enemy and made it more difficult for Gorbachev to prevail. In this context, Gorbachev needed to already have a keen awareness of the USSR's predicament. Ultimately, it is in the internal conditions of the Soviet system that one finds the most compelling reason for perestroika: the declining performance of the Soviet economy. For this, the Reagan administration can claim little credit.

It should be borne in mind that when Gorbachev came to power, the overall situation in the USSR was difficult, to be sure, but the Soviet regime and its alliance system were not on the verge of collapse. The Gorbachev administration had a fair amount of maneuvering room in both domestic and foreign policy matters. That is why the course on which they embarked and to which they held surprised most political observers.

In this chapter, I have investigated the relationship between the ideas of Gorbachev's circle (their beliefs, views and expectations concerning international processes) and their patterns of behavior. These ideas were by no means entirely contingent.

As has been noted, the Soviet leadership underwent a social-democratic mutation, under the sway of an intellectual elite that had already been "social-democratized" to a large extent. This "social democratization" is not an accident in the history of Marxist, and later Leninist, parties. It is the result of the relative success of parliamentary democracy and the liberal economy, and their capacity to adapt. From the beginning of the century, reformism began to win over Marxist-based revolutionary parties. The split in the socialist movement and the polarization resulting from the appearance of Leninist parties helped accelerate the process in the non-Leninist parties. Since one of the main reasons for their existence was to fight the reformism of social democracy, the Leninist parties' penetration by "social-democratization" was much slower. In the West, the most remarkable case was that of the Italian Communist Party under Enrico Berlinguer in the late 70s and early 80s. In the East, social-democratization first won over the most European of the ruling Communist Parties, the Polish and Hungarian parties in 1956 and the Czechoslovak party in 1968. In those cases, the process was of course interrupted by Soviet pressure or military intervention. While there was nothing inevitable about the timing, the CPSU finally went through "social-democratization" as a way out of its growing problems.

The critical phase in a Communist Party's transition to social-democracy is often marked by the strongest dose of political idealism, and this is no coincidence. Initially, the social-democratic transformation is rarely recognized as such by its proponents. Informed by an all-embracing vision of international and social processes, imbued with a heroic mission, a Leninist Party cannot abandon its old standards without pursuing new, more promising objectives that are as galvanizing as the goals that appear to be out of reach or discredited. The old goals are not completely abandoned but continually diluted into new "syntheses," seen as both novel and promising. This explains the PCI's proposed "historic compromise" of the 1970s, which was supposed to fundamentally transform Italy's political life and put it on a qualitatively new track, initially conceived as altogether different from social-democracy. In proposing an accommodation with Christian Democracy, the PCI accepted a transformation of the Party, but with the conviction that it would keep the best of itself, and that Christian Democracy would also be transformed in the process. Similarly, the

Prague Spring of 1968 sought to reconcile socialism and democracy, planning and the market, in a new synthesis that would renew socialism's attraction. The project of European and global reconciliation advanced by the USSR in 1988 and 1989 was all the more impressive since it came from a nuclear superpower, and was centered precisely on disarmament.

Paradoxically, while the messianic ambitions were indeed pursued with determination and conviction, they essentially accompanied a process of adaptation. That is why we have defined the worldview and the vision of social processes in question as a transitional ideology. As we have seen, for Gorbachev and his circle the socialist idea became ever more open-ended. In the search for a new synthesis, osmosis was first effected with social democracy, which was perceived as less and less alien.

The space of time between the conquering, promising phase of Gorbachev's ambitious plan, when his project for a new synthesis seemed to be on track, and its rapid unraveling after the fall of the Berlin Wall, was extremely short. Consequently, the process of adaptation was very difficult and traumatic for the Soviet leaders. But adaptation did carry the day. At the end of 1989, events were spiraling out of control on all sides. The leaders had burnt their bridges. But ecumenicalism, the conviction that the former adversary would be at least partially transformed by the new relationship, the certainty that ultimately something of the initial project would be saved—all these contributed to the refusal to resort to even a demonstration of force, to the decision not to block an agreement on German reunification.

There can be little doubt that the underlying tendency in Eastern Europe in 1989 was toward the dismantling of the Communist regimes. But it did not have to take the form of the precipitous collapse that did occur. As we have argued, a more interventionist policy and less vacillation by Gorbachev in promoting reforms in East Germany or Czechoslovakia could have bought him a little more time. A somewhat slower transition in Berlin and Prague (which would have had a restraining effect on developments in Poland and Hungary) would have allowed Gorbachev to push ahead with his European policy. His prospects were excellent in the summer of 1989. What he was lacking was time, and above all a minimally stable alliance through which to advance his plan. To be sure, such an ambitious and messianic project could not have been realized in its totality. But, messianic and ambitious though it may have been, the project was not wholly devoid of realism, and it did embody political aspirations that had currency in both the East and the West. It was only after the fact—after the failure—that the illusions turned out to have been just that. Was it then entirely illusory to have expected Mazowiecki's Poland to remain in the Warsaw Pact for two or three more years?

Leninism's departure from the European stage could have left a more stable European order in its wake, one that would have been worthy of the historic opportunity presented by 1989. On this count, as on many others, Gorbachev was poorly rewarded.

However, what is most noteworthy and important here is that Leninism, which had been a ruthless dictatorship, left Europe so peacefully. This remains a masterwork of history and a legacy of hope for the future of humankind.

Notes

1. The Brezhnev Doctrine, also called the doctrine of "limited sovereignty," is a Western term used to characterize the USSR's official justification of its military intervention in Czechoslovakia in 1968. The Soviet leaders did claim that the leadership of a given socialist country was responsible not only before its own people but also before the whole socialist community. Therefore, it was claimed to be the right and duty of the USSR and other socialist states to intervene when they deemed socialism to be threatened in a given member-country of the community.

2. See the statements of V. Kryouchkov (KGB chief under Gorbachev), D. Yazoz (Minister of Defense), O. Shenin (Politburo member) and other leaders who took part in the putsch against Gorbachev in August 1991, in the transcripts of the Moscow Conference of June 1999, organized by the Mershon Center, Ohio State University in cooperation with the Institute of Contemporary History of the Russian Academy of Sciences.

3. Mikhail Gorbachev, *Perestroika: vues neuves sur notre pays et le monde* (Paris: Flammarion, 1987), p. 197.

4. The fact that many features of the "old" thinking coexisted with the emerging new concepts accounts for some of the skepticism with which the new thinking was received for some years.

5. For a consistent exposition of the tenets of the "Common Home," see the article by the director of the Institute of Europe of the Academy of Sciences: V. Zhurkin, "Obshtchii dom dlia Evropy" [A common house for Europe], *Pravda,* May 17, 1989.

6. Alexandr Yakovlev recounted to this writer a private conversation he had with Erich Honecker in 1989. To Honecker's question about why the CPSU's leadership had begun and was continuing down the path of dangerous policies, Yakovlev responded that "it is not a question of choice or political options, but one of objective, unavoidable necessity." He added: "Without *perestroika* [I told Honecker] we would eventually be confronted with a revolution that could be as violent as the October Revolution." *Interview with Alexandr Yakovlev,* Moscow, November 8, 1994.

7. *K Strategii Otnoshenii z Evropeiskimi Sotsialisticheskimi Stranami* [Towards a strategy for relations with European Socialist states], pp. 11–12. (Unpublished document, now available at the National Security Archive, Washington.)

8. For a discussion of the expectations of Communist reformers in Eastern Europe's more conservative regimes and their disappointment with Gorbachev, see Jacques Lévesque, *The Enigma of 1989: The USSR and the Liberation of Eastern Europe* (Berkeley: University of California Press, 1997), chapters 3, 8, and 9. This chapter draws heavily on the analyses and sources cited therein.

9. Ibid., pp. 86–90.

10. *New York Times,* November 5, 1987, cited by Glenn Chafetz, *Gorbachev, Reform and the Brezhnev Doctrine: Soviet Policy toward Eastern Europe, 1985–1990* (Westport: Praeger, 1993), p. 71.

11. Interview with Valeri Leonidovich Musatov (Deputy-director of the International Department of the CPSU Central Committee, in charge of socialist countries in 1989), Moscow, November 4, 1991.

12. See Antonio Rubbi, *Incontri con Gorbaciov—i colloqui di Natta e Occhetto con il leader sovietico* (Rome: Editori Riuniti, 1990), p. 246.

13. We suggested this hypothesis to Alexandr Yakovlev, and he expressed total agreement. Interview with Alexandr Yakovlev, Moscow, November 8, 1994

14. A few months earlier, at the 19th Party Conference, he had stated that the principle of "freedom of choice, occupies a key place [*klyuchevoe mesto*] in the new thinking. We believe in the universality of this principle for international relations. [. . .] In this situation, foreign imposition of a social system or a lifestyle through any method, and even more so through military measures, is a dangerous way of acting from the past." (*Pravda,* June 28, 1988.)

15. Polish United Workers Party, was its official name.

16. *Izvestia,* April 6, 1989.

17. *Kommunist,* for example, wrote that "the Polish Party's experience carries significance not only for Poland, but also for the other countries. . . ." See "Novyi etap v zhizni Pol'shi" [A new stage in the life of Poland], *Kommunist,* May 7, 1989, pp. 94–99.

18. *K Strategii Otnoshenii z Evropeiskimi Sotsialisticheskimi Stranami* (op. cit.) February 1989

19. He said: "The political and social order in one country or another has changed in the past and can also change in the future. Still, it is exclusively up to the peoples themselves. It is their choice. All interference, whatever its nature, in the internal affairs of a state to limit its sovereignty, even from a friend or ally, is inadmissible." (*Pravda,* July 7, 1989).

20. Gorbachev's popularity was due to his dramatic disarmament proposals, and to the special sensitivity of this issue in Germany, given that the largest quantities of both alliances' weapons were on German soil. On the eve of his visit to Bonn, opinion polls showed that 47 percent of Germans considered the USSR to be the "principal force" working for world peace, while only 22 percent gave that role to the United States. (*Washington Post,* May 30, 1989, quoted by Michael Sodaro, *Moscow, Germany and the West: From Khrushchev to Gorbachev* (New York: Cornell University Press, 1990), p. 353.

21. The Hungarian Socialist Workers Party was its official name.

22. "A coalition government as the result of an election (not later than June 1990) appears to be a real possibility, with the (now reformed) Communist Party exerting a kind of leading role, in virtue of its better performance in the elections." Vladimir Kusin, "The Changing Parties," *Background Report* (Radio Free Europe), 138, August 4, 1989.

23. Interview with Andrei Grachev (Deputy Director of the Central Committee's International Department in 1989, and Gorbachev's official spokesman in 1991), Paris, March 2, 1993.

24. Interview with Vadim Zagladin (Gorbachev's presidential adviser in 1989), Moscow, April 29, 1993.

25. *Pravda,* June 27, 1989.

26. See Lévesque, *The Enigma of 1989* (op. cit.), pp. 139–140.

27. The testimony of his closest aides, given nearly ten years later, is very clear on this: "He believed in the possibility of reform socialism up until the very end, until everything began falling apart." (Anatoly Chernyaev)

    "When we are talking about socialism, we need to define what we have in mind. Gorbachev meant everything good and healthy that was in our system. [. . .] In other words, if you do not take the stiff model that developed in our country as the example, but if you take what we have now lost, or are in the process of losing—free health care, free public education, the large network of institutions that were designed to take care of people, and which are being missed now, including the resort facilities, sanatoriums, day care facilities, nurseries, and so on—we are longing for these now, we should have preserved all of them. That is also socialism. [. . .] That is what Gorbachev wanted to preserve." (Georgy Shakhnazarov).

The End of the Cold War in Europe, 1989: "New Thinking" and New Evidence, Transcript of proceedings of the Musgrove Conference, St. Simon's Island, GA, May 1–3, 1998, pp. 36 and 38 (National Security Archive, Washington).

28. Interview with Peter Hardi (Director of the Hungarian Institute of International Affairs in 1989), May 4, 1992.

29. A few weeks after Rezsö Nyers and Grósz met with Gorbachev in Moscow, Nyers summarized Gorbachev's views and concerns in these terms: "Gorbachev shares our own fears and preoccupations, which are: that the road to reforms not end in anarchy; that the HSWP (Hungarian Socialist Workers Party) remain *one of the essential forces* in the renewal of society; and that Hungary not abandon its friendship with the Soviet Union in *a unilateral movement toward the West.*" *Corriere della Sera,* September 9, 1989. Emphasis added.

30. Speaking to Gorbachev in September 1989, "in a very confidential manner," as she said, Margaret Thatcher told him, long before the fall of the Berlin Wall "We are very concerned with the processes that are underway in East Germany. [. . .] Britain and Western Europe are not interested in the unification of Germany. [. . .] We are not interested in the destabilization of Eastern Europe or the dissolution of the Warsaw Pact either. Of course the internal changes are ripe in all the countries of Eastern Europe. However, we are in favor of those processes remaining strictly internal, we will not interfere in them and spur the decommunization of Eastern Europe. I can tell you that this is also the position of the US President." *Record of Conversation Between Mikhail Gorbachev and Prime Minister of Great Britain Margaret Thatcher. September 23, 1989.* Archive of the Gorbachev Foundation, Moscow (copy at The National Security Archive, Washington.)

31. See M. R. Beschloss and Strobe Talbott, *At the Highest Levels* (Boston: Little Brown, 1993), pp. 82–93.

32. Wojciech Jaruzelski, *Les chaînes et le refuge—Mémoires.* Paris: Jean-Claude Lattès, 1992, p. 337. The outcome of the election was made possible by the abstention of several Solidarity members and the deliberate absence of several others.

33. Ibid., p. 92.

34. *Izvestia,* July 16, 1989.

35. Interview with M. Rakowski, Warsaw, March 3, 1993.

36. See the confidential memorandum sent by the Institute on the Economy of the World Socialist System to A. Yakovlev in his capacity as Chairman of the International Commission of the CPSU Central Committee, in February 1989: *Peremeny v Vostochnoi Evrope i ikh Vliyane na SSSR* [The changes in East Europe and their influence on the USSR]. (Unpublished document, now available at the National Security Archive, Washington.)

37. See Lévesque, *The Enigma.* op. cit. pp. 149–54.

38. See Beschloss and Talbott, op. cit., p. 134.

39. See Charles Van Der Donckt's chronology, *Six mois qui ébranlèrent le monde* (Québec: CQRI, 1990), p. 148.

40. See Anatoly Cherniaev, *Shest' let s Gorbachevym: po dnevnikovym zapisiam* [Six years with Gorbachev: After Notes from a Journal]. (Moscow: Progress Kultura, 1993), p. 307.

41. See Lévesque, *The Enigma.* op. cit., pp. 69–74, 97–98, and 144–46

42. See Georgi Shakhnazarov, *Tsena svobody: reformatsiia Gorbachev glazami ego pomoshchnika* [The Price of Freedom: Gorbachev's reformist undertaking through the eyes of his assistant] (Moscow: Rossika Zevs, 1993), p. 440.

43. See Peter Rutland, "Solving the Puzzle," *Transitions* 5 (7) (July 1998), pp. 82–85

44. Mikhail Gorbachev, *Erinnerungen* [Memoirs]. (Berlin, Siedler Verlag, 1995), pp. 925–26; translated from German by Laure Castin. (Emphasis added).

45. M. S. Gorbachev, *Otvety na voprosy professora J. Leveka* [Responses to questions from prof. J. Lévesque], Moscow, July 12, 1995.

Chapter 6

German Unification

James W. Davis and William C. Wohlforth

Introduction

Encouraged by Mikhail Gorbachev's policies of reform, rapprochement, and nonintervention, Hungary and Poland initiated democratic reforms in the summer of 1989. In September, thousands of East Germans fled to the Federal Republic of Germany (FRG) over the newly opened Austrian-Hungarian border, and tens of thousands began demonstrating for democratic reforms in the German Democratic Republic (GDR) itself. Under pressure from Gorbachev and challenged within his own Socialist Unity Party (SED), hard-line leader Erich Honecker stepped down in October 1989. Desperately seeking to stabilize its rule by appeasing the population's growing demands for reform, the new SED leadership dropped travel restrictions and called for free elections. But within weeks of the fall of the Berlin Wall on November 9, support among East Germans for unification grew, the GDR failed to stabilize, and German unity became the epicenter of world politics.

West German Chancellor Helmut Kohl seized the initiative in late November with a Ten-Point Plan for German unity, provoking the irritation of the victorious World War II allies, save the United States. The plan—which envisaged a slow transition from a vaguely defined "treaty community" linking the two German states to "confederative structures" (rather than a confederation)—was soon overwhelmed by events on the ground as the economic, political, and social collapse of the GDR generated a massive westward flight of refugees and a pro-unity consensus among the new East German democratic parties. In early February, the four World War II victors with occupation rights in Berlin—the United States, USSR, France, and Great Britain—and both German states set up the Two-Plus-Four talks to negotiate the international terms of a settlement. Kohl and his party, the Christian Democratic Union (CDU), pushed for rapid unification via the incorporation of the GDR *Länder* (states) into the FRG via Article 23 of the Basic Law.[1] The East German CDU and its allies won the first free GDR elections in March on a platform of rapid unity. With the momentum toward unity building weekly, the East and West German governments worked to persuade their allies and, especially, the Soviet leadership, that a united Germany should be a member of NATO. In dramatic summit encounters with American President George H.W. Bush and Kohl in May and July 1990, Gorbachev agreed to NATO membership in exchange for financial support for the withdrawal of Soviet troops from East Germany. The Two-Plus-Four talks concluded in September, and reunification took place on October 3, 1990.

The emergence of a unified German state in the middle of a transformed Europe was a major, if not *the* major, turning point in the end of the Cold War. It easily meets the essential criteria set forth by Herrmann and Lebow in that it was a change "of significant magnitude . . . that would be difficult to undo." Moreover, designating German unification as a turning point is not in any meaningful sense a "subjective judgment." Policymakers and scholars on all sides and of nearly all intellectual persuasions do not dispute the event's seminal importance and irreversibility.

German unification is so clearly a turning point because all the relevant actors saw it as such at the time. It is not an artifact of hindsight or theoretical reinterpretation. Other events in the larger East-West relationship, for example the "arms-control détente" of January 1989, were regarded at the time as deeper versions of familiar Cold War easings of tension. Despite all the changes, the fundamentals of the Cold War international system were still in place: two superpowers heading two alliances, and managing their security relations through arms control summitry.

Until the rapid and successive collapse of communist regimes across Eastern Europe, critical actors still debated whether or not the Cold War was really ending. As Jacques Lévesque shows in chapter 5, Gorbachev himself continued to believe in the possibility of reform socialism and a new pan-European security system, even as East European regimes began to tumble. It was only in the spring and summer of 1990, as the terms of German unification were settled, that actors on all sides saw not only that the Cold War was ending, but the geopolitical terms of its conclusion. In Washington, the prospect of a unified Germany in NATO suggested to many that the United States and its European allies were about to "win" the Cold War. In Moscow, the realization that the Soviet Union was about to lose the most important symbol of its long struggle and eventual victory over Hitler, as well as one of its most strategically important

Warsaw Pact allies, sparked the first real, open, and concerted challenge to Gorbachev's foreign policy. Everyone recognized that a united Germany meant the dawn of a new era in Europe and that a return to familiar Cold War patterns was impossible.

German unification represents a *political* turning point of the first order. The product of Great Power bargaining, the Two-Plus-Four Treaty represents the founding event of the post–Cold War international system. It is our Vienna, our Versailles: the event that definitively ended the previous international order and ushered in a new one. It was during the crucial early months of 1990 that the fundamental outlines of the post–Cold War U.S. and West European grand strategy were defined: the adaptation and expansion of existing U.S.-dominated Cold War institutions to the new circumstances rather than the true creation of a new world order based on new institutions. This basic strategic choice is still with us and it is important to understand its origins.

Finally, there are strong *theoretical* justifications for regarding German unification as the key turning point in the end of the Cold War. Unification is variously held to have reflected, caused, and codified massive changes in the distribution of material capabilities in Europe. Soviet armed forces were redeployed from the Elbe River, the old dividing line between East and West Germany, back to the Eurasian steppe, and Germany's geographic, population, and potential economic base was dramatically enhanced. Moreover, the process and form of German unification—the accession of the GDR to the Federal Republic and the continued membership of the FRG in NATO—reflected the preferences of the Germans themselves and the triumph of the idea of self-determination over calls for a new, Great Power–negotiated grand design for post–Cold War Europe.

For scholars who highlight the importance of the distribution of material resources in international politics, German unification and the retreat of the Red Army resulted from fundamental change in the balance of power. For theorists who emphasize the autonomous influence of ideas, German unification marks a break with ideational structures based on competing ideologically constituted spheres of influence and the legitimacy of two German states. Most theories of international politics expect changes of this magnitude in the international system to come as a result or consequence of major war.[2] The peaceful end of the Cold War thus represents a major puzzle for international relations scholarship, and German unification is the turning point within the larger event that presents this puzzle in its sharpest form.

Explaining German unification is important and inevitably controversial, and all efforts necessarily have to draw on the four generic kinds of explanation that frame this volume: material incentives, ideas, domestic politics, and leadership. Our purpose in this chapter is to mine the latest evidence in a careful assessment of the strengths and weaknesses of these four explanatory themes. In each of the following four sections, we summarize the standard arguments, models, or causal mechanisms associated with each type of explanation. In the conclusion, we offer our best judgment of the strengths and limitations of each kind of explanation, and the ways in which all four causes worked together to produce the outcome.

Because German unification is an event of daunting complexity, we restrict our focus to central puzzles that are closest to the concerns of this volume. Why was the question of German unification on the agenda? Why was there no use of force to prevent or stall the drive to unity? Why did unification occur in the manner it did—via the absorption of the GDR by the FRG and the inclusion of the newly unified Germany in NATO?

Material Incentives

The root material change underlying the end of the Cold War was the relative economic decline of the Soviet Union and its Central European allies.[3] While the Soviet economy grew at impressive rates in the 1950s, and registered respectable performance in the 1960s, beginning in the 1970s it entered a period of stagnation, underperforming its main rivals (the United States, Western Europe, and Japan). In the 1975–80 period, Soviet relative decline became particularly acute, and in the 1980s the systemic decline spread to all of Moscow's allies in Central Europe. And such quantitative measures understate decline, since Soviet-type economies were notorious for low quality and inefficiency. Indeed, the Soviet Union's longstanding technological lag began to worsen in the mid-to-late 1970s, as the productivity of labor, capital, and research-and-development expenditures all declined, while the Western economies and Japan began to enter the postindustrial revolution in information and communications technology. At the same time, numerous other indicators—on demographic trends, public health, and the environment—all trended dramatically downward in precisely this period.

In short, by the early 1980s the Soviet economy was losing the capacity to generate the resources needed for the leadership's three central objectives: a minimally acceptable standard of living; traditional foreign policy goals; and sufficient investment to ensure future growth. In the 1970s, the crisis was delayed somewhat by massive windfall oil profits, which the Brezhnev leadership used to improve consumer welfare slightly and attain overall military parity with the United States. But those policies were achieved only by squeezing investment, which appears to have contributed to the new slowdown in growth in the 1976–82 period. When the Soviet economy plunged into recession in 1980–82, Siberian oil production began to decline in 1983, and world oil prices plummeted in 1985, two powerful consequences for Soviet foreign policy followed.

First, economic decline created strong incentives for the Soviet Union to reverse the growth in the costs of its global position. This implied the need to limit Moscow's intervention in the domestic affairs of its Central European allies. The more the Soviet Union and its dependencies declined, the higher the marginal cost of maintaining Russian influence over the domestic choices of Central European states, and the greater the incentives to devolve authority. Decline also increased the incentives for engagement with the West, not only to reduce the costs of confrontation but also to reap the potential gains from increased trade and, especially, foreign direct investment (FDI) from rich Western partners.[4] These incentives figured especially powerfully in relations with West Germany, which was the Soviet Union's number one trade partner, source of FDI, and government and private creditor.[5]

The connection between decline and policy change is not mechanistic, however. Material change must be perceived to affect policy. An economic downturn may initially be seen as temporary, and only after it persists is it seen as a trend. Soviet policymakers thus only began to agonize over relative decline in the early 1980s, after several years of poor economic performance.[6] And, once a trend is recognized, it always takes some time to formulate and effect a response, given the standard institutional and organizational lags that characterize any modern polity. Hence, in the Soviet case we see a two-to-three year lag between recognition of the systemic trend and the new policy response.

When Gorbachev assumed office, the Soviet Union had been growing on average 1 percent per year slower than the United States for a decade. Defense claimed at least 15–20 percent of GDP, and the defense burden was rising measurably and steadily in the 1975–88 period.[7] The Central European allies were a large and dramatically growing drain on resources.[8] The United States was ramping up the arms race to a new technological level, and the Soviet military was clamoring for scarce technological resources to meet the challenge. Unless the material trends were reversed, at some moment in the future the Soviet Union would lack the capability to maintain the Cold War status quo.

Soviet retrenchment and engagement were not the only possible responses to decline, but explanations based on material incentives suggest that these policies were the most likely responses. What were the alternatives? By 1985–87, there was no evidence that just clinging to the status quo and hoping trends would miraculously reverse themselves would be a sustainable policy over the long run. A renewed assault on the West would only increase the economic burden Moscow already faced and cut off all hope of obtaining gains through economic interaction. Given the United States' economic and military ascendancy, higher tensions only reinforced its dominance over its own alliance and hence its ultimate superiority over Moscow. U.S. superiority, nuclear deterrence, and the declining economic value of territory made preventive war out of the question. Given that the status quo or a new offensive were off the table, that left as the only realistic policy reducing the economic burden of the Cold War and restoring the economic competitiveness of the Soviet Union.

The second major consequence of changing material incentives is that they affected the bargaining outcome once the GDR began to collapse—partly itself an unintended consequence of the Soviets' effort to revitalize their domestic institutions while cutting back the costs of empire. German unification occurred in the manner most congenial to the preexisting preferences of the U.S. and West German governments because they were by far the most powerful players. The key here is that both the Soviet Union and the GDR turned out to be far worse off economically than observers recognized before 1989. Failure to predict the precipitous decline of the Soviet Union and the GDR does not impugn explanations rooted in material incentives: the fact that observers were not aware of decline is not evidence that it was unimportant.

This explains the puzzle of the dramatically skewed terms of the settlement. The relevant actors learned suddenly and quickly in 1989 and early 1990 just how exhausted the material resources of Moscow and Berlin really were, and changes in the bargaining over terms reflected quick updating of actors' assessments of relative power. West Germans and Americans proposed, and the Soviets (and French and British) accepted terms that reflected their assessments of who would suffer the most if negotiations broke down.

In 1989, the Soviet economy entered a devastating crisis, with no growth, a ballooning deficit, rampant inflation, and a burgeoning foreign exchange crisis.[9] In late October, both Moscow and Berlin learned just how impoverished was the GDR—keystone of Moscow's Central European arch—when East German Planning Minister Gerhard Schürer produced a report that concluded that the economy was shattered.[10] Aside from declining living standards and abysmal productivity, the most pressing crisis was servicing the foreign debt: the country was headed for bankruptcy. Without new capital from the west, stemming the tide of indebtedness for the next year would require an immediate drop of the people's standard of living by 25 to 30 percent, which would make the GDR "ungovernable." The report proposed a profound economic reform that would require an infusion from West Germany of DM 2–3 billion *above* the existing line of credit.

On November 1, East German leader Egon Krenz met Gorbachev in Moscow, informing his Soviet ally of the GDR's crisis. Gorbachev was "astonished" to learn of the extent of the GDR's economic crisis.[11] His response was that the East Germans should get more credits from Bonn and initiate reforms to win over the disaffected masses. The Soviet Union would try to live up to existing agreements,

Gorbachev explained, but in view of its own problems, no increase in aid or sub-sidies would be forthcoming. In what must have come as a rude awakening for Krenz, Gorbachev noted that Moscow was at the very moment gearing up to ap-proach the Bonn government and financial sector for closer ties and increased credits. In short, as the GDR entered its terminal crisis, *both* Berlin and Moscow were seeking increased favors from Bonn. To put it mildly, this did little to en-hance their bargaining leverage on inter-German issues.

The regime of Erich Honecker had been systematically deceiving the West, the Russians, its own people, and perhaps even itself, about the economic con-dition of the GDR.[12] While a "Potemkin village" strategy can work in the short run, barring an economic turnaround it is eventually doomed. In Honecker's case, the economy did not turn around; it continued to decline. Leadership turnover sparked by social unrest created the incentives to collect and dissemi-nate relatively accurate data on the country's deteriorating economic situation. It took time for the reality of the depth of East Germany's problems to penetrate the minds of Soviet and Western officials. Once the Wall came down, however, each day brought more evidence that the country could not be rescued, and, even if it could, the West Germans were unwilling to foot the bill without at-taching conditions that further undercut the Berlin government. Recently re-leased documents clearly show that the Soviets at last recognized in December–January 1989–90 that the assumptions underlying their European policy were no longer valid: reform socialism was collapsing; Washington and Bonn were moving toward "blatant intervention in the internal affairs of the GDR" in support of unification; and London and Paris lacked the power to do anything to stop it.[13]

Once the depth of decline was understood, the punishingly high costs and low benefits of using force to prevent East Germany's collapse were appar-ent—and not just to Gorbachev and the new thinkers, but to most "old thinkers" in the Soviet Union as well. Large-scale use of force would have ended the detente with the West, increased the West's allocations for defense, closed off all credits to a Soviet economy in desperate need, and shut down all technology transfers or joint ventures. Moreover, intervention would imply the assumption of direct responsibility for the GDR's foreign debt, whose ser-vicing would have added massive burdens on the Soviet economy; or, of course, a default, which would have further closed Western markets. Had it intervened, Moscow would then have had to establish a new client regime whose obvious dependence on the Soviet Union would imply even higher gov-ernance costs for the Soviet budget than the old GDR. A major use of force would, in short, have entailed Soviet isolation unseen since the 1950s, and it would have required Moscow to extract 1950s-level sacrifices from its own population. But in the 1950s, the Soviet economy was growing at 8 percent yearly, and Russian rulers had a rational confidence in their system. Fifteen years of decline had sapped that confidence, and with it the willingness to die, kill, and impose material hardship in the name of socialism. Given these material trends, it is not surprising that no old thinker advocated the use of force in 1989, and none has since suggested that such a decision would have served Soviet interests.[14]

Given the immense costs of using its military muscle in Central Europe, Moscow had limited bargaining room. Indeed, only two concrete alternatives to capitulation have emerged from the documents—both of which were based on impossibly optimistic assumptions. In November 1989 the Soviet ambassador in Bonn suggested that the GDR seize the initiative with a plan for a state-to-state confederation, preserving the Warsaw Pact and NATO. The proposal assumed that the Berlin government possessed the capability and organizational coherence to retain power democratically and pursue a concerted international initiative.[15] More important, it assumed that Bonn would fork over new billions of Deutschmarks to continue to prop up the GDR. Neither assumption was remotely plausible.

In February 1990 veteran Soviet arms negotiator Oleg Grinevsky vetted the idea that Moscow should immediately support unification but insist on a neutral, demilitarized Germany. This assumed that Moscow had the power and legitimate rights of a victor over a vanquished state.[16] But West Germany and the United States were the victors in the Cold War, not the Soviet Union. A Soviet assertion of power or residual rights over Germany would probably have had to face an overwhelming diplomatic countercoalition. According to Western officials, Washington and Bonn had contingency plans in case the Soviets balked and asserted their residual four-power rights from World War II.[17] The Western three would simply have unilaterally withdrawn their rights, leaving Moscow alone against the Germans. Few policymakers in Moscow thought the Soviet Union could prevail if the West was truly willing to risk a return of Cold War confrontation rather than acquiesce to German neutrality. If negotiations broke down—or if Moscow simply announced "our troops are not leaving until you accept our terms"—the likelihood was that the Soviets' bargaining position would only deteriorate with time as the Soviet and Eastern German economies continued their precipitous decline. Meanwhile, the West German government was in effect beginning to provide governance for the Eastern German territory. Moscow simply lacked the resources to counter this influence—unless it was truly willing to crack down forcefully and assume full responsibility, something no one in Moscow wanted to contemplate.

Relationships of power and wealth—and rational expectations of which side could prevail if negotiations broke down, as well as which side could offer more material rewards in return for concessions—account for the puzzle of Gorbachev's sudden acquiescence to unified Germany being a member of NATO in the spring of 1990. Gorbachev seems to have concluded that as much as he opposed the expansion of NATO, a concession on this issue would pay off in the future in terms of better relations with the new Germany. He was reluctant to endorse any diplomatic ploy that banked on the GDR, which by January he had concluded was doomed, or which risked spoiling the emerging relationship with Germany.[18]

Ideas

Few proponents of materialist explanations of political outcomes argue that ideas don't "matter." Rather, ideas are more often held to "track" shifts in material incentives, to provide explanations for the timing or tactics of policy shifts that by necessity lag behind material change.[19] Such arguments, however, can often be turned around. Thus, in response to the argument that long-term Soviet economic and military decline confronted Gorbachev with a material fact that demanded a change in policy, one could argue that the decline was the result of, and lagged behind, ideologically informed choices of the Soviet elite. The methodological problem confronting any effort at constructing a causal explanation for complex social processes and outcomes is deciding where to "cut in" to a chain of historical events, a choice that will often bias the relative weighting of favored causal factors.

Scholars who stress the autonomous role of ideas in the processes that led to peaceful German reunification start from the basic premise that the implications of material decline were not self-evident, and that a variety of responses were available to Soviet leaders. Had the Soviet leadership been persuaded of a different set of ideas, they would have made different strategic choices and the course of history would have been quite different. The question we ask is: Given decline, how did ideas affect the course of events that led to German unification?

In analyzing the course and content of unification, three sets of ideas stand out as important independent variables: Soviet ideas on the legitimacy and effectiveness of the use of force in Eastern Europe; Soviet and West German ideas on the right of East German citizens to self-determination; and, within Germany, nationalism as a unifying principle. Each of these ideas appears to have been either independent of material factors or at least not easily reducible to or implied by a particular material condition. Moreover, each was to some extent contested; that is, other sets of ideas were available to guide the choices of decision makers or inform the preferences of public opinion.

Non-use of Force

Popular uprisings in the streets of East Germany's largest cities and the subsequent breaching of the Berlin Wall on November 9, 1989, raised the question in Western policymaking circles of whether the Soviet Union would resort to military intervention in an effort to restore order, as it had during the East German workers' protests in 1953 or the uprisings in Hungary in 1956 and Czechoslovakia in 1968. The Soviet Union's rejection of a military response to instability in the GDR was certainly crucial to the chain of peaceful events that led to unification. As both Soviet and Western leaders recognized at the time, a resort to force would have stopped the reform process in the Soviet Union, brought a halt to further progress on arms control, and prolonged the Cold War.

There is ample evidence suggesting that new thinkers, with Gorbachev and Shevardnadze at the fore, regarded the use of force as illegitimate and counterproductive as a means of coping with political dissent across Eastern Europe. Andrew Bennett argues that both Gorbachev and Shevardnadze developed strong aversions to the use of force as means of coping with political dissent in the wake of the Soviet interventions in Hungary and Czechoslovakia. Failures of Soviet-backed rebellions in the Third World as well as the Soviet military defeat in Afghanistan only strengthened their longstanding antipathy.[20]

Bennett's argument that Gorbachev came to power already skeptical of the utility of military force to achieve political ends is supported by Gorbachev's own writings. In his memoirs, Gorbachev claims to have used the occasion of Chernenko's funeral in March 1985 to inform the East European leaders that the Soviet Union would no longer intervene in their domestic affairs and that the national communist parties would be responsible for maintaining political order, in effect renouncing the Brezhnev Doctrine.[21] Writing in 1987, Gorbachev asserted that military power was of limited utility for the long-term political subordination of other nations.[22] Repeated public and private declarations of a change in Soviet doctrine took concrete form with the unilateral reduction of Soviet forces in Eastern Europe announced by Gorbachev in a speech before the UN General Assembly in December 1988. The 500,000 Soviet troops to be withdrawn from Eastern Europe included 5,000 tanks and 50,000 related personnel deployed in Hungary, Czechoslovakia, and the GDR. These forces had served as a constant reminder of Soviet dominance over Eastern Europe, and their withdrawal represented a dramatic shift in Soviet foreign policy, making any future use of force in Eastern Europe both less likely and more costly.

But to what extent can it be argued that the non-use of force was a function of ideas and not a choice dictated by material constraints? Gorbachev had strong, long-term financial incentives to reduce the Soviet troop presence in East Europe. And because perestroika's success was premised upon an accommodation with the West, an accommodation that a military crackdown in Eastern Europe would jeopardize, one could argue that Gorbachev's range of foreign policy options was constrained by the very real need to effect domestic economic reform. This was widely recognized among Soviet leaders.[23]

The strong argument for a link between the declining material fortunes of the Soviet Union and the rejection of force as a means of ensuring political stability and Moscow's influence in Eastern Europe is not entirely persuasive. As Bennett's research documents, Mikhail Gorbachev and the new thinkers he elevated to positions of authority had rejected the use of force as a means of redressing political instability in the Soviet sphere of influence largely independent of their growing awareness of the Soviet Union's declining material fortunes. Whether Gorbachev, as General Secretary of the Communist Party of the Soviet Union, would have prevailed in a counterfactual Politburo debate over the use of force as a response to instability in the GDR is unknown. But given the dominant position of the General Secretary in the Soviet system, one could make the case that Gorbachev's preferences would have carried the day. Indeed, even the conservative leaders of the attempted August 1991 coup d'état admitted to having regularly deferred to the wishes of Gorbachev, who they subsequently criticized for having increasingly centralized and insulated the decision-making process.[24]

The puzzling fact of the matter is that the use of force to restore order in the GDR and to prevent the unification of Germany was never discussed in the Politburo. It is doubtful that no one in the leadership of the military or KGB thought about the use of force as a means to slow down the pace of change and regain Soviet influence over the course of events in the GDR. That such ideas were not raised with Gorbachev is probably due to the fact that Gorbachev's views on the use of force were widely known. As Gorbachev's foreign policy advisor Anatoly Chernyaev put it: "I know for a fact that Marshall Yazov, who was defense minister at the time, never even asked Gorbachev [about the use of force]. He couldn't afford to ask that question, because he knew what the answer would be, that Gorbachev would never allow any kind of use of Soviet troops that were at that time in Germany."[25]

Perhaps the strongest evidence for rejecting material decline as a sufficient explanation for the Soviets' non-use of force in East Germany is that the Soviet leadership was willing to use force after the collapse of pro-Soviet regimes across Eastern Europe. In January 1991, 14 people were killed and over 600 injured when Soviet troops engaged Latvian citizens who had established defensive positions around the Vilnius television and radio tower in an effort to stop the Latvian communists and their Black Beret mercenaries from closing down independent news broadcasts. And with the launching of the anti-Gorbachev coup by the State Committee for the State of Emergency on August 19, 1991, Soviet General Fedor Kuzmin announced that the Baltic military district was taking over control of the Baltic republics.[26] Even in the face of ever-increasing material constraints during an accelerated economic and military decline, the Soviet leadership adopted a different response to civil unrest in the Baltics than they had in the GDR. And the rapid effort to impose martial law in the Baltics during the August coup suggests that the anti-Gorbachev hard-liners would have been even less resistant to seeking military solutions to political and civil unrest had their coup been successful.

Self-determination

Having ruled out the use of force as a response to popular uprisings in the GDR and the steady flow of East German citizens into the Federal Republic of Germany, Gorbachev was forced to come to terms with the political impulses to which these developments gave rise. Although unification was certainly on everyone's mind, neither Moscow nor Bonn regarded unification as a near-term prospect.[27] For Gorbachev, the immediate question was how to respond to the demands of the East German masses for political reform. Was the future of the GDR a matter for the "fraternity of socialist states" to determine, or in the first instance a question for the East Germans themselves?

For his part, Chancellor Kohl consistently maintained that the East Germans' right to self-determination was guaranteed by the Helsinki Final Act (1975), a position that was echoed by American President George H. W. Bush.[28] Gorbachev explicitly recognized the Germans' right to self- determination on the occasion of Kohl's visit to Moscow on February 10, 1990. The move was significant. By granting the Germans the right to decide their own future, Gorbachev reduced the risks that either half of Germany would face Soviet retribution in the event that the two states should pursue the goal of national unification. It is in this context that the February 12 announcement of the Two-Plus-Four—rather than Four-Plus-Two, or Four-Plus-Zero—mechanism for negotiating the terms of unification is important.[29] Though certainly not a sufficient cause of German unification, the outcome of East German demands for political reform would quite likely have been different had the norm of self-determination been absent and the World War II allies insisted on their rights to negotiate a peace treaty with the erstwhile vanquished foe.

Like material constraints, however, international norms rarely prescribe precise political outcomes. In the process leading to German unification, the norm of self-determination set the terms of debate, but not the outcome. A number of outcomes would have been consistent with the norm of self-determination, including the establishment of a reform communist or a non-communist, yet independent, East German state. How did self-determination come to mean national unification?

"*Wir sind* ein *Volk*"

That the East Germans had a right to decide their political future on their own was widely accepted, but this is not to say that the key external players did not have clear preferences on the course and content of self-determination. Despite the accelerating pace of events in the GDR, Gorbachev appears to have believed as late as October 31, 1989, that reform communism could take hold in East Germany and the Warsaw Pact.[30] If there were any doubts that Chancellor Kohl's ultimate aims were unification, they were dispelled on November 28, 1989, when he presented his ten-point plan to the Bundestag. But German public opinion, both in the West and East, was divided over reunification.

Important members of the West German Social Democratic Party (SPD) were opposed to Kohl's plans for unification, as were eminent members of the intelligentsia, such as Günther Grass and Walter Jens, who regarded unification as a "chimera blind to history."[31] Similar arguments were aired in the GDR. In November 1989, leading members of the East German intellectual avant-garde warned against unification, suggesting that the GDR had a choice of either "a society of solidarity in which peace and justice, individual freedom, freedom of movement and the preservation of the environment are guaranteed . . . [or] a sellout of our values."[32] However, it was popular opinion in the GDR that gave self-determination its national character and provided the necessary momentum for unification.

Popular sovereignty and the right to self determination were clearly reflected in the original slogan of the mass demonstrations across East Germany: "Wir sind das Volk!" (We are the people). However, on November 19, demonstrators in Leipzig began to chant a new slogan that rapidly displaced the first in protests across the GDR: "Wir Sind ein Volk!" (We are one people). The discursive shift was consequential, for it signified a move from merely a demand for popular sovereignty in the GDR to an assertion of the national unity of all Germans.[33] Without a strong reserve of nationalism, unification would not have occurred in 1991.[34]

Domestic Politics

Even if we restrict our analysis to the power, preferences, and strategies of states, domestic processes must figure in any explanation of German unification. First, domestic processes strongly affect state capacity, and thus the systemic distribution of capabilities. Second, politicians' essential motivation to retain office influences their foreign policy. And third, domestic institutional and political arrangements channel international bargaining toward particular solutions.

Domestic Processes are Endogenous to the Balance of Power

The capacity of a state to coerce or entice others is critically dependent on the efficacy of its domestic institutions and the outcomes of crucial choices over domestic policies. The Soviet Union was in decline in part because of changes in the international system, but also because of deficiencies intrinsic to its domestic institutions. More important for our case, the Soviet Union's "power" in 1989–90 was influenced critically by Gorbachev's domestic policies. He initially chose to reinvigorate the Soviet economy in the belief—widely held among party officials of Gorbachev's generation—that it could be competitive if the proper set of incentives could be put in place. However, the policy was a catastrophic failure, generating massive fiscal imbalances, no upsurge in growth, and the beginnings of a breakdown in the command system.[35] Gorbachev's response to this failure was to revamp the political system to undercut the "conservatives" who he thought were sabotaging perestroika. These reforms further destabilized the system, and by the winter of 1989–90, Soviet politics were in a chaotic transitional state. In short, the weak, confused, and incoherent Soviet Union that Bonn and Washington dealt with in the negotiations over German unification was partially the product of Gorbachev's domestic gambles.

There were alternatives to Gorbachev's choices, of course, but it is important to be careful in considering the counterfactuals associated with them. The two most plausible alternatives—the strategy of "optimizing the planning mechanism" favored by more conservative officials such as Nikolai Ryzhkov and Yegor Ligachev, and the strategy of rapid marketization pushed by liberals like Yegor Gaidar and Grigory Yavlinsky—were both weighted even *more* heavily toward cutting back the imperial burden.[36] Both Ryzhkov and Gaidar—coming from two very different perspectives—had the same fundamental criticism of Gorbachev: that he failed to rein in government expenditures (including on defense) fast enough to establish the macroeconomic stability true reform demanded. And this raises a critical point with which all such counterfactuals must contend: that the Soviet Union's material decline was closely connected to the high and growing economic costs of its international position.

In a counterfactual involving Soviet adoption of either the conservative or the liberal alternatives to the course Gorbachev chose, the Soviets would have been even *more* sensitive to the costs of holding on to the GDR than they were in reality. Moreover, there is little reason to believe that either plan would have restored growth to the Soviet economy by 1989–90. Thus, counterfactuals that portray an economically viable Soviet Union in 1990 require heroic assumptions and find little empirical support. On the other hand, it is much easier to imagine a counterfactual Soviet Union of 1989–90 still backward, weak, declining, and dependent on the West but nonetheless with its traditional political institutions intact. And that imaginary Moscow would have been in a much better position than was the real one to conceive and implement a proactive policy on Germany.

Political Incentives Affect Strategic Choices

Leaders may select a foreign strategy with an eye toward maintaining or enhancing their domestic authority. This is arguably the most common argument concerning the effect of domestic politics in the international relations literature. In the case of the Soviet Union and German unification, Gorbachev argues that his policies were constrained by the domestic standoff between radicals and conservatives, which prevented the kind of flexible approach that might have won Moscow better terms on German unification.[37] Soviet military and Party hard-liners, the argument goes, were so viscerally opposed to any compromises that Gorbachev could not offer early concessions on Germany that might have allowed Moscow to seize the initiative despite material constraints by linking early Soviet acquiescence to German unity to insistence on neutrality. Such ploys would have required Gorbachev to clarify his stance on Germany publicly, which would have hastened the mobilization of conservatives against him. In other words, domestic polarization demanded that Gorbachev maintain ambiguity on Germany, even though this ambiguity was suboptimal from the point of view of Moscow's bargaining interests.

It is difficult to verify this argument, but Gorbachev's behavior is consistent with it. Central to Gorbachev's leadership style was the maintenance of strategic ambiguity about his real preferences in order to keep supporters on board while keeping opponents too uncertain to take decisive action against him. By January 1990 Gorbachev appears to have concluded that unity was inevitable, and that Moscow was in no position to oppose a strong Western preference for German membership in NATO. However, he felt unable to express these arguments publicly. By offering one fateful concession after another in high-stakes summits with Western leaders, and then pretending to back away, he in effect enlisted the Americans and Germans to bludgeon his own bureaucracy and public opinion into agreement. On Germany, as on so many other issues, Gorbachev engineered faits accompli that his opponents only recognized as such after it was too late to change course.

While domestic politics may have constrained Gorbachev from following the strategically optimal policy on Germany, the same pattern of behavior is consistent with both the argument that Gorbachev was merely ambivalent or incompetent, as hard-liners allege, and the argument that Gorbachev rationally responded to material trends and incentives and the uncertainty concerning whether his leverage would improve or decline with time. Domestic polarization may have had nothing to do with it. The standard domestic politics hypothesis is thus precisely the sort of argument whose resolution requires much more access to internal documents than we presently enjoy.

Domestic Politics Channel International Bargaining

That the course and content of German unification reflected the preferences of the more powerful of the two German states can be seen as supporting evidence for the materialist argument. However, the precise nature of the settlement of the German issue can only be explained by considering preexisting political arrangements and domestic political processes.

Chancellor Kohl's ten-point plan of late November 1989 was as much an effort to set the terms of debate within Germany as it was a blueprint for the diplomacy of unification.[38] By conditioning continued economic assistance to fundamental economic reform and political change in the GDR, including free elections, Kohl made clear that he intended to use West Germany's economic strength to influence the course of reform and the process of unification. Insofar as the remaining points were largely devoted to enumerating the possible stages on the path to that end, he assured that the principal issue in any GDR elections would be the larger question of German unification.

Given the ongoing mass migration of East Germans (almost 50,000 per month) to the West and the further collapse of the East German economy, the election of a new East German parliament (*Volkskammer*) quickly turned into a referendum on the terms of reunification: quick accession via Article 23, or the slower creation of a new German state under Article 146. Opinion in both German states was deeply divided on the issue of the constitutional question. Proponents of unification on the basis of Article 146 tended to support a "third way" for Germany, a constitutional structure that would create a state that was less capitalist and individualist than the Federal Republic but more democratic than that of the GDR. Kohl's plans for rapid unification under Article 23 came under constant attack from the West German Social Democratic Party (SPD) and the Greens. SPD leader Oscar Lafontaine warned against the massive costs of reunification and argued that an eventual unification should occur under the terms of Article 146. For their part, the Greens supported a confederation of the two German states.

Characterizing Lafontaine and the SPD as out of touch with the will of the East German population, Kohl appealed to the East Germans to adopt the *Königsweg* (a king's path) to unification offered through Article 23.[39] Many in the East German social movements thought that elections were coming too fast: the citizenry was not adequately prepared, East German party structures were too weak, and the potential influence of Western money was too great.[40] As the March elections approached, the West German parties became extremely active in supporting the further organization and financing of their counterparts in East Germany.[41]

The faster the process of unification, the more Kohl controlled it. He repeatedly exploited the powers of his office to influence public opinion in the GDR, for example announcing a plan for an economic and currency union with the GDR popular with East Germans. Kohl was also successful in raising millions of marks from private sources to support the East German CDU. On March 18, the day of the elections, East German voters were confronted with a choice between parties supporting rapid unification and currency union or those promoting a slower course, with the terms to be negotiated. In overwhelming numbers they chose the first option, surprising nearly everyone.[42]

The East German elections were clearly a turning point in the process that led to unification. Had the SPD, whose views on the pace and form of unification converged to a large extent with those of Gorbachev, won a clear majority, the Soviet Union would in all likelihood have had a better chance to influence the terms of unification. And an SPD victory in the GDR might well have strengthened the SPD in the Federal Republic.[43]

The overwhelming victory of the Alliance and the subsequent formation of a coalition government under the premiership of CDU-member Lothar de Maizière meant the broad outlines of the endgame were clear. Two German states, each led by parties favoring rapid unification on the basis of Article 21 of the Basic Law of the Federal Republic, would negotiate the specifics of that outcome. On March 18, the fortunes of the Soviet Union sank with those of the East German Social Democrats.

Any complete account of German unification or explanation for why one set of ideas triumphed over others requires an analysis of domestic politics and pre-existing institutional arrangements such as the Basic Law. Precipitous Soviet decline, the GDR's collapse, and the Soviets' recognition that any solution to their problems required Western economic assistance, do not provide a sufficient explanation for the developments of 1989–90. Relative decline did not prescribe the precise terms of East German reform or the future relations of the two German states. Unification was but one of a number of possible outcomes (another being the establishment of a confederate union with continued Western subsidies for the GDR) that were discussed both among the Four Powers and the Germans themselves. East Germany's economic weakness provided Bonn with an opportunity to influence the terms of GDR reform and German unification through the use of financial incentives and linkage politics. And Helmut Kohl aggressively exploited that opportunity. However, given the prevailing views in the West German SPD and Green Party, the nature of that linkage might well have been different had a "red-green" coalition governed in Bonn.[44] It is thus misleading to speak of unification on the basis of West German preferences. Rather, the outcome reflected the preferences of the ruling coalition, with Kohl at the top.

Leadership

The end of the Cold War has spawned a new scholarly interest in the study of leadership.[45] Concerning German unification, the boldest leadership argument is that some other plausible Soviet leader besides Gorbachev might have prevented further Soviet decline and succeeded in holding on to the Central European socialist allies. Such arguments place great demands on counterfactual analysis and are extraordinarily hard to tame empirically and analytically. There is no way to establish without serious scholarly controversy the availability of alternative policies that would have reversed Soviet decline or dramatically decreased the economic drain of Moscow's main dependencies. Any such program would have had to confront the costly imperial burden imposed on the Soviet Union by its position in the international system. No evidence has come to light that Gorbachev's domestic opponents entertained any strategies that had a plausible chance of turning Soviet fortunes around. Available evidence shows that, even earlier, the Brezhnev leadership was sensitive to the costs of maintaining suzerainty in Central Europe and deeply reluctant to use force to maintain it in the early 1980s.[46] And, the evidence indicates that hard-liners like Kryuchkov and Yazov were also unwilling to contemplate the large-scale use of force to rescue the GDR in 1989. All of these patterns of evidence make it harder to sustain the counterfactual that German unification would not have happened had Gorbachev not been in power.

Much more tractable and better supported empirically are three more modest arguments about leadership effects in 1989. First is the argument that a more conservative leader than Gorbachev would not have reacted to the failure of the initial reform package in 1988 by deepening and extending "democratization" reforms. Since those reforms arguably contributed mightily to the weakness and incoherence of Soviet policy in the winter of 1989–90, had a counterfactual Soviet leader attempted to keep the old totalitarian institutions intact after 1988, Moscow would still have been declining, reluctant to use force, and deeply in need of detente and retrenchment. But it would have been far better able to control information and coordinate an effective policy response. This is plausible if the radicalization of perestroika in 1988 was Gorbachev's own brainchild as opposed to the product of a more complex domestic political process. In assessing the role of leadership in this instance, it is important to bear in mind that at that time many Soviet officials and analysts shared Gorbachev's belief that democratization was necessary to break the grip of conservative bureaucrats and push through the reforms that the Soviet Union needed to restore economic growth. Thus the fateful push for political reforms is not entirely the idiosyncratic product of one man's vision.

A second argument concerns the evolution of trust between decision makers. This factor is often stressed by former policymakers themselves, and it also figures in scholarly analyses.[47] But trust was quite slow in developing. Indeed, on the available evidence, the process of the dissolution of communism in Central Europe was well along before relations of trust appeared to take hold among Kohl, Gorbachev, and Bush.[48] In other words, trust emerged when the material fortunes of the Soviets collapsed, and they agreed to Western terms. It is thus difficult to disentangle the importance of interpersonal synergy from dictates of dire necessity, in the case of Gorbachev, and the delights of getting exactly what one wants, in the case of Bush and Kohl.

The most popular leadership argument is that Kohl, Bush, and their respective policymaking teams were more effective strategists than their counterparts in Moscow, Paris, and London. In responding quickly to surprise developments and formulating effective responses, Kohl was clearly way ahead of the pack, with Bush close behind. Mitterrand, Thatcher, and Gorbachev were well behind the German-American duo. The West Germans clearly had a better reading on the evolving situation in the GDR than any of the other major players. From November 1989 on they were always quicker to see the GDR's decline and the possibilities it implied than were any of their Great Power interlocutors.

If the pattern in Soviet policy on German reunification was inconsistency, the pattern in West German policy was a consistent interpretation of all signals as green lights for unification. Each demonstration in the GDR, each increase in East German emigration, every Soviet statement—all evidence was interpreted as indicating the necessity and desirability for pushing forward unification, and the sooner the better. The pattern suggests a policy—at first perhaps implicit and even subconscious but later carefully orchestrated—of driving unification forward by systematically destabilizing the GDR.[49] Thus, one explanation for why Kohl and his aides were consistently more accurate in reading events in the GDR was that they were doing everything they could to cause those events to occur in the first place—in short, that Kohl and his aides were exercising leadership.

The second claimant for the mantle of leadership during these events is George H. W. Bush. The Bush administration assumed office convinced that although Moscow was "in general retreat" worldwide, Gorbachev had managed to seize control of the global agenda.[50] They believed that it was imperative to regain the initiative. Bush announced a new policy of "going beyond containment toward the integration of the Soviet Union into the international system" in a speech at Texas A&M University on May 17, 1989. The fundamental logic of the policy was to establish conditions Moscow would have to meet to be admitted into the U.S.-led international political and economic system. Spelled out formally in National Security Directive 23 (September 1989), the new approach called for "the integration of the Soviet Union into the existing international system," which required "fundamental alterations in Soviet military force structure, institutions, and practices that can only be reversed at great costs, economically and politically, to the Soviet Union."[51] The centerpiece of the new initiative was to go on the offensive in Europe by playing to U.S. and Western strengths and focusing on the fundamental weaknesses of Moscow's position in East-Central Europe. Bush countered Gorbachev's vision of a "common European home" with his own catch-phrase: "a Europe whole and free." Bush scheduled visits to Poland and Hungary, and began subtly to change his rhetoric on the German question.

By the late summer and fall of 1989, however, it became clear to Bush and his top aides that major change was afoot in Central Europe. Their initial reaction was careful; their basic impulse was to support stability and shy away from anything that might provoke the Soviets. When the crisis spread to the GDR, however, the prospects for stability dimmed. Kohl made the initial move in August, declaring that German reunification was "back on the international agenda." As the crisis intensified in October, Bush made a point of telling reporters, "I don't fear German reunification."[52]

The available evidence suggests that Bush's forthcoming public stance on reunification reflected his private convictions. While he did not think it was in the U.S. interest to push the issue before October, he had no principled objection to German unification as long as Moscow could swallow it and Germany's commitment to NATO was secured. By November he was intellectually ready to make one of the most important foreign policy decisions of his presidency: to back Helmut Kohl's reunification drive to the hilt.[53] Although the U.S. government was divided on the issue, Bush made his preferences known and he deserves the credit for placing America's chips on Bonn early and decisively.

Thus, the case for the effective leadership of Kohl and Bush is strong. Yet, it needs to be tempered by three caveats. First, both leaders followed such coherent policies because they both knew exactly what they wanted—to have their cake and eat it, too. That is, they both wanted both unification and NATO. They did not want to have to face any trade-offs between these two aims—the easiest route for any politician, and the one requiring the least creativity. Once they settled on taking the easiest intellectual route to the new situation—namely, adapting existing institutions to the new circumstances—it was comparatively easy to ensure that the vast decision-making bureaucracies in both capitals followed a clear and well-orchestrated line. All the intellectual rationales were already in place.

Second, the Soviet Union, France, and Britain lacked the power to force Kohl and Bush to face the trade-offs inherent in their policies. The two leaders most praised for their statesmanship happened to head the states that had the most power in Europe. The fact that their preferences prevailed owed more to the material resources than to the intellectual firepower at their disposal.

Third, they both "fudged" the critical question of integrating Moscow into the new European order, an oft-stated commitment of American and West German leaders that was contradicted by their policies. The essence of the choice they made for Europe was exclusionary. Some would be in NATO; others had to be out. To have reached another solution would have required facing tough trade-offs and rethinking cherished precepts and practices. It would have required thinking long and hard about whether NATO really was the conditio sine qua non of the U.S. presence in Europe. It would have demanded *real* leadership.

Conclusion

In this chapter, we asked why Germany reunified peacefully on mainly Western terms in 1990. Our analysis suggests that changing material incentives in the 1980s made peaceful unification on Western terms the most likely outcome. Material shifts seem to offer the most leverage on the case and to a large extent underpin other causes. Absent decline, ideas, leaders and domestic politics could not have had the effect they had with decline. "Freedom of choice" is a very convenient idea for an imperial leader who lacks the resources to enforce or entice compliance from his dependencies. That is not to say that the idea is reducible to material constraints. It is just that one cannot analyze the effect of the idea without paying heed to the fact that it did "fit" with material incentives. The same goes for leaders. Gorbachev may have desired reform and entente with the West for purely normative reasons. But he could not have been a reform *leader*—that is, he could not have persuaded others to follow him—unless he could point to undeniable material trends. Leaders can effect major change against entrenched interests in part because material shifts undermine opposition to change

Our conclusion that changing material incentives offer the most leverage on the explanation of this turning point must be qualified in several ways. First, the fact that changing material incentives appear to make some outcome probable does not mean it is the "only" possible outcome. Nor does it establish the timing of events with any precision. To get from material shifts to "unity in 1990 on these exact terms," we need to consider ideas, domestic politics, and leaders. A more conservative Soviet leader may (at least) have delayed matters by concealing decline and hoping for the best, and (at most) tried to use force. A Soviet leader less hemmed in by domestic pressures might have made a more proactive offer on the German Question earlier and gotten better terms. A Soviet leader with a less theoretical and a more pragmatic and strategic mindset might also have wrenched better terms from the West. A Kremlin leader with different causal beliefs about the instrumental utility of democratization and glasnost for economic revival might not have opted for those kinds of reforms, and thus led a more authoritarian and unitary (though still declining) Soviet Union in 1989–90. A less conservative East German leadership might have opted for reform earlier and prolonged—or shortened—GDR's lease on life. Or, events might simply have gotten out of control in the GDR, shots fired, powerful emotions raised, and quantities of blood spilled. Counterfactuals such as these can be spun out at length, and there is nothing in our basic finding that can rule them out categorically—although it does cast doubt on the more extreme versions (such as the argument that the Cold War could have continued essentially unchanged for decades under another leader).

Second, processes and outcomes were highly path dependent. Leadership choices appear to have magnified the effects of material change. Gorbachev's initial decisions to reform powerfully influenced subsequent interactions. The Soviet empire was strongly destabilized—in hard-to-reverse ways—by the reform effort at center. The reforms corroded the ancien regime's mechanisms for ensuring compliance from its agents throughout the economy and society without establishing functioning alternatives. Although it is hard in hindsight to think of remotely plausible policies that would have held things together, one must acknowledge that what Gorbachev actually did was deeply destabilizing.

Third, ideas and identities appear to have intensified the causal effects of material changes. Indeed, the way we framed the case may have privileged material incentives. We accepted as unproblematic givens the actors (states and the people who made decisions on their behalf), their identities and interests, and the history of their interaction as of the early 1980s. In addition, we framed the task as one of causal explanation, and thereby accepted the injunction "you can't explain change with a constant." Accepting these restrictions means that many factors and conditions that were clearly necessary and important for understanding the case do not explain it because they were relatively constant for years and even decades before the events transpired. So, new thinking ideas, as well as ideas of freedom, democracy, and self-determination did not vary, and so do not explain the case. Numerous scholars have documented how these reform ideas incubated in the Soviet Union from the 1950s onward.[54] They would not have become politically salient in the 1980s if the Soviet Union and its socialist allies had not been mired in a deepening and systemic economic decline. Similarly, the GDR had always been unfree. And the Germans were as much "ein Volk" in 1970 or 1960 as they were in 1989. What changed was not these background ideas but the Berlin regime's economic capacity to resist them.

Though these ideas are not "variables" in the case as we construed it, their existence is necessary to understand the outcome. The very identities of GDR and USSR in many ways magnified the impact of material changes. Their socialist ideologies were explicitly materialist. They had set themselves up as competitors to the West and defined their own legitimacy in amazingly explicit material terms. If they could not credibly promise to deliver on their explicit pledge to provide military and economic security superior to the West, and prosperity at least broadly comparable to the West, their legitimacy was vulnerable to challenge. For the Soviet Union in particular, the state's official identity demanded comparison to the United States—not just militarily but overall. Only given this prior condition did relative decline have the strong effect we observed in this case. Similarly, the GDR was the "socialist" Germany, where socialism was equated with certain material rewards and expensive egalitarian policies. If the regime could not deliver on these promises, then its reason for being was called into question in an unusually direct way. Thus, even though in this case material pressures were not as dire as in other cases (e.g., North Korea), their effects were powerful owing in part to these received social understandings. Sensitivity to this is crucial, lest we facilely apply "lessons" of German unification or the end of the Cold War to other cases.

In sum, we bracketed the case—as any analyst somehow must do. And, we sought to adjudicate among classes of causes—as nearly all social science and policy analysis must do. And we found that material incentives gave us great purchase explaining the case. However, this does not mean that material changes will always have this kind of effect in other cases, nor that social science "laws" can be derived from this and other cases. Material changes may have had powerful effects in this case because of social and ideational preconditions that are only beginning to be understood by international relations scholarship today.

Notes

1. Reflecting the conviction that the division of Germany was a provisional state of affairs, the founding document of the Federal Republic was not a constitution but rather the Basic Law adopted in 1949. The goal of unification was articulated in the preamble, which called on all Germans to strive for national unity. Two means for establishing a unified German state were also set forth. Article 23 provided for the accession of additional *Länder* to the Federal Republic, whereas Article 146 provided for the replacement of the Basic Law with a constitution adopted by a national constitutional convention upon unification.

2. This is true for both materialist and constructivist theories. See Jack Levy, "Declining Power and the Preventive Motivation for War," *World Politics* 40 (October 1987), pp. 82–107; and J. Samuel Barkin and Bruce Cronin, "The State and the Nation: Changing Norms and the Rules of Sovereignty," *International Organization* 48 (1) (Winter 1994), pp. 107–30.

3. In this chapter, we define as "material" incentives those arising from economic or security constraints. The data on economic decline in this and the next paragraph are detailed in Stephen G. Brooks and William C. Wohlforth, "Power, Globalization and the End of the

Cold War: Reevaluating a Landmark Case for Ideas," *International Security* 25 (3) (2000/2001), pp. 5–53 from which this section draws. See also Vladimir Kontorovich, "Economists, Soviet Growth Slowdown and the Collapse," *Europe-Asia Studies* 53 (5) (July 2001), pp. 675- 95.

4. For more, see Brooks and Wohlforth, "Power, Globalization and the End of the Cold War," and Dale Copeland, "Trade Expectations and the Outbreak of Peace: Détente 1970–1974 and the end of the Cold War 1985–1991," *Security Studies* 9 (1/2) (Winter-Spring 1999–2000), pp. 15–58.

5. For the data, see Alan B. Sherr, "Foreign Direct Investment in the Soviet Union; Status and Trends," Briefing Paper No. 5, Project on Soviet Foreign Economic Policy and International Security, Center for Foreign Policy Development, Brown University, 1991.

6. See Mark Kramer, "Ideology and the Cold War," *Review of International Studies* 25 (4) (October 1999), pp. 539–76

7. Note that these calculations are based on CIA estimates that overstate real Soviet economic performance. See John Howard Wilhelm, "The Failure of the American Sovietological Economics Profession," *Europe-Asia Studies* 55 (1) (January 2003), pp. 59–74. On defense spending: Noel E. Firth and James H. Noren, *Soviet Defense Spending: A History of CIA Estimates, 1950–1990* (Houston: Texas A&M Press, 1998).

8. See Randall Stone, *Satellites and Commissars: Strategy and Conflict in the Politics of Soviet-Bloc Trade* (Princeton, NJ: Princeton University Press, 1996).

9. See Sergei Germanovich Sinel'nikov (-Murylev), *Biudzhetnyi krisis v rossii, 1985–1995 gody* (Moscow: Evraziia, 1995), chap. 1.

10. The document is excerpted and analyzed in Hans Hermann Hertle, "Staatsbankrott: Der ökonomische Untergang des SED-Staates," *Deutschland Archiv* 25 (10) (October 1992), pp. 1019–30. See also, Hans Hermann Hertle, "'Das reale Bild war eben katastropha!' Gespräch mit Gerhard Schürer," *Deutschland Archiv* 25 (10) (October 1992), pp. 1031–39. Subsequent research indicates that Schürer's report was, if anything, understated. See Albrecht O. Ritschl, "An Exercise in Futility: East German Economic Growth and Decline, 1945–89," in *Economic Growth in Europe since 1945,* Nicholas Crafts and Gianni Toniolo eds. (Cambridge: Cambridge University Press, 1996). For illuminating accounts of the GDR's demise and German reunification that establish the lack of viable options, see Charles Maier, *Dissolution: The Crisis of Communism and the Collapse of East Germany* (Princeton, NJ: Princeton University Press, 1997); and Hannes Adomeit, *Imperial Overstretch: Germany in Soviet Policy from Stalin to Gorbachev* (Baden Baden: Nomos Verlagsgesellschaft, 1998); and, for an account of the collapse of the GDR's military that similarly documents social and economic constraints, see Dale R. Herspring, *Requiem for an Army: The Demise of the East German Military* (New York: Rowman & Littlefield, 1998).

11. "Niederschrift des Gesprächs des Genossen Egon Krenz, General Sekretär des ZK der SED und Vorsitzenden des Staatsrates der DDR, mit Genossen Michail Gorbatschow, General Sekretär der ZK der KPSU und Vorsitzender des Oberste Sowjets der UdSSR am 1.11.89." Typescript in author's possession.

12. For a brilliant analysis, see Jeffrey Kopstein, *The Politics of Economic Decline in East Germany, 1945–1989* (Chapel Hill: University of North Carolina Press, 1997).

13. The recognition is expressed clearly in, for example, Gorbachev's conversations with Genscher on December 5, 1989, and with Mitterrand on December 6, and in Memo. From CC CPSU International Department, "Towards a New Concept" (January 5, 1990), Doc. Nos. 70, 71, and 74 in National Security Archive, "The End of the Cold War in Europe: 1989."

14. For a review of the evidence on this point, see Andrew O. Bennett, "Trust Bursting Out All over: The Soviet Side of German Unification," in Wohlforth, ed., *Cold War Endgame: Oral History, Analysis, Debates* (University Park, PA: PennState University Press, 2003).

15. Julij A Kwizinskij, *Vor dem Sturm: Errinerungen eines Diplomaten* (Berlin: Siedler, 1993).

16. Ambassador Grinevsky's proposal—quashed by Shevardnadze—is outlined in Grinevsky, "Kak nachilos' germanskoe ob"edinenie," unpub. MS., in authors' possession.

17. Philip Zelikow and Condoleeza Rice, *Germany Unified and Europe Transformed: A Study in Statecraft* (Cambridge: Harvard University Press, 1995), pp. 245–46.

18. See notes from the critical Politburo meeting on Germany in Chernyaev, *Shest' let.* Anatoly, Chernyaev, *Shest' let s Gorbachevym: Po Dnevnikovym Zapisiam* (Moscow: Progress, 1993).

19. The argument can be found in William C. Wohlforth, "Ideology and the Cold War," *Review of International Studies* 26 (2) (April 2000), pp. 327–31.

20. See Andrew Bennett, "Ideas, Learning and the Soviets' non-use of Force in 1989," draft chapter for Tanenwald and Wohlforth, eds., *Ideas and the End of the Cold War,* book manuscript in progress; and Bennett, *Condemned To Repetition? The Rise, Fall, and Reprise of Soviet-Russian Military Interventionism, 1973–1996* (Cambridge, MA: MIT Press, 1999), chapter 7.

21. Michail Gorbatschow, *Erinnerungen* (Berlin: Siedler Verlag, 1995), chap. 30.

22. Mikhail S. Gorbachev, *Perestroika: New Thinking for Our Country and the World* (New York: Harper & Row, 1987), p. 138.

23. See Jacques Lévesque, *The Enigma of 1989: The USSR and the Liberation of Eastern Europe* (Berkeley: University of California Press, 1997), chapter 5.

24. Based on their comments at the Moscow oral history conference in May 2000, co-organized by the Mershon Center and the Institute of General History.

25. Conference transcript reprinted in William C. Wohlforth, ed., *Cold War Endgame,* chap, 2.

26. See Juris Dreifelds, *Latvia in Transition* (Cambridge, UK: Cambridge University Press, 1996), pp. 76–80.

27. Gorbachev claims that he regarded unification as a prospect for the twenty-first century. See Michail Gorbatschow, *Wie es war. Die deutsche Wiedervereinigung* (Berlin: Ullstein, 1999), p. 83. In discussions with U.S. President Bush at this point, Kohl indicated that unification could not be considered for at least two years. See Horst Teltschik, *329 Tage* (Berlin: Siedler Verlag, 1991), p. 63; Angela E. Stent, *Russia and Germany Reborn: Unification, the Soviet Collapse, and the New Europe* (Princeton, NJ: Preinceton University Press, 1999), pp. 98–100.

28. The Helsinki Final Act brought to a close the Conference on Security and Cooperation in Europe held in the Finish capital. Thirty-five European and North American signatories pledged to respect a number of basic human rights. For a discussion of the relevance of Helsinki to the thinking of Bush and Kohl, see Zelikow and Rice, *Germany Unified and Europe Transformed,* pp. 111–18; and George Bush and Brent Scowcroft, *A World Transformed* (New York: Knopf, 1998), p. 200.

29. The authorship of the Two-Plus-Four mechanism has given rise to much debate. See Zelikow and Rice, *Germany Unified and Europe Transformed,* chapter 5; Wohlforth *Cold War Endgame,* chap 2; Kiessler and Elbe, *Ein runder Tisch mit scharfen Ecken* (Baden-Baden: NOMOS, 1993), pp. 86–89; Chernyayev, *Shest' let s Gorbachevym,* pp. 346–47.

30. Stent, *Russia and Germany Reborn,* p. 92.

31. Quoted in Lothar Probst, "German Pasts, Germany's Future: Intellectual Controversies since Reunification," *German Politics and Society* 30 (Fall 1993), p. 21.

32. See Appel *"Für Unser Land,"* issued November 26, 1989. See too Stefan Heym, "Aschermittwoch in der DDR," *Der Spiegel* 49 (December 4, 1989), p. 58.

33. See Maier, *Dissolution,* esp. pp. 108–67 and 192–93.

34. Although the data for East Germany suffer from certain methodological shortcomings, survey research conducted by both East and West German research institutes in the late 1980s repeatedly found that 80 percent of East Germans considered the Germans to be one nation. The figure for West Germans was 75 percent. See See Manuela Glaab, "Ein-

stellung zur deutschen Einheit," in Werner Weidenfeld and Karl-Rudolf Korte, eds., *Handbuch zur deutschen Einheit: 1949–1989–1999* (Bonn: Bundeszentrale für politische Bildung, 1999), pp. 313–15.

35. In addition to Sinel'nikov, *Biudzhetny krizis,* see David Kotz, with Fred Weir, *Revolution from Above: The Demise of the Soviet System* (London: Routledge, 1997).

36. On the "Ligachev/Ryzhkov alternative," see Jerry F. Hough, *Democratization and Revolution in the USSR, 1985–1991* (Washington, DC: Brookings, 1997). On the liberal-market option, see Yegor Gaidar, *Days of Defeat and Victory,* trans. Jane Ann Miller (Seattle: University of Washington Press, 1999).

37. See Gorbachev, *Erinnerungen,* and "'Schön, ich gab die DDR weg.' Michail Gorbatschow über seine Rolle bei der deutschen Vereinigung," *Der Spiegel* 40 (1) (1995), pp. 66–81.

38. See Teltschik, *329 Tage,* pp. 52–58.

39. Gregg O. Kvistad, "Parties and Citizens in the Western German Unification Debate," *German Politics and Society* 30 (Fall 1993), pp. 34–48.

40. See Maier, *Dissolution,* pp. 198–200.

41. See Volkens and Klingemann, "Die Entwicklung der deutschen Partein im Prozeß der Vereinigung," p. 195–97. Also Ulrich Eith, "Parteien," in Weidenfeld and Korte, eds., *Handbuch zur deutschen Einheit,* pp. 558–70; and Petra Schuh and Binanca M. von der Weiden, *Die deutsche Sozialdemokratie 1989/90: SDP und SPD im Einigungsprozess* (München: Forschungsgruppe Deutschland, 1997).

42. Teltschik, *329 Tage,* p. 173.

43. That the Kohl team feared the effects of an SPD victory on West German domestic politics is clear in the diary entries of Horst Teltschik. See *329 Tage,* pp. 176–77.

44. During the commemoration of the tenth anniversary of unification in the fall of 2000, Helmut Kohl's assertion that a red-green coalition would in all likelihood pursue a radically different path in 1989–90 sparked vitriolic interparty debate.

45. In addition to the Breslauer and Lebow and Brown chapters in this volume, see Fred I. Greenstein, "Reagan and Gorbachev: What Difference did They Make?" in William Wohlforth, ed., *Witnesses to the End of the Cold War* (Baltimore: Johns Hopkins University Press, 1996); and Vladislav Zubok, "Gorbachev and the End of the Cold War: Different Perspectives on the Historical Personality," in Wohlforth, ed., *Cold War Endgame;* and Mark Allmond, "1989 without Gorbachev," in Niall Fergusen, ed., *Virtual History* (New York: Basic Books, 1997)

46. See Vojtech Mastny, "The Soviet Non-Invasion of Poland in 1980–81 and the End of the Cold War" (Washington, DC: Cold War International History Project Working Paper No. 23, 1998); and Mark Kramer, *Top-Secret Documents on Soviet Deliberations during the Polish Crisis, 1980–81. Special Working Paper No 23* (Washington, DC: Woodrow Wilson Center, 1999).

47. On the former, see Wohlforth, ed., *Witnesses to the End of the Cold War;* scholarly treatments include Breslauer and Lebow, Greenstein, "Reagan and Gorbachev"; Risse, "Let's Argue!: Communicative Action in World Politics"; Andrew Kydd, "Trust, Reassurance, and Cooperation," *International Organizatio* 54 (2) (2000), pp. 325–57; Deborah Welch Larson, *Anatomy of Mistrust: U.S.-Soviet Relations During the Cold War* (Ithaca, NY: Cornell University Press, 1997); and Derek Chollet and James Goldgeier, "Once Bitten, Twice Shy? The Pause of 1989," in Wohlforth, ed., *Cold War Endgame.*

48. And relations were quite testy up to that point. For Bush and Gorbachev, the key moment appears to have been the Malta Summit meeting in December 1989. See *A World Transformed;* Chernyaev, *Shest' let';* and the participants' recollections reported in Wohlforth, *Cold War Endgame,* chap. 1; while between Kohl and Gorbachev personal relations remained frosty until May or June 1990. See Gorbachev, *Erinnerungen.*

49. See Doris G. Wolfgramm, *The Kohl Government and German Reunification: Crisis and Foreign Policy* (Lewiston, NY: Edwin Mellen Press, 1997).

50. Bush and Scowcroft, *A World Transformed,* p. 65.

51. NSD 23 (9/22/89), "United States Relations with the Soviet Union," Doc. No. 52 in National Security Archive, "The End of the Cold War in Europe."

52. Quoted in Zelikow and Rice, *Germany Reunified,* p. 81.

53. See ibid., chap. 4; Bush and Scowcroft, *A World Transformed,* chap. 8; "Cold War Endgame," transcript, chap. 2.

54. See Robert D. English, *Russia and the Idea of the West: Gorbachev, Intellectuals and the End of the Cold War* (New York: Columbia University Press, 1999) and other treatments cited therein.

Part II

Comparing Turning Points and Causes

Chapter 7

Leadership and the End of the Cold War

A Counterfactual Thought Experiment

George W. Breslauer and Richard Ned Lebow

> *Hinkley's bullet still lodged in Reagan's heart. Doctors foresee little chance of recovery. Vice President Bush assumes presidential authority.*
>
> —AP Bulletin, March 21, 1981

> *Central Committee of the Communist Party of the Soviet Union has unanimously elected comrade Viktor Grishin as General Secretary.*
>
> —Pravda, March 6,1985

If the news reports above had been real, there might have been no "Gorbachev phenomenon," and glasnost and perestroika might not have become households words. Led by cautious and conservative General Secretary Grishin, the Soviet Union might have shunned serious reform at home and continued to regard the West as its principal foreign foe. The United States, led by an equally cautious and conservative President Bush, would almost certainly have responded in kind. In this counterfactual world, the Berlin Wall would still be in place and communist parties still in power in Moscow and Eastern Europe. The Warsaw Pact and NATO would be preparing to deploy a new generation of weapons because of the continuing deadlock in their arms control talks.

If this counterfactual—or some variant of it—seems plausible, it is because we recognize that leaders often make a difference, and sometimes make a huge difference. A Soviet Union without Gorbachev, and a Soviet-American relationship without the personal empathy and trust that developed between Reagan and Gorbachev, and between Secretary of State George Schultz and Foreign Minister Eduard Shevardnadze, might not be identical to the world depicted above, but it almost certainly would have been very different from the world that actually took shape between 1985 and 1991. The willingness of most political analysts and commentators to recognize the importance of leaders stands in sharp contrast to many theories of international relations. These theories typically rely on "structural" variables for their analytical power, and downplay, or downright ignore, the power of agency. To explain the Gorbachev foreign policy revolution, realists invoke the international balance of power, or expectations of impending shifts in that balance. Liberals attribute the change to the interaction between state structures and ideas, and downplay the independent role of leaders, contingencies, and accidents.[1]

International relations theorists generally seek to understand the most critical driving forces behind events; they almost invariably do so after the fact, when the outcome is known. The process of backward reasoning tends to privilege theories that rely on a few key variables to account for the driving forces allegedly responsible for the outcomes in question. Since, for the sake of theoretical parsimony, the academic discipline generally favors independent variables that are "structural" in nature, the entire endeavor has a strong bias toward deterministic explanations, thus distorting our understanding of the causes of events or accounts that are products of complex, conjunctional, indeterminate causality.[2]

In retrospect, almost any outcome can be squared with any theory unless the theory is rigorously specified. The latter requirement is rarely met in the field of international relations, and its deleterious effect is readily observed in the ongoing debate over the end of the Cold War. Various scholars, none of whose theories predicted a peaceful end to that conflict, now assert that this was a nearly inevitable corollary of their respective theories.[3] The disciplinary tendency to privilege structural explanations is reinforced by the well-documented human bias to exaggerate in retrospect the probability of an observed outcome.[4] By working back from the outcome, and from the known path to that outcome, we diminish our sensitivity to alternative paths and consequences.

In our opinion, both structure and agency are important. The challenge for analysts and theorists alike is not to choose between them but to develop a better understanding of their interaction. With this end in mind, we examine the role of leadership in ending the Cold War and do so through the use of two counterfactual thought experiments that are based on a sober assessment of the strength of structural constraints on leadership choices. We do not claim that "anything was possible," for counterfactual speculation must be disciplined by a realistic appreciation of the historical context that helped shape the observed outcome. We ask three questions: Would different leaders in Washington and Moscow, operating under the same domestic and international constraints as Gorbachev, Reagan, and Bush, have adopted different foreign strategies and tactics? Would those choices have led to different patterns of interaction between the Soviet Union and the United States and between both of them and important third parties? Would this have made any difference for the trajectory of evolution of the superpower relationship?

Our counterfactual thought experiment addresses only the short- to middle-term: the five years following the death of General Secretary Konstantin Chernenko in March 1985. The longer-term prospects of a Soviet Union that avoided disintegration in 1990–91 are another matter. It is conceivable that the collapse of communism in Eastern Europe, the dissolution of the Warsaw Pact, and even the breakup of the Soviet Union would ultimately have occurred regardless of the strategies of the post–Brezhnev era leadership. But even structural determinists will concede that there was nothing inevitable about the way in which these developments occurred or about their timing. We believe that process and timing were critical for the peaceful transition that occurred and the nature of subsequent relations between Russia and the West.

Method

Counterfactual analysis introduces variation through thought experiments that add or subtract contextual or other factors and analyze how these changes might have influenced subsequent events. Thought experiments provide researchers with surrogates for the kinds of controls normally available only in the laboratory. They suffer from the obvious drawback that it is impossible to know with certainty the consequences of the variation introduced by the experimenter.[5] The uncertainty increases dramatically when one considers the longer-term consequences of a counterfactual. This has led some historians to dismiss the exercise as little more than a "parlour game."[6]

The Epistemology of Counterfactual Reasoning

We disagree strongly with that judgment, on epistemological grounds. Counterfactual analysis is not based on mere speculation; in fact, it may be as richly documented as "normal" history. The controversy over France and Britain's response to Hitler is a case in point. The failure of appeasement is undeniable, but the putative efficacy of deterrence as an alternative rests on the counterfactual that Hitler would have been restrained if France and Britain had demonstrated willingness to go to war in defense of the territorial status quo. German documents make this an eminently researchable question, and historians have used these documents to try to determine at what point Hitler could no longer be deterred.[7] Their research has important implications for the historical assessment of French and British policy and the broader claims made for the strategy of deterrence.

Even when such evidence is meager or absent, the difference between counterfactuals and normal history may still be marginal. Documents are rarely "smoking guns" that allow researchers to establish motives or causes beyond a reasonable doubt—even when actors leave evidence about the motives behind their policy choices, and historians must decide how much of their testimony is credible. More often historians infer motives from what they know about actors' personalities and goals, their past behavior, and the constraints acting on them. When we move up the levels of analysis from individual actors to small groups, elites, societies, and states to regional and international systems, the balance between evidence and inference shifts dramatically in the direction of the latter. This is especially true of structural arguments based on simple conceptual abstractions.

For the most part, then, arguments in history and social science are a chain of inference that use selected "principles" (e.g., the balance of power) as anchor points. Documents or other empirical evidence, when available, may be used to try to establish links between these principles and behavior. But even in the best of cases these links are indirect and presumptive, and can be corroborated only obliquely and incompletely. Frequently, evidence is not available or not exploited. Readers evaluate these arguments on the seeming "reasonableness" of the inferences being made, the quality and relevance of the evidence offered in support, and the extent to which that evidence permits or constrains alternative interpretations. Our receptivity to competing arguments is also significantly influenced by the seeming plausibility of the underlying political and behavioral "principles" in which the inferences are rooted. When these "principles" run counter to both beliefs and the reigning orthodoxy, the arguments in question may be dismissed out of hand regardless of the evidence. Counterfactuals are even more vulnerable to this problem, and for this reason, Tetlock and Belkin suggest that counterfactuals should be consistent with well-established theoretical laws. This is not possible, as there are not established laws in international relations or political science more generally; all theories are controversial, and generally indeterminate in their predictions.[8] The best we can do is to be explicit about the principles or judgments that underlie our counterfactual arguments.

Counterfactual thought experiments can be fundamentally similar to "factual" modes of historical reconstruction. The importance of Mikhail Gorbachev for the ending of the Cold War can be evaluated by studying the probable career and policy orientations of other likely candidates (Grishin, Romanov, Ligachev) to have succeeded Chernenko. Their likely policies can be inferred from their past preferences and commitments, the political environment in 1985, and the general domestic and foreign situation of the Soviet Union. There is considerable documentary evidence that sustains informed arguments about the kind of domestic and foreign policies these other leaders might have pursued.

In the final analysis, counterfactual arguments, like any other historical argument, are only as compelling as the logic and evidence mustered by the researcher to substantiate the links between hypothesized antecedents and expected consequences. Every good counterfactual thus rests on multiple "factuals," just as every factual rests on counterfactual assumptions. The difference between good "factual" and "counterfactual" arguments is one of degree, not of kind.[9]

Criteria for Plausible Counterfactual Rewrites

The counterfactual thought experiments we propose must be based upon "minimal rewrites" of history. More specifically, to be treated as plausible, rather than fanciful, counterfactual rewrites must be disciplined by a realistic appreciation of the historical context that shaped the observed outcome.[10] Toward this end, we offer a threefold test for the alternative policies we will consider: their intellectual availability, practicality, and political feasibility.

Intellectual availability means that policymakers depend on the state of social knowledge at the time to make sense of the world and the information they receive about it. Since the industrial revolution, governments might have been able to spend their way out of recessions and depressions through a program of public works, selective investment, and tax cuts, but this strategy was not intellectually available until the twentieth century. Since the 1970s, many governments have been attempting to coordinate their policies to deal with looming threats to the global environment; the intellectual grounding for such efforts was not available in the 1950s. To be sure, such knowledge is rarely consensual, definitive, or universally accepted. Hence, the availability of a body of knowledge does not ensure its acceptability. But absent its availability, counterfactual thought experiments, to be plausible, cannot posit a rewrite of the historical context that stipulates the presence of social knowledge that did not yet exist.

Practicality means that while a strategy or policy might be intellectually available, it is impractical in light of the resources available at the time. Those resources are technological, organizational, cultural, economic, and the like. To be plausible, counterfactual reconstructions must not be based on technological anachronism; neither the Soviet Union nor the United States had the capability to deploy a space-based anti-missile system in the 1980s. Organizational, cultural, and financial constraints are nicely illustrated by Norman Naimark's research on Soviet policy in eastern Germany after World War II. Stalin did not have the option of employing a strategy analogous to that which the West employed in western Germany: of winning the hearts and minds of the population through an expensive policy of economic assistance. Naimark contends that Stalin's reliance on coercion and brutality to establish and maintain Soviet influence was not a choice but a necessity given the political-economic limitations of the Soviet system.[11]

The observer can stipulate the limits of practicality only within general bounds. Some technological anachronisms are obvious; some economic limitations are also relatively "hard" constraints. But other technological and economic constraints may be less "hard," while many organizational and cultural constraints can be "softer" and more ambiguous, subject to being changed or avoided by policies crafted for that purpose. Bold campaigns to overcome alleged constraints may marshal resources and attain ends previously thought impractical. Stalin's first Five Year Plan and John Kennedy's effort to land a U.S. astronaut on the moon within the decade are cases in point.

Such campaigns may also fail, and thereby demonstrate the intractability of the constraints in question. But it is important not to assume that policymakers will define what is practicable in the same way as will scientific observers. The "fact" that something is impractical does not mean that policymakers won't try it. Khrushchev misjudged the ability of the Soviet Union to deploy missiles in Cuba without their being detected by the United States. American and Soviet leaders miscalculated the ability of their respective armed forces to prevail in Vietnam and Afghanistan. Similarly, the fact that something is practical and desirable does not mean that policymakers will necessarily recognize its practicality. For example, early in the Berlin crisis of 1948–49, the White House and State Department thought there was no way an airlift to Berlin could deliver enough food, fuel, and medicine to support the city, and were therefore prepared to give in to Stalin's demands. Only when the U.S. Air Force demonstrated its airlift capability did minds change about the limits of the practical.[12]

Thus, if our purpose is to explain how different policymakers might have behaved, or how the same policymakers might have behaved differently from the way they did, we have to consider both the limits of the "hard," practical constraints within their environment and the factors that might induce them to test the limits of hard constraints, to stretch the limits of the softer constraints, or to miscalculate by overestimating or underestimating their practical capabilities.

Political feasibility means that many policies that are intellectually available and manifestly practical are impractical for political reasons. Most leaders will only sponsor major departures from established policies, or ways of conducting them, when they believe there is a real need to do so and think they have, or can muster, political support for these changes. The presence or absence of political support may seem obvious to the outside observer in extreme circumstances: for example, it is likely that no American president could have sustained or built support for near-term conciliation of the USSR following the invasion of Afghanistan; similarly, it would have been extremely difficult for any Soviet leader to justify a strategy of conciliating the United States following the bombing of Hanoi and Americanization of the Vietnam War in 1965. But political feasibility is often a softer constraint than that, and can depend on the skills of the leader in building support for alternative policies. Moreover, a leader's ability to wield these resources can be affected by fortuitous circumstances, whether stochastic events (e.g., the Chernobyl meltdown) or changes in other policy realms (e.g., good economic news).

The concept of political feasibility also encompasses the beliefs and personalities of the leaders in question. A leader's personal opposition to an initiative for which political support might have been (or had been made) available will often doom such an initiative. For example, it is hard to imagine either Leonid Brezhnev or George H. W. Bush committing themselves to minimal deterrence and the radical reduction of nuclear weapons it would have involved, or to the strategy of "GRIT" and the initial, unilateral concessions necessary to set it in play.[13] Leaders will adopt policies because they are compatible with their goals, views of the world, and interests—or because they judge them tactically necessary to achieve more important goals, such as staying in power. They may or may not be able to create or sustain political support for their policies. Hence, that which is deemed politically feasible at a given point in time will depend on its acceptability to both the leaders in question and their actual or potential support bases.

When we posit different leaders pursuing different policies, we must also ask whether the leader would have had the skills to exploit beneficial circumstances. And we must recognize that political factors may push leaders to undertake initiatives they would have otherwise not chosen to pursue. Thus, just as the judgment of practicality combines elements of the objective and subjective, so judgments of political feasibility are indeterminate to some extent.

Plausible Rewrites: Altering the Leadership Equation

To carry out our counterfactual experiment we need to substitute other leaders for Ronald Reagan and Mikhail Gorbachev. These leaders—George H. W. Bush or a Democratic President in the United States, and Viktor Grishin, Grigori Romanov, or Yegor Ligachev in the Soviet Union—cannot arbitrarily be inserted into power by us. We must introduce plausible rewrites of history to arrange for their accession to power. In the case of George Bush, this is a relatively straight-forward matter. If Hinkley had been "lucky" and assassinated Reagan, Vice President Bush would have moved into the Oval Office in accord with the provisions of the Twenty-Fifth Amendment to the Constitution. We would not have to introduce any changes in the domestic and foreign political context, although under a new, unelected President who assumed office almost at the outset of a new administration, both would have been different.

Substituting a Democrat for Reagan requires more serious political intervention. Walter Mondale, or some other prominent Democrat, would have had to have won the 1984 presidential election, the first election following the attempted assassination of Reagan. Any number of developments could have led to this outcome, and the simplest scenario continues to rely on John Hinkley's bullet. A few millimeters' difference in its trajectory might have brought Bush to office in March 1981 and then three years in which to alienate enough of the electorate for a Democratic opponent to unseat him. Or, Reagan might have survived, but have been seriously impaired, and stepped down after one term, giving the voters a choice between a popular Democrat and a Republican who had spent four years in the relative obscurity of the vice presidency. Or, Reagan might have decided to run for a second term, but have been rejected by voters in favor of a younger, more vigorous challenger.

How might we imagine a Soviet Union more or less the same but without Gorbachev at the helm? The easiest counterfactual to imagine is to extend the life of Andropov or Chernenko another five or six years. But we can go beyond this pathway, and eliminate generational continuity from our counterfactual scenarios. Gorbachev could have been chosen General Secretary but been assassinated shortly thereafter. This is not far-fetched; there were assassination attempts on several Soviet Party leaders, including Gorbachev, and any one of them might have succeeded.[14]

The Politburo could also have chosen someone other than Gorbachev in March 1985. This is a bit more difficult to imagine in light of recent evidence. The Kremlinological literature of the late 1980s generally described the selection of Gorbachev as a close call, with Viktor Grishin and Grigori Romanov regarded as the main competitors. This judgment was based on the limited, indirect evidence available at the time, coupled with mistaken assumptions about voting norms and voting behavior within the Soviet leadership.[15] More recent literature, based on the extensive memoirs by Gorbachev's associates, tends toward the conclusion that Gorbachev won easily and quickly.[16] To change this outcome, we would probably have to change the participants in the process. Defense Minister Dimitri Ustinov, a conservative and one of the most powerful members of the leadership in the early 1980s, died suddenly in December 1984. If we posit his survival and involvement in the decision-making processes of

March 1985, we may plausibly change the equation sufficiently to produce an-other outcome. We can readily imagine a coalition of aged Prime Minister Niko-lai Tikhonov, Foreign Minister Andrei Gromyko, and Defense Minister Ustinov teaming up to block Gorbachev and to support someone from the "younger" generation whom they perceived as less likely to oust them from their jobs. In this circumstance, it is at least plausible that the Politburo could have been in-duced to choose either Grishin or Romanov as a "neo-Brezhnevite" successor. Alternatively, the Politburo could have dipped into the ranks of recently pro-moted regional secretaries for a "neo-Andropovite" successor like Yegor Lig-achev, who had a reputation for being incorruptible. Any of these alternative leaders could have served as General Secretary for at least five to ten years.

To run a controlled counterfactual thought experiment, we need to hold do-mestic constraints and opportunities and the foreign environment constant and vary only the leaders in power. But any of the scenarios that would make a Democrat President in January 1985 or bring to office a different Soviet Gen-eral Secretary seven weeks later require changes, some of them significant, in the political context in the two countries. We need to acknowledge the nature of these alterations, and take them into account as best we can as we conduct our thought experiments. What other changes might our alterations have brought about—second-order counterfactuals—and how might they have altered the domestic and foreign policy environment or the consequences of any of the al-ternate strategies chosen by our substitute leaders?

The Superpowers' Policy Repertoires

To avoid embracing fanciful counterfactuals, we must explore the range of gen-eral options available to each superpower leader by the early 1980s. By that time, the Cold War had been raging for more than three decades. Many efforts at de-tente had been attempted and had collapsed, though with legacies that left cer-tain agreements and institutions in place (e.g., the Helsinki Accords, the ABM Treaty, and other agreements). By 1980–81, the United States had reverted to a posture of irreconcilable antagonism, while Soviet leaders, confused and con-cerned, were searching for a response. To understand what policies at the time were intellectually available, capable of being implemented, and politically fea-sible within each capital, we need to explore the general options or postures available at the time.

Realistic Soviet Options

When Ronald Reagan was elected President in November 1980, Mikhail Gor-bachev was almost four-and-a-half years away from being chosen General Secretary.

Indeed, Gorbachev would not become the Soviet leader until seven weeks into Reagan's second term. President Reagan's first term in office was marked instead by his having to deal with three aged and sickly Soviet leaders: Leonid Brezhnev (until November 1982); Yuri Andropov (until February 1984); and Konstantin Chernenko (until March 1985). During these years, Soviet leaders tried a series of approaches to parry, counter, or defuse the threat from Reagan's conventional, nuclear, and space-based military buildup, his active support for anti-communist insurgencies in the Third World, and his apocalyptic rhetoric.[17] At various times, and in varying combinations, they pursued five types of policies:

(1) *Confrontation*—answering militancy with militancy and confronting the adversary with the potentially escalatory costs of intransigence. The Soviets repeatedly threatened to match Reagan's military buildup in kind or with countermeasures. They boycotted arms control talks beginning in November 1983. In spring 1984, they initiated a series of incidents with escalatory potential: maneuvers by the largest Soviet fleet ever seen assembled in the Norwegian Sea and North Atlantic; a buildup of missile-bearing submarines off the East Coast of the United States; ramming of an American naval vessel on the high seas; mugging of an American consular official in Leningrad; interference with air traffic in the Berlin corridor; and others.[18]

(2) *Competition*—attempts to avoid direct confrontation while promoting initiatives intended to undermine the adversary's positions, weaken and divide its alliances, and undercut political support for its policies. During 1981–83, for example, the Soviets sought to mobilize and sustain peace movements in Western Europe in their opposition to the deployment of cruise missiles and Pershing-II intermediate range ballistic missiles.

(3) *Temporization*—watching and waiting while doing nothing likely to escalate or de-escalate the confrontation. This strategy assumes that with time the situation may clarify or even turn to one's advantage. In the meantime, leaders do nothing that incurs great risks or costs. This was essentially the Brezhnev leadership's response in 1981–82 to the Reagan arms buildup.[19]

(4) *Retrenchment*—selectively cutting losses in realms that are not central to the conflict. Shortly after the KAL airliner incident in September 1983, in which a Soviet interceptor destroyed a Korean passenger plane, Andropov initiated a behind-the-scenes review of Soviet foreign policy, especially policy toward the West. Although he did not live to implement the results of that critical review, Andropov intended to use it as a prelude to retrenchment.[20]

(5) *Conciliation*—offering concessions to the adversary in the main realms of superpower relations in order to break the confrontational deadlock and foster cooperation. The Brezhnev, Andropov, and Chernenko administrations all offered partial concessions in their terms for nuclear arms control agreements in

hopes of inducing Western compromises. President Reagan still found their terms unacceptable.

Behind the scenes in Moscow during the early 1980s, all five options were being discussed and advocated by powerful political actors. These options were not mutually exclusive. One strategy could be pursued in one realm of foreign policy (e.g., retrenchment in the Third World) and another elsewhere (e.g., political competition in Europe and military confrontation in arms control). Strategies could also be sequenced within the same policy realm. A leader might consider following either retrenchment or confrontation with conciliation if the first strategy influenced the adversary to be more receptive to the proposed terms for cooperation.

By the time Chernenko lay dying in January-February 1985, none of these approaches had yielded fruit for Moscow. President Reagan had won reelection in a landslide; the deployment of cruise missiles and Pershing IIs in Western Europe was proceeding apace, and the Western European peace movement against deployment had failed; the more general Reagan military buildup had been financed and sustained by Congress, and the Strategic Defense Initiative ("Star Wars") remained in place; the Soviet Union was more deeply mired in Afghanistan, with no victory in sight; and Soviet policy in the Third World was increasingly controversial within the policymaking elite. Even the conciliation strategy, limited by the Brezhnevite premise of "offensive detente," had found no taker in Reagan.[21] It would be reasonable to suppose that the Soviet establishment would be collectively primed for, and consensually receptive to, some new thinking.

This was not the case. In February 1985, Gorbachev and Politburo member Romanov engaged in polemics over what should come next in Soviet policy toward the United States. Gorbachev alluded to the necessity for and feasibility of cooperation; Romanov spoke of the irreconcilability of Western imperialism with Soviet-style communism, and the inevitability of confrontation.[22] Gorbachev's perspectives were consistent with a strategy of conciliation intended to break the dangerous deadlock in superpower relations. Romanov's perspectives implied some combinations of confrontation, competition, and retrenchment. Many others within the leadership were fence-sitters, who shied away from either escalation or far-reaching conciliation, and who would likely have settled, at least in the near term, for a strategy of temporizing.

Realistically, then, three, not five, general strategies for dealing with the U.S.-Soviet deadlock were being advocated within the Soviet leadership in March 1985 when Gorbachev came to power. These were: (1) a hard-line strategy of confrontation and competition, accompanied perhaps by selective cutting of losses (retrenchment) in some Third World hot spots; (2) a temporizing strategy of selectively cutting losses while avoiding any sharp turns toward either confrontation or conciliation in the principal theaters of confrontation: Europe and arms control; and (3) an accommodative strategy that combined conciliation and retrenchment. For ease of reference, we will refer to these three options as confrontation, temporization, and conciliation. These same general strategies were also being debated in Washington at the time.

The three foreign policy strategies we described were not unrelated to different orientations toward key domestic issues. In the Soviet Union, the confrontational strategy tended to correlate with advocacy of hard-line domestic policies: continuing crackdown on political dissent, disciplinary-mobilizational policies toward labor, anticorruption campaigns among officials, and budgetary aggrandizement of the military-industrial complex. The conciliatory strategy tended to correlate with selective liberalization of the polity and economy. The temporizing strategy was consistent with a wide range of domestic policies, including a hold-the-line strategy in defense of central planning and party control, or a "Chinese model," which combined partial liberalization and opening of the economy with the maintenance of tight political controls. Within the Soviet political establishment in 1984–85, advocates of all of these approaches could be found.[23]

Realistic American Options

Ronald Reagan was elected President in November 1980 promising to rebuild U. S. defense capability and to reassert the country's standing as a global superpower. His perspective on international affairs was a reaction against the so-called post-Vietnam syndrome of the 1970s. Nor was this sentiment confined to the Republican Party. In the wake of the Soviet invasion of Afghanistan in December 1979, President Carter had begun a defense buildup, embargoed grain sales to Moscow, and endorsed other confrontational and competitive initiatives. With the exception of his reversal of the grain embargo, President Reagan continued and intensified his predecessor's policy of confrontation by keeping diplomatic contacts limited, using more offensive rhetoric, accelerating the arms buildup, and publicly considering disavowing previous arms control treaties and agreements.[24]

If our thought experiment is based on the plausible counterfactual that Hinkley's bullet ended Reagan's life or incapacitated him just two months after he became President, we have to ask whether George Bush's policies of 1981–85 would have been any different from Reagan's determinedly confrontational line.[25] It seems likely that Bush, whose temperament, beliefs, self-confidence, and political authority within the Republican Party were quite different from Reagan's, would have responded in a more differentiated way than did Reagan. Like his Soviet counterparts, Bush would have had five strategies from which to choose: confrontation, competition, temporization, retrenchment, and conciliation. He was more cautious and insecure, both personally and politically, than Ronald Reagan, more ambivalent as a personality, and a more complex, but less visionary, thinker than Reagan.[26] Hence, he would have been unlikely to initiate any major policy departure on his own, and been slower than Reagan in reciprocating a Soviet strategy of accommodation. He would have been likely to have responded in kind to a Soviet strategy of competition or temporization, but could have replied to Soviet retrenchment with a strategy of either competition or temporization. Each of these options was intellectually available and practicable: they were all part of the repertoire of postures the United States had adopted in some policy realms at various stages of the Cold War. None of them exceeded U.S. capabilities in 1981–85.

Their political availability, however, is less certain. Anti-Soviet sentiments surged among the U.S. public and Congress following the Soviet invasion of Afghanistan, further fanned by Carter's reaction to the invasion and Reagan's campaign rhetoric.[27] Reagan came into office after a landslide victory, promising to turn the tide in world affairs. All this, plus the sentiment generated by Reagan's hypothetical death or incapacitation in March 1981, would have made it difficult, perhaps prohibitive, for his Republican successor to embrace a strategy of conciliation, even if he were so inclined.

While it seemed unlikely that Bush would pursue a strategy of conciliation, four alternatives remained available to him. His ambivalence, moderate Republicanism, and lesser popularity might have inclined him toward a less sweeping strategy of confrontation, less extreme rhetoric ("evil empire") and policies (Star Wars), and, perhaps, toward selective reciprocation of Soviet temporization. Reciprocation might have been more attractive after Brezhnev's death in November 1982 and Andropov's initial softening of Soviet terms for an arms control agreement and signaling that a reconsideration of Soviet Third World policy was underway. The growing strength of peace movements in Western Europe and the related worries of key West European leaders about the domestic consequences of bellicose American rhetoric and policies would have added another point of pressure on hypothetical President Bush to avoid confrontation, to temporize on matters like Euromissiles, and perhaps cautiously to explore the intent behind Soviet conciliatory gestures. By contrast, President Reagan dug in his heels in the face of all these obstacles and held out for maximal Soviet concessions. He announced his Strategic Defense Initiative only four months after Andropov came to power and pushed forward vigorously with deployment of the Pershing–II and a new generation of cruise missiles in Western Europe.

There was considerable diversity within the Republican Party and the Reagan administration by the time Gorbachev came to power in early 1985. Like the Gorbachev Politburo, officials within the Reagan administration—and leading Republicans more generally—advanced quite different policy agendas and not infrequently worked at cross-purposes with one another.[28] Gorbachev was perceived by some members of the Reagan administration as a skillful and dangerous master of public diplomacy whose goals were fundamentally similar to those of his predecessors: undermining the Western alliance. As "Gorbymania' swept Europe and North America, those officials worried that the Atlantic Alliance would weaken and that American public support would diminish for nuclear weapons, large military budgets, and the hard-line policies they thought essential to constrain and weaken the Soviet Union. Confrontation was also advocated by a minority of officials who acknowledged Gorbachev's interest in some kind of meaningful accommodation. Like Eisenhower and Dulles in 1953–54, they read Soviet gestures as driven by weakness and considered it useful to hold out for more far-reaching Soviet concessions.[29] Still another group of officials in the second Reagan administration, and much of the conservative media, doubted that Gorbachev's initiatives were "for real." They perceived them as, at best, temporary measures dictated by political circumstances and intended to strengthen the Soviet Union and permit renewed confrontation. These officials recommended a "wait and see" attitude—a strategy of temporization. And it took Ronald Reagan himself several years before he concluded that Gorbachev's foreign policy concessions and domestic liberalization had gone far enough to warrant treating them as significant changes.

The diversity of perspectives and personalities within the government would have provided a hypothetical President Bush with some wiggle room to pursue a less confrontational approach toward the Soviet Union in 1981–84. The temper of American politics, as well as Bush's personality, however, probably would have ruled out a substantially conciliatory U.S. response to Soviet gestures. Given the history of the Cold War to that point, it is also unlikely that any reduction of tensions—or mutual forbearance—in the early 1980s would have broken down the Cold War system or significantly altered the interests and ideologies in both countries that sustained that conflict. The Soviets under Brezhnev, Andropov, and Chernenko would not have abandoned "old thinking" or reduced the budget of the military-industrial complex. Nor would the United States, given the temper of the times. However, a President inclined toward conciliation—whether a reelected George Bush or a newly elected Walter Mondale—might increasingly have regained his freedom of action as a result of Gorbachev's domestic and foreign initiatives and the overwhelmingly favorable reaction they elicited from the American electorate and European leaders.

Alternative Scenarios of Interaction

We now formalize and extend some of these scenarios by looking beyond the specific strategies available to each superpower to examine alternative scenarios of bilateral interaction among them. For the sake of convenience, and because several strategies could be pursued simultaneously in different realms of policy, we collapse the five strategies into three: confrontation (a combination of confrontation and competition); temporization (a combination of temporization and retrenchment); and conciliation. We play off each of the three Soviet strategies with their three American counterparts, for a total of nine possible combinations (see table), and analyze the likely consequences of these different combinations for the course of East-West relations from 1985 to 1990. We also discuss how subtraction of Gorbachev or Reagan—or both—from the equation might have influenced the acceptability and political availability of each of the strategies. The stage is set by Reagan's (or, hypothetically, George Bush's) first term as president, and by the assumption that the American strategy during that term was, and would have been, largely confrontational. Our combinations therefore begin with Soviet policy following Chernenko's death in March 1985.

Strategies	*Short-Term Outcomes*
Soviet confrontation vs. U.S. confrontation	Possible intensification of the Cold War
Soviet confrontation vs. U.S. temporization	Possible intensification of the Cold War
Soviet temporization vs. U.S. confrontation	Possible intensification of the Cold War
Soviet temporization vs. U.S. temporization	No change
Soviet temporization vs. U.S. conciliation	Amelioration of relations
Soviet conciliation vs. U.S. temporization	Amelioration of relations
Soviet conciliation vs. U.S. conciliation	Amelioration of relations
Soviet conciliation vs. U.S. confrontation	Unpredictable
Soviet confrontation vs. U.S. conciliation	Fanciful counterfactual

Soviet Confrontation and American Confrontation

A Soviet leader other than Gorbachev—Romanov, for example—might have responded to "evil empire" Reagan or "enough is enough" George H. W. Bush with a strategy of confrontation, based on a determination to confront the adversary, "tit-for-tat," with the costs of its intransigence.[30] Politically, this strategy would have been most appealing to a general secretary who considered Cold War tensions a useful means of building political support at home, keeping dissidents in line and deflecting attention from the Soviet Union's many structural problems. Soviet confrontation could have taken many forms: an extension of the war in Afghanistan that included attacks against guerrilla training bases in Pakistan; increased harassment of domestic opponents and American media and diplomatic representatives; the use of force against nationalist and anti-communist movements in Eastern Europe; acceleration of the arms race—all accompanied by a drum-beat of anti-American and "anti-imperialist" rhetoric.

Under this scenario, the Cold War almost certainly would have intensified, to the advantage of the military-defense establishments of both superpowers. There would have been few contacts between leaders of the superpowers—basically, the state of affairs during Reagan's first term—and certainly no arms control negotiations, let alone agreements. Continued East-West confrontation, made more acute by mutual arms buildups, could have led to a crisis of the magnitude of Berlin in 1961 or Cuba in 1962. Suppose that Reagan or his successor had broken out of the ABM Treaty and proceeded to deploy components of a space-based anti-missile system. Gorbachev, who was publicly committed to oppose any such deployment, worried that such a challenge could lead to a Cuban missile crisis in reverse.[31]

Soviet Confrontation and American Temporization

This is the flip side of Reagan's first term, when the Soviets generally temporized in the face of an American political-military challenge. Temporization might have been judged an appropriate response by a President who believed that reciprocal confrontation would only make the Cold War worse, strengthen hardline forces in Moscow, and risk drawing the superpowers into a war-threatening crisis. At best, it would have bought time and facilitated the return of a more moderate leader to the Kremlin. Given the nature of American politics, temporizing in the face of repeated Soviet provocations would have been extremely difficult to justify to the American people.

Soviet Confrontation and American Conciliation

Some conflict-management strategies like GRIT (Gradual Reduction in Tensions) recommend cooperation as a possible response to defection. But it seems implausible that a president would have wanted to or could have pursued the strategy of conciliation in a sustained way. A Democratic president would have been accused of appeasement, and a Republican president would have confronted great opposition from within his own party and administration.

Soviet Temporization and American Confrontation

This was the reality of Reagan's first term. Relations deteriorated between the superpowers and between the United States and its allies, particularly the Federal Republic of Germany. Soviet temporization was based on the premise that little could be accomplished with a hard-line, hostile president. It also reflected the stasis of Brezhnev's last years and the fragile health of his successors. If Gorbachev, or some other successor to Chernenko, had continued to pursue a strategy of temporization after 1985, it seems unlikely that much, if any, progress would have been made in East-West relations. As part of a strategy of temporization, Soviet leaders likely would have sought to exploit politically growing disagreements within the Western alliance, and might have selectively cut Soviet losses in Third World hot spots. The net result might have been to raise the heat on an intransigent American president from critics within Congress and Western Europe, especially if the campaign were waged by a Soviet leader with the public relations savvy of a Gorbachev.

In this scenario, the Cold War would have remained very much alive, but its focus would have shifted to the political arena and could have put a hard-line American administration with a penchant for bellicose rhetoric very much on the defensive. Given the political weight of Cold War constituencies in the United States and Western Europe at the time, however, it is difficult to imagine an American president—be it Reagan, Bush, or Mondale—being forced into unwanted, significant concessions on arms control and other issues central to the relationship in the absence of concrete and far-reaching Soviet concessions in arms control negotiations.

Soviet Temporization and American Temporization

An American policy of temporization might have been the fall-back position in the face of Soviet temporizing in response to an American policy of confrontation. This combination could have developed out of the previous scenario. The political heat generated in Washington from a successful Soviet political campaign and selective retrenchment in the Third World might have encouraged an American president to back away from confrontation when he came to realize that it played into his opponent's hand. Allied leaders, especially in Western Europe, would undoubtedly have pushed for such a change when they found themselves stretched between their commitment to NATO and a public increasingly disenchanted with the United States.

Alternatively, leaders of both superpowers could simultaneously have chosen to pursue wait-and-see strategies in early 1985, motivated by domestic or foreign calculations. Pressing domestic concerns unrelated to Cold War issues might have led them to keep foreign policy issues on the back burner. Leaders might also have chosen to temporize if they believed that the other side was uninterested in accommodation, and that they could only lose politically at home by pursuing a strategy of conciliation. Arms competition and the struggle for global influence would probably have continued in a muted way unless the independent action of third parties created some kind of undesired crisis. But such mutual temporization would likely have been temporary, as the growing costs of an arms race led to growing pressure on one or the other side to "do something" of either a confrontational or conciliatory nature to break the logjam.

Temporization characterized much of Gorbachev's policy toward the United States in 1985. The response of the Reagan administration was to continue the policies of confrontation the president had pursued in his first term until Moscow became conciliatory. It is conceivable, however, that a President Bush or President Mondale would have been more inclined to temporize instead. This response would have provided more maneuver room for Gorbachev.

Soviet Temporization and American Conciliation

Soviet temporizing could have prompted an American strategy of conciliation. If the political heat from within Western Europe threatened a crisis within the alliance, and that pressure was intensified by Soviet cutting of losses in the Third World, as well as the realization that the Soviets had not chosen to match the American military buildup of Reagan's first term, an American president might have chosen to respond to Soviet temporizing with genuinely conciliatory measures. The result of this interaction might have been Soviet adoption of a conciliatory strategy and a "virtuous circle" of mutual accommodation.

But American efforts at conciliation could have elicited other responses depending on the underlying reasons for Soviet temporization. If Soviet caution had been motivated by doubts about the United States being a willing or reliable partner, presidential efforts at conciliation could have reassured a Soviet leader and helped him to build domestic support for reciprocal gestures. If temporization was primarily a response to domestic considerations, conciliatory policies could have created something of a dilemma for a relatively new general secretary in the process of consolidating his power, all the more so if he derived support from more conservative elements within the Communist Party. For a general secretary committed to shifting resources from national security to other sectors of the economy, however, American efforts at conciliation would have been helpful.

It is unclear whether, in the mid-1980s, a U.S. president would have been inclined to adopt a strategy of conciliation absent a Soviet conciliatory posture. Perhaps it is plausible to contend that neither President Bush nor President Mondale would have had the self-confidence that Reagan had to stand fast until his maximal demands were met. Either of them might have responded to growing domestic and European demands for progress in U.S.-Soviet relations with a policy of conciliation in response to the growing political costs to the U.S.

president of a successful Soviet strategy of temporization. Absent a rapid Soviet reciprocation of that conciliation, however, it is difficult to imagine this strategy being sustained.

Soviet Conciliation and American Confrontation

This was the state of U.S.-Soviet relations in 1986–87. Soviet conciliation amounted to movement toward acceptance of unequal terms in arms control treaties, liberalization of human rights policies, and movement toward retrenchment or cutting of losses in the Third World, including Afghanistan. If President Reagan had responded to Soviet conciliation by continuing to raise the ante in negotiations, by refusing to strike deals that would abandon U.S. military deployments, and by continuing to increase the military pressure on Soviet positions in the Third World—and some of his advisors urged him to do this—it seems unlikely that the Cold War would have moved rapidly toward resolution. Gorbachev might have found it difficult to maintain support within the Politburo for a sustained policy of unreciprocated conciliation. Hard-liners might have found it easier to mobilize support within the leadership against domestic changes that threatened to weaken the Soviet Union. In every way, Gorbachev would have been more constrained, and might have had to fall back on a foreign policy of temporization. Or, worse, he might have been replaced by a hard-line leadership that promptly abandoned both domestic reform and foreign accommodation.

It also seems clear that domestic and European opposition to an American posture of confrontation would have risen greatly and rapidly. The Reagan administration would have found it increasingly costly politically to continue its all-around confrontation of the Soviet Union in the face of Gorbachev's conciliatory behavior and clever public relations. "Gorbymania" would have put considerable pressure on first Reagan and then Bush to adopt more conciliatory policies.

This scenario is counterfactual in the sense that it alters the actual American response to Soviet conciliation. Another counterfactual alters the actual leadership equation by subtracting both Gorbachev and Reagan. It is difficult to imagine a Romanov or any other Soviet old-guard leader embracing a strategy of conciliation in 1986–87. It is easier—but still not easy—to imagine Bush or Mondale resisting the pressure to reciprocate Soviet conciliation, or at least to temporize in the face of it. If either man was insecure about his political authority and less than self-confident about his image within the United States, he might have been tempted to sustain a posture of American confrontation and deny the reality of Soviet conciliation. In that case, the explanation for Ronald Reagan's refusal to go this route, and, instead, to test the sincerity of Soviet conciliatory policies, would be his greater political security and sense of identity combined with his visionary urge to go down in history as a great peacemaker.

Soviet Conciliation and American Temporization

Soviet conciliation might have encouraged an American president to back away from a policy of confrontation in the expectation that a softer line would facilitate further Soviet retreat. There is evidence that Gorbachev's retrenchment and conciliation, coupled with his moves to liberalize the Soviet political system, had precisely this effect. Initially uncertain about Gorbachev's broader goals, and disinclined for domestic and foreign reasons to take many risks, the Reagan administration chose to temporize. The president became more forthcoming when given the prospect of a favorable arms control treaty. If he had not done this, it might have been difficult for Gorbachev to continue his increasingly concessionary foreign policies. Gorbachev could have become more cautious about concessions in arms control, or simply drawn out the process of East-West accommodation for long enough that the German problem was still unresolved by the time his power waned.

In reality, in 1989, President Bush initially thought that Ronald Reagan had gone too far to accommodate Gorbachev; he accordingly temporized during his first year in office. Temporization is usually a short-term strategy, and Bush, like his predecessor, gradually moved toward conciliation. It is interesting to speculate about what would have happened had either president continued to temporize; it could have led to a very different end to the Cold War. It could have encouraged Gorbachev to try to cut a separate deal with Germany. Unification, even if it required a neutral Germany or special status for the East—as Gorbachev initially demanded—could have appealed to West German Prime Minister Helmut Kohl and his foreign minister, Hans-Dietrich Genscher.

Soviet Conciliation and American Conciliation

After the Geneva summit, Gorbachev's policy toward the West became increasingly conciliatory on all fronts. As noted, both American presidents temporized and then adopted conciliatory policies. This was the path through which the Cold War came to an end, at the time it did, and on the terms it did.

Leader Indispensability?[32]

The only peaceful route to resolution of the Cold War was through an iterative process of mutual conciliation. How essential were Mikhail Gorbachev and Ronald Reagan to the adoption of sustained, mutually conciliatory postures?

In the case of Gorbachev, we encounter a Soviet leader who made a conscious decision to reject the ideological assumptions that supported the "anti-imperialist" struggle, the Cold War international order, and the domestic Soviet institutions whose identities were defined by this approach to international politics.

He came eventually to a conscious decision to transform Soviet domestic politics in a liberalizing, democratizing, and Westernizing direction.[33] He articulated a vision of a transformed domestic and international order and managed to justify his conciliatory posture with reference to that new way of thinking. He was able to sell the approach to key audiences within the Soviet political establishment because he articulated a seemingly compelling political-economic rationale. His doctrinal innovations were ingenious syntheses of old and new precepts that appeared faithful to the Marxist revolutionary tradition while rejecting core features of the Leninist approach to international relations.[34] Gorbachev also had the kind of self-confident and assertive personality that could dominate small-group decision-making processes, and possessed the political skills to exploit opportunities created by stochastic events. He used the Chernobyl accident as a springboard to rein in the censorship authorities and exploited the landing on Red Square of Matthias Rust's Cessna as a pretext to purge the military command. At least from early 1985 through early 1989, before he lost control of events, he had an outstanding sense of timing, was highly articulate in small-group debate, and knew how to seize the initiative from prospective skeptics.[35]

To be sure, Gorbachev was not a magician; he was operating in a context that facilitated his efforts. A good deal of individual and collective learning had taken place behind the scenes of Soviet politics during the 20 years before Gorbachev came to power. By the 1980s, party intellectuals and officials in growing numbers had sensed that something fundamental had to give—that the Soviet Union was approaching a cul de sac in both its domestic evolution and foreign relations.[36] Their foreboding was far from a majority position, but it did provide an opening for an entrepreneurial political leader ready to exploit new ideas and build a new political base.[37] Then, too, very large numbers of party officials who resisted this pessimistic conclusion had nonetheless lost confidence in their ability to justify their right to rule—to themselves and the populace at large—and worried about how long they could sustain their domination. Gorbachev was able to exploit these changes in both the intellectual and the psychological context, and to use his formidable political skills to maintain support—if only passive support in many instances—for the determined strategy of conciliation he had embraced.

There is no evidence to suggest that anyone else in the Soviet leadership possessed Gorbachev's flexible intellect, personality, and political skills. Reformist advisors such as Anatoliy Chernyayev and Georgy Shakhnazarov, along with other reformists in the journalistic and academic establishments, provided important ideas for Gorbachev to wield, but themselves could not have become Party leaders at the time. Men like Aleksandr Yakovlev and Eduard Shevardnadze matched Gorbachev in intellect; but neither of them were in a position to be elected General Secretary in 1985, and neither had Gorbachev's personality and political skills. Other supporters, like Vadim Medvedev, fell short on all three counts, and could not have been elected in any case. Other members of the Politburo did not display the inclination to heed the radical advice being offered by "new thinkers" within the establishment or to conciliate the United States under the circumstances of the mid-1980s, though several of them might have been pragmatic enough to engage in retrenchment from positions of overextension in the Third World. In short, any counterfactual that eliminates Gorbachev from the scene in March 1985 leads to the conclusion that it is highly unlikely that Soviet foreign policy would have been redirected toward conciliation, and would have sustained that orientation in the face of initial American temporization.

Was Ronald Reagan equally necessary for the realization of a virtuous circle of mutual conciliation? Did his personality and perspectives uniquely facilitate East-West accommodation? Reagan had a deep abhorrence of nuclear weapons and, with it, a growing commitment to find a way out of the East-West impasse. There is some evidence that Reagan's commitment intensified in early 1984 after his briefing on a president's possible responses to a Soviet nuclear attack, and the Soviet Union's overreaction to the American "Abel Archer" nuclear exercise. These events seem to have "primed" Reagan to initiate efforts to reestablish better communications with Moscow and, possibly, to respond more favorably to the overtures toward accommodation that Gorbachev would later make.[38]

Ronald Reagan held strong views on many subjects and had little knowledge to back up those views. He repeatedly demonstrated his ignorance of the Soviet Union, in public and private. Reagan had a much less complex cognitive schema about the Soviet Union than did his advisors, or some other contenders for the presidency. Laboratory experiments indicate that people with different levels of complexity react differently to information at odds with their beliefs and expectations. People with less developed schemas are initially more likely to maintain their schemas intact in the face of discrepant information, but to change them dramatically in the face of a consistent stream of discrepant information. People with more complex and developed schemas are more likely to find ways of interpreting discrepant information in a manner consistent with their schemas, or of making small, incremental changes in their schemas to accommodate this information.[39] It is not surprising that Reagan, who entered office with the most fervently anti-Soviet views, retired as the biggest dove in his administration. Reagan's advisors had far more elaborate schemas of the Soviet Union, and these schemas allowed them to explain away Gorbachev's reforms and interest in arms control and accommodation as clever, duplicitous, and seeking to weaken the West by appealing to the antiwar sentiments of European and American public opinion. They remained doubting and dubious longer than most Americans. As we have noted, as late as 1989, Vice President Bush claimed to be still unconvinced of Gorbachev's sincerity when he actually assumed the presidency.

Reagan's dramatic about-face may also have been facilitated by his propensity—noted by many of his confidants—to reduce issues to personalities. If he liked and trusted someone, he was more prone to give credence to the policies they espoused. Reagan's closest advisors testify that his personal meetings with Gorbachev at Geneva in November 1985 and at Reykjavik in November 1986 made a big impact on him; he came away impressed by the General Secretary and his seeming commitment to reduce the nuclear danger and tensions between the superpowers.[40] We can speculate that Reagan's assessment of Gorbachev created considerable cognitive dissonance for him because he liked and respected the leader of what he had called the "evil empire." Once he accepted Gorbachev as sincere, he worked with him to bring about the accommodation both men desired. By the time of the 1988 Moscow summit, when a newsman reminded Reagan of his earlier depiction of the Soviet Union as an "evil empire," the President chuckled and replied, "I was talking about another time, another era."[41] It seems unlikely another president, and certainly not George Bush, would have undergone such a transition.

The Reagan-Gorbachev Relationship

Was there something about the personal rapport between these two leaders that encouraged conciliation and helped them to sustain the momentum of that process once it had begun?[42] We think the answer is "yes." Gorbachev shared Reagan's horror of nuclear weapons.[43] The fact that both men happened to share a vision of a world without nuclear weapons was salutary to the process of mutual conciliation. That they were in power at the same time was a remarkable and perhaps even necessary coincidence.

Reagan and Gorbachev had the right chemistry. Both men were self-confident idealists unprepared to bow to political expediency. They "immediately sensed this" about each other, former Soviet Foreign Minister Aleksandr Bessmertnykh observed, and "this is why they made 'good partners.'"[44] Confronted with a different general secretary, who had neither Gorbachev's personality nor his commitment to reduce the nuclear threat, Reagan might well have remained an anti-Soviet ideologue. Given his commitment to holding out for asymmetrical, indeed maximal, Soviet concessions in all realms, the Cold War might well have remained unresolved and a more complicated legacy for his successor. On the other hand, confronted with a different American President, Gorbachev might well have impressed and converted him with his willingness to make so many unilateral concessions. But the lesser resolve and greater political insecurity of a George Bush or Walter Mondale might have made it less attractive tactically and more difficult politically for Gorbachev to justify such far-reaching concessions. The perception that a Bush or Mondale would have settled for less could have led Gorbachev to demand a more balanced compromise. Had Gorbachev not transcended such a perspective, intellectually or politically, he might have participated in a more drawn-out process of negotiation that could have become the basis for mutual disillusionment—as it did in the 1970s—or, further down the line, a Cold War settlement different in scope and form. Paradoxically, then, it is worth considering the proposition that it was Reagan's maximalism and resolve, coupled with his willingness to strike deals and abandon hostile rhetoric when his maximalist demands were met, and the personal rapport and vision he shared with Gorbachev, that ended the Cold War when and how it did.

Thus, when we examine the mutual conciliation that led to the end of the Cold War in finer detail, we discover that it was more than a simple, iterative process of strategic interaction. The results could not have been predicted by knowing only the strategies and preferences of the actors. After the first iteration, the adoption of follow-on strategies can be influenced, perhaps decisively, by the personal chemistry and trust—or lack of it—that develops between leaders and between negotiators. That chemistry and trust can reshape preferences, commitments, and expectations of reciprocity. It can, in other words, make the difference between breakdown and further iterations of the game. This highlights, in turn, the likely indispensability of both Gorbachev and Reagan to the ending of the Cold War in the late 1980s and early 1990s.

Notes

1. Kenneth N. Waltz, "The Emerging Structure of International Politics," *International Security* 18 (Fall 1993), pp. 5–43; Kenneth Oye, "Explaining the End of the Cold War: Morphological and Behavioral Adaptations to the Nuclear Peace?," in Richard Ned Lebow and Thomas Risse-Kappen, *International Relations Theory and the End of the Cold War* (New York: Columbia University Press, 1995), pp. 57–84; and Wohlforth, "New Evidence on Moscow's Cold War." For a critique of the realist argument, see Richard Ned Lebow and John Mueller, "Realism and the End of the Cold War," *International Security* 20 (Fall 1995), pp. 185–86. Representative liberal literature includes Michael W. Doyle, "Liberalism and the End of the Cold War," and Thomas Risse-Kappen, "Ideas Do Not Float Freely: Transnational Coalitions, Domestic Structures, and the End of the Cold War," in Lebow and Risse-Kappan, *International Relations Theory*, pp. 85–108 and 187–222; Matthew Evangelista, *Unarmed Forces: The Transnational Movement to End the Cold War* (Ithaca, NY: Cornell University Press, 1999). The literature on the end of the Cold War, including constructivist interpretations, is reviewed by Matthew Evangelista, "Internal and External Constraints on Grand Strategy: The Soviet Case," in *The Domestic Bases of Grand Strategy*, eds. Richard Rosecrance and Arthur Stein (Ithaca, NY: Cornell University Press, 1993), pp. 154–78, and Richard Ned Lebow, "The Rise and Fall of the Cold War," *Review of International Studies* 25 (5) (December 1999).

2. On conjunctional causality, see Charles C. Ragin, *The Comparative Method: Moving Beyond Qualitative and Quantitative Strategies* (Berkeley: University of California Press, 1987), pp. 25–26.

3. William Wohlforth, in "New Evidence on Moscow's Cold War: Ambiguity in Search of Theory," *Diplomatic History* 21 (Spring 1997), pp. 229–42, reviews this literature and criticizes realists for explaining ex post facto what none of them predicted ex ante.

4. Baruch Fischoff, "Hindsight is not Equal to Foresight: The Effect of Outcome Knowledge on Judgment under Uncertainty," *Journal of Experimental Psychology: Human Perception and Performance* 1 (2) (1975), pp. 288–99; S. A. Hawkins and R. Hastie, "Hindsight: Biased Judgments of Past Events after the Outcomes are Known," *Psychological Bulletin* 107 (3) (1990), pp. 311–27. The tendency was earlier referred to as "retrospective determinism" in comparative-historical studies by Reinhard Bendix, *Nation-Building and Citizenship* (New York: Wiley, 1964).

5. On counterfactuals, and their applicability to history and international relations, see Max Weber, "Objective Possibility and Adequate Causation in Historical Explanation," in *Max Weber on the Methodology of the Social Sciences*, eds. Edward A. Shils and Henry A. Finch (Glencoe: Free Press, 1949), pp. 164–88; Nelson Goodman, *Fact, Fiction, and Forecast* (Cambridge, MA: Harvard University Press, 1983); John Elster, *Logic and Society: Contradictions and Possible Worlds* (New York: John Wiley, 1978); Robert Fogel, *Railroads and American Economic Growth: Essays in Econometric History* (Baltimore: Johns Hopkins University Press, 1964); G. Hawthorn, *Plausible Worlds: Possibility and Understanding in History and the Social Sciences* (New York: Cambridge University Press, 1991); James D. Fearon, "Counterfactuals and Hypothesis Testing in Political Science," *World Politics* 43 (January 1991), pp. 169–95; Philip E. Tetlock and Aaron Belkin, "Counterfactual Thought Experiments in World Politics: Logical, Methodological, and Psychological Perspectives," in *Counterfactual Thought Experiments in World Politics: Logical, Methodological, and Psychological Perspectives*, eds. Philip E. Tetlock and Aaron Belkin (Princeton, NJ: Princeton University Press, 1996); Henry Ashby Turner, Jr., *Geissel des Jahrhunderts: Hitler and seine Hinterlassenschaft* (Berlin: Siedler, 1989); Philip E. Tetlock, Richard Ned Lebow, and Geoffrey Parker, *Unmaking the West: Counterfactual Thought Experiments in History* (forthcoming).

6. See E. H. Carr, *What is History?* Second ed. (New York: Vintage, 1961), p. 127. According to A. J. P. Taylor, "a historian should never deal in speculation about what did not happen," in *Struggle for the Mastery of Europe, 1848–1918* (London: Oxford University Press, 1954); see also E. P. Thompson, *The Poverty of Theory and Other Essays* (New York: Monthly Review Press, 1978), p. 300. M. M. Postan writes: "The might-have beens of history are not a profitable subject of discussion," quoted in J. D. Gould, "Hypothetical History," *Economic History Review*, 2nd ser. 22 (August 1969), pp. 195–207. See also David Hackett Fischer, *Historian's Fallacies* (New York: Harper Colophon Books, 1970), pp. 15–21; Peter McClelland, *Casual Explanation and Model-Building in History, Economics, and the New Economic History* (Ithaca, NY: Cornell University Press, 1975).

7. Yuen Foong Khong, "Confronting Hitler and Its Consequences," in *Counterfactual Thought Experiments in World Politics*, eds. Tetlock and Belkin, pp. 95–118.

8. Tetlock and Belkin, *Counterfactual Experiments in World Politics*, pp. 27–30.

9. For a fuller elaboration of this argument, see Richard Ned Lebow, "What's so Different about a Counterfactual?" in *World Politics* 52 (July 2002), pp. 550–85.

10. Philip Tetlock and Aaron Belkin (eds.), *Counterfactual Thought Experiments in World Politics*, ch. 1 and *passim*.

11. Norman N. Naimark, *The Russians in Germany: A History of the Soviet Zone of Occupation, 1945–1949* (Cambridge, MA: Harvard University Press, 1995).

12. Lucius D. Clay, *Decision in Germany* (New York: Doubleday, 1950), pp. 365–66.

13. "Graduated Reciprocation in Tension-Reduction," a concept and strategy first suggested in Charles E. Osgood, "Suggestions for Winning the Real War with Communism," *Jour-*

nal of Conflict Resolution, 3 (1959), pp. 295–325. The strategy calls for making unilateral concessions and maintaining that posture, at least initially, even if the concessions are not reciprocated; in short, "don't take 'no' for an answer." This was the approach that Gorbachev embraced, though without necessarily being aware of Osgood or GRIT per se.

14. A man tried to shoot Gorbachev on November 7, 1990, but as he pulled the trigger a police sergeant deflected his rifle. There was apparently an attempt to poison Gorbachev in September 1987, and the Gorbachevs were apparently shot at in September 1986. The KGB claimed in 1990 that it stopped attempts on Kremlin officials monthly. Similarly, someone shot at Brezhnev during a parade with four cosmonauts in January 1969. See Elizabeth Shogren, "Gorbachev's Would-Be Assassin," *Los Angeles Times*, November 25, 1990: A4; Philip Taubman, "Gorbachev Reappears At Kremlin," *New York Times*, September 30, 1987: A4; Antero Pietila, "Plot on Gorbachevs Rumored," *The San Diego Union-Tribune*, September 18, 1986: A25; "KGB Tells of Foiling Kremlin Attacks," *Los Angeles Times*, March 30, 1990: A14; "Assassinations and Attempts," *New York Times*, January 24, 1969: A6; and Werner Wiskari, "Brezhnev is Among World's Well-Wishers," *New York Times*, April 1, 1981: A21, respectively.

15. For an early sorting of Western speculation on this matter, and citations to the large Kremlinological literature on Gorbachev's rise to power, see George W. Breslauer, "From Brezhnev to Gorbachev: Ends and Means of Soviet Leadership Selection," in *Leadership Change in Communist States*, ed. Raymond Taras (London: Unwin Hyman 1989).

16. Archie Brown, *The Gorbachev Factor* (Oxford, UK: Oxford University Press, 1996), pp. 82–88; Jerry F. Hough, *Democratization and Revolution in the USSR, 1985–1991* (Washington, DC: The Brookings Institution, 1997), ch. 3.

17. For a detailed chronicle of Soviet policy in the early 1980s, see Raymond L. Garthoff, *The Great Transition: American-Soviet Relations and the End of the Cold War* (Washington, DC: Brookings, 1994), chs 1–4. Conceptualization and categorization of types of policies pursued, however, is our own.

18. Some of these incidents are discussed in Garthoff, *The Great Transition*, pp. 149–51.

19. Although Brezhnev's policies toward the U.S. from 1980 to 1982 included elements of competition and conciliation, in general during this period Brezhnev temporized in order to wait and see what course the new Reagan administration would take. Brezhnev and other senior Soviet leaders hoped that Reagan would prove a second "Nixon," a conservative capable of salvaging detente. Garthoff, *The Great Transition*, pp. 54–74, esp. pp. 57, 60, and 67. See also Garthoff, *Détente and Confrontation: American-Soviet Relations from Nixon to Reagan*, rev. ed. (Washington, DC: Brookings, 1994), pp. 1101–19.

20. Garthoff, *The Great Transition*, pp. 131–36. Georgi Arbatov, *The System* (New York: Random House, 1992) pp. 276–77.

21. Jack Snyder, *Myths of Empire: Domestic Politics and International Ambition* (Ithaca, NY: Cornell University Press, 1991), pp. 246–50.

22. *Moskovskaya pravda*, February 22, 1985; *Leningradskaya pravda*, February 15, 1985.

23. See Jerry F. Hough, *Democratization and Revolution in the USSR, 1985–1991* (Washington, DC: Brookings, 1997), pp. 96–97; Anders Aslund, *Gorbachev's Struggle for Economic Reform*, 2nd ed. (Ithaca, NY: Cornell University Press, 1991).

24. On Reagan's approach to the Soviet Union in his first term, see George P. Schultz, *Turmoil and Triumph: My Years as Secretary of State* (New York: Charles Scribner's Sons, 1993), chs. 8, 12, 17–18, 25–26, and 30; Garthoff, *The Great Transition*, chs. 1–4; *Witnesses to the End of the Cold War*, ed. William C. Wohlforth (Baltimore: Johns Hopkins University, 1996).

25. We have decided not to pursue consideration of the counterfactual scenario that keeps a physically weakened Ronald Reagan in office and then has him win or lose the 1984 election, since we do not know how to estimate the likely behavior of a partially incapacitated Reagan.

26. Our image of George Bush is shaped by the following sources: George Bush and Brent Scowcroft, *A World Transformed* (New York: Knopf, 1998); James A. Baker III with Thomas M. DeFrank, *The Politics of Diplomacy: Revolution, War and Peace, 1989–1992* (New York: G. P. Putnam's Sons, 1995); Philip Zelikow and Condoleezza Rice, *Germany Unified and Europe Transformed: A Study in Statecraft* (Cambridge, MA: Harvard University Press, 1995); Michael Beschloss and Strobe Talbott, *At the Highest Levels* (London: Little, Brown, 1993); and *The Political Psychology of the Gulf War: Leaders, Publics, and the Process of Conflict,* ed. Stanley A. Renshon (Pittsburgh: University of Pittsburgh Press, 1993).

27. Helen Dewar, "Senate Joins House in Backing Boycott of Moscow Olympics," *The Washington Post,* January 30, 1980: A8. Peter Osnos, "Detente Is Dead," *The Washington Post,* December 30, 1979: A1; Robert G. Kaiser, "Afghanistan: End of the Era of Détente," *The Washington Post,* January 17, 1980: A1.

28. Schultz, *Turmoil and Triumph,* chs. 27, 29, 30, and 34; Garthoff, *The Great Transition,* chs. 5 and 6; Robert M. Gates, *From the Shadows* (New York: Simon and Schuster, 1996), chs. 18, 19, and 21.

29. Matthew A. Evangelista, "Cooperation Theory and Disarmament Negotiations in the 1950s," *World Politics* 41 (July 1990), pp. 502–28.

30. Reference is to Bush's comment about President Manuel Noriega of Panama just before deciding to invade that country to seize Noriega and bring him to the United States for trial.

31. Lebow interview with Mikhail Gorbachev, Moscow, May 1989.

32. The concept, "leader dispensability," was first suggested by Alexander George.

33. Witness, for example, two of Gorbachev's relatively early speeches: in his "Report to the Central Committee of the CPSU," Moscow, January 27, 1987, Gorbachev declared that "we need democracy like air. If we fail to realize that, or if we realize it but make no real serious steps to broaden it, to advance it and to draw the country's working people extensively into the reorganization process, our policy will get choked. . . ." Also, in his 1986 Party Congress speech, he stated that "democracy is the wholesome and pure air without which a socialistic public organism cannot live a full-blooded life." Mikhail Gorbachev, "Speech to the Twenty-seventh Congress of the CPSU," Moscow, February 25, 1986. See also Archie Brown, *The Gorbachev Factor,* pp. 89–97; Robert G. Kaiser, *Why Gorbachev Happened* (New York: Simon and Schuster, 1991), pp. 76–77; and Thomas H. Naylor, *The Gorbachev Strategy* (Lexington, MA: D.C. Heath, 1988), pp. 215–17.

34. See George W. Breslauer, "How Do You Sell a Concessionary Foreign Policy?" *Post-Soviet Affairs* 10 (July-September 1994), pp. 277–90.

35. Beschloss and Talbott, *At the Highest Levels,* pp. 11, 29–30, 452–54; John Miller, *Mikhail Gorbachev and the End of Soviet Power* (New York: St. Martin's, 1993), pp. 54–55. Christian Schmidt-Häuer, *Gorbachev* (Topsfield, MA: Salem House, 1986), pp. 115–22.

36. See Brown, *The Gorbachev Factor;* Hough, *Revolution and Democratization; Learning in US and Soviet,* chapters by F. Griffiths, R. Legvold, and G. Breslauer.

37. Arbatov, p. 294. Kaiser, pp. 62–73.

38. The strongest statements for the view that Ronald Reagan deserves credit as the initiator of the overtures of conciliation that led to the end of the Cold War are found in Beth A. Fischer, *The Reagan Reversal: Foreign Policy and the End of the Cold War* (Columbia: University of Missouri Press, 1997); and Jack F. Matlock, Jr., *Autopsy on an Empire: The American Ambassador's Account of the Collapse of the Soviet Union* (New York: Random House, 1995).

39. H. M. Schroder, M. J. Driver, and S. Streufert, *Human Information Processing* (New York: Holt, Rinehart & Winston, 1967); and S. Streufer and S. C. Streufert, *Behavior in the Complex Environment* (New York: Wiley, 1978).

40. Nancy Reagan, *My Turn: The Memoirs of Nancy Reagan* (New York: Dell, 1989), pp. 370–71; Wohlforth, *Witnesses to the End of the Cold War,* pp. 164–65, 170, 180 (com-

ments by Aleksandr Bessmertnykh); Schultz, *Turmoil and Triumph,* pp. 996 and 1138; Anatoly Dobrynin, *In Confidence* (New York: Random House, 1995), p. 504; Brown, *The Gorbachev Factor,* pp. 231–33.

41. Dan Oberdorfer, *The Turn: From the Cold War to a New Era: The United States and the Soviet Union, 1983–1990* (New York: Poseidon Press, 1991), p. 299; see also Beschloss and Talbott, *At the Highest Levels,* p. 132.

42. The argument is also made by Fred I. Greenstein, "Ronald Reagan, Mikhail Gorbachev, and the End of the Cold War: What Difference Did They Make?" in *Witnesses to the End of the Cold War,* ed. William C. Wohlforth (Baltimore: Johns Hopkins University Press, 1996), p. 216.

43. Brown, *The Gorbachev Factor,* pp. 230–31.

44. In Wohlforth, *Witnesses,* p. 107; See also the observation of Frank Carlucci, a cabinet member in the Reagan administration (in *Ibid.* pp. 102–03): "And the amazing thing is that the alchemy between these two disparate personalities seemed to work, that it somehow came together. There is no question that Ronald Reagan was very taken by Gorbachev; that he understood that Ronald Reagan was very taken by Gorbachev; that he understood this was a new figure in the Soviet Union; that this was a historical moment. And as our former Soviet friends have said, there's no question that Gorbachev recognized that this was a new, unique opportunity to establish a personal relationship and change the whole dynamic of the relationship."

Chapter 8

Understanding the End of the Cold War as a Non-Linear Confluence

Richard Ned Lebow and Janice Gross Stein

The end of the Cold War changed the world and the way we think about it. It ushered in a profound transformation of the international system, and has already become a critical case for the generation and testing of theories about conflict resolution and international relations more generally. The policy and theoretical lessons we draw from the largely peaceful end to a conflict that threatened the survival of humankind depend on the explanations we develop for this surprising but welcome development. The introduction to this volume voiced our concern about the predilection of scholars and policymakers alike to reason backwards and offer explanations for the end of the Cold War that are consistent with and supportive of their preferred theories and foreign policies. To combat this tendency and lay the groundwork for more persuasive treatments of the events of 1986–91, the Mershon Center and its collaborators ran a series of conferences to bring policymakers and scholars together and to provide new documentary evidence on the basis of which they could collectively attempt to reconstruct the important decisions that led to the end of the Cold War.

We structured our book around four generic explanations for the end of the Cold War: capabilities, ideas, domestic politics, and leaders. To what extent could they singly or in combination produce compelling accounts for the five turning points we identified as critical steps leading to this outcome? Our assumption from the outset, which was borne out in practice, is that none of these explanations alone can provide a compelling account for the end of the Cold War. We need to combine explanations to account for individual turning points and for the end of the Cold War as a whole, and this requires adequate conceptual tools for bridging levels of analysis. This chapter will take a step in that direction by examining four models of causation, two of them nonlinear, to see how they capture our understanding of the Cold War's end. It will also argue that the end of the Cold War was highly contingent, and that the uncertainty and unpredictability of its outcome, the shape it took, and its timing offer additional, cautionary lessons to the academic and policy communities.

Causes and Turning Points

The five turning point chapters reach some common conclusions. All their authors find it difficult to establish appropriate boundaries for the competing explanations. In the absence of clear boundaries we invite a game of leapfrog. Individual explanations, especially capabilities and ideas, can claim to account for all turning points because they also claim to account for each other. Realists explain Gorbachev's strategy of retrenchment and accommodation as a response to declining Soviet capabilities relative to the West. That decline is generally attributed by Soviet specialists to the command economy that Stalin imposed on the Soviet Union and that his successors maintained. Scholars who posit the power of ideas invoke ideology to explain Stalin's choice and the survival of the command economy long after it proved grossly inefficient. Invoking the Gerschenkron thesis, realists could respond that the command economy, and indeed, the Leninist system itself, were a response to late industrialization and thus ultimately a response to a relative disadvantage in capabilities.[1] To avoid this kind of infinite regress, we disallowed leapfrogging and insisted that our contributors use variants of the four explanations to account directly for their turning points, not indirectly through any capacity to account for other explanations.

Our contributors found it difficult to distinguish among competing explanations. Capabilities, ideas, domestic politics, and leaders are concepts that we impose on the external world, and even precise definitions of these concepts do not make it easy to discover their boundaries or determine whether they should be regarded as causes or effects. Consider, for example, the concept of ideas. It is often invoked to explain domestic political differences, and certainly distinguished Gorbachev and the reformers around him from their more conservative opponents. But political factions also mobilize ideas in support of goals they seek for other reasons. Matthew Evangelista documents this phenomenon in the case of the Reagan administration's espousal of the "double zero" proposal for theater arms control. When leaders' policies are motivated by a particular vision, ideas may distinguish them from other leaders. But those ideas may only affect policy because a leader committed to them comes to power. Richard Herrmann argued that this is what happened in the Soviet Union; the Soviet elite as a whole did not adopt a new set of ideas, but a group of individuals with ideas and a vision different from the predecessors gained control over the levers of power. To disaggregate competing explanations, Herrmann suggests that we distinguish between driving forces and enabling conditions.

A third common finding is that no single explanation provides a satisfactory explanation for any turning point, let alone all of them. Each of the authors—their arguments are reviewed below—found it necessary to invoke all four explanations to explain the specific nature, timing, and implications of their turning point. Davis and Wohlforth rightly observe that the utility of any explanation depends on what we expect of it. Few if any social scientists would claim that a single causal factor would account in detail for any complex outcome. But it might explain more of the variance than other factors and be the most useful starting point for a more comprehensive explanation. Indeterminacy in their view is not a fair ground for rejecting an explanation. Scholars who work on questions with complex causes need to establish *levels* of indeterminacy and use them to assess the relative merit of competing explanations.

Davis and Wohlforth develop such a framework to sustain their claim that a decline in material capability—gradual up to 1989, and precipitous after that—was the single most important cause of Soviet retrenchment and accommodation and, by extension, of the unification of Germany. They recognize that other responses to decline were possible, although less rational in their view. They acknowledge that the timing of events, Moscow's refusal to use force to prevent or stall the German drive to unity, and the particular form of unification—absorption of the DDR by the FRG and its incorporation in NATO—can only be explained with reference to explanations at other levels of analysis. They acknowledge that Gorbachev's refusal to consider the use of force to maintain Soviet client regimes in Eastern Europe is better explained by ideas than by material forces.

Jacques Lévesque uses a similar framework to reach different conclusions about his turning point. He acknowledges that the decline in Soviet material capabilities was an important underlying cause of change. He believes it highly unlikely that a Soviet leader would have wanted to retreat from Eastern Europe, or would have had the political freedom to do so, if the Soviet Union had been a rising and the United States a declining power. But Soviet decline neither made this retreat necessary or probable. Ideas were the key determinant of this policy choice, especially the belief shared by Gorbachev and his top advisors that reformed socialism was both advisable and feasible in Eastern Europe. Acting on this conception, Gorbachev set in motion a chain of events that narrowed his subsequent choices and led to the demise of communism throughout the region. To understand how these events played out, it is necessary to look beyond ideas to Gorbachev's idiosyncrasies, leadership style, and the domestic political pressures acting on him.

Herrmann and Evangelista reject this kind of layered approach. They contend that military capabilities had not changed in any significant way, and thus cannot account for movement toward their turning points. At the most, material factors provide a context—but not an underlying cause—for what happened. They maintain that ideas were the central driver of Soviet policy change. Third World conflicts had no intrinsic, only symbolic value. They were important when the Cold War was understood as a global contest. Once Moscow and Washington restructured their relationship, the struggle for influence in Asia, the Middle East, and Latin America lost its perceived purpose. For Gorbachev and his advisors, arms control and a unilateral withdrawal of conventional forces from Eastern Europe were expressions of their commitment to reduce the offensive potential of Soviet armed forces and emphasize their defensive purpose. This goal was partly motivated by their overarching objective of promoting a new system of common security under which East and West would have closer political and economic relations. Herrmann and Evangelista recognize the role of domestic politics, but even more, that of leaders, in shaping the specific forms and timing of their turning points.

Several of our authors use counterfactuals to establish the relative importance of different explanations. Brown contends that the Soviet system could only have been dismantled from inside, and that no other possible leader would have attempted this task.[2] He also argues that Gorbachev had to hide his domestic and foreign policy goals, and proceed incrementally, in fits and starts. Had he openly espoused in 1985 or 1986 the policies he implemented in 1988 or 1989, he would have been removed from office. Herrmann considers what might have happened in the absence of Gorbachev and Reagan, and concludes that the selection of Gorbachev was all-important because there were no other reform-minded leaders on the Soviet side. On the American side Reagan was less important because other leaders might have cooperated with Gorbachev and facilitated Soviet disengagement from Afghanistan, Angola, and Nicaragua. Evangelista offers the counterfactual of an earlier INF agreement to show that what counted was the meaning of that agreement for leaders, and it was the worldview and goals of Gorbachev and his advisors that made INF a turning point. It only became a turning point in retrospect for the American side, and that was after they looked back on it as part of a broader strategy by Gorbachev to restructure East-West relations.

Lévesque uses the counterfactual of extended socialist rule in Eastern Europe to probe the role of Gorbachev and the latitude open to Soviet leaders in general. He suggests that if Gorbachev had made the suggestion in 1989 or earlier

that the Prague Spring be reassessed, Alexander Dubcek would have been reha-
bilitated and he and his followers would have rapidly taken over leadership of
the Czechoslovak Community Party and could handily have won a free election.
Lévesque constructs a similar scenario for East Germany, with more important
political consequences. If Gorbachev had pressed for the replacement of Erich
Honecker by Hans Modrow, the preferred candidate of the reformers, and had
he made overtures to the opposition, as he likely would have, events in Germany
and Eastern Europe in general would have unfolded differently. The DDR
might have remained independent for some time—all the existing opposition
forces were in favor of its continuation—and ultimately might have been unified with the Federal Republic rather than absorbed. The new governments in
Poland and Hungary in the summer of 1989 did not call for an end to the Warsaw Pact and reserved a major and crucial role of their communist parties. It was
the sudden collapse of the DDR and calls for German unification that upset the
equilibria in Poland and Hungary and made dominoes fall in Bulgaria, Czechoslovakia, and Rumania, and, with them, the Warsaw Pact.[3]

Breslauer and Lebow devote their entire chapter to counterfactual analysis.
They imagine East-West relations without Gorbachev, Reagan, or Bush to make
the case for the determining role of leaders. They explore the possibility of different leaders on both sides and the consequences of their likely interactions,
with outcomes that range from an intensified Cold War through detente to a
more rapid end of the Cold War that might even have preserved the Soviet
Union. In a second experiment, they keep the historical leaders in place and ask
how much of context they would have to change to prevent key turning points
from taking place or others that did not happen from occurring (e.g., a far-
reaching arms control agreement at Reykjavik). Building on the counterfactuals
suggested by the authors of the turning point chapters, they argue that the end
of the Cold War was highly contingent.

All of our authors attempt to situate their explanations in broader historical
perspectives. Brown describes the growing dissatisfaction of intellectuals with
the current state of domestic and foreign affairs and the evolution of new
thinking and how these attitudes facilitated the kind of transformation Gorbachev envisaged. Herrmann examines Third World conflicts as an extension
of the core conflict in central Europe, and explains how those conflicts have
waxed and waned as a function of how the core conflict was understood by the
superpowers. Evangelista also situates the development and regulation of strategic weapons in historical context. Both authors show how these relationships
were interactive and reinforcing throughout the Cold War. Herrmann and
Evangelista make parallel arguments about how disengagement in the Third
World and arms control made the core conflict easier to ameliorate, and how

progress here facilitated further accommodation in the periphery and arms control.

Two sets of authors offer perspectives that go beyond the Cold War. Davis and Wohlforth consider the end of that conflict as another manifestation of the realist "law of uneven growth" For realists, the primary cause of international change is the uneven growth of material capabilities among states. It leads to a redistribution of power in the international system that can undermine the status quo. New political, economic, and territorial arrangements arise, or are imposed, through war or diplomacy, to reflect the new distribution of power. The retreat of the Soviet Union from the Third World and Eastern Europe and its subsequent fragmentation were a dramatic instance of this process, as was the unification of Germany within NATO and the eastward extension of that alliance.[4]

Jacques Lévesque attributes the end of the Cold War to the delayed triumph of revisionism in the Soviet Union. Much of the Soviet political elite became "social democratized" and sought to make domestic and foreign policy consistent with their ideology. Thus, the collapse of communist regimes in Eastern Europe did not lead to the demise of the USSR, but rather the reverse. Lévesque attributes the appeal of revisionism to the relative success of liberal democracy in the West and the improvements in material conditions and dignity this brought to the working class. Socialist parties in the West did not so much abandon their goals as they found ways to reformulate their objectives and work within the existing political system. In the 1970s and 1980s most West and Eastern European socialist parties had embraced social democracy, and the conversion of Leninist parties, as in Italy, accelerated the process in the Soviet Union. Lévesque finds that the critical phase of a communist party's conversion to social democracy is often marked by intense political idealism. This was characteristic of Gorbachev and his advisors and helps to explain their naive belief that a smooth and controlled process of change was possible in Eastern Europe.

The key cleavage between our contributors is the weight they give to material capabilities and ideas as the principal agents of change. Davis and Wohlforth privilege material capabilities, while the other authors award pride of place to ideas. In a recent article on the end of the Cold War, Wohlforth develops the framework that informs his analysis. He maintains that relative power and material interests "strongly determine" which ideas gain acceptance; ideas have no independent power, but follow and reflect powerful group interests and material conditions.[5]

The clash between material forces and ideas is a long-standing and deeply rooted debate, and our evidence cannot be determining. However, in this particular case, idea-based explanations appear to offer a more comprehensive account of the end of the Cold War and appear central to all the turning points. The first criterion for judging our four explanations is how they make use of the written and oral evidence generated by our project and by other scholars. The Davis-Wohlforth chapter, which makes the strongest case for material forces, marshals considerable evidence to document the Soviet economic decline and how much more precipitous it had become after 1989. This is the first step in their argument. The second, and critical step, is their assertion that Gorbachev's policy toward Eastern Europe and Germany was a direct response to decline *and* was motivated by the concern for preserving as far as possible Soviet power and influence in the world. Davis and Wohlforth offer no evidence in support of these contentions from official records, memoirs, or interviews—in contrast to their analysis of the policies of Bush and Kohl.

The materialist argument appears to offer limited help in explaining the other turning points. Archie Brown is adamant that in 1985 the Soviet Union faced a slow decline rather than an imminent collapse, and could have pursued the same kinds of foreign and domestic policies for at least several more decades. Richard Herrmann argues that costs, direct or indirect, cannot explain the Soviet Union's retreat from Afghanistan, Angola, or Nicaragua. Neither the Soviets nor their clients had been defeated on the battlefield, and withdrawal did not save Moscow much money. Gorbachev substantially increased military and economic aid to Afghanistan after withdrawing Soviet forces. The claim that American support of the mujahadeen, UNITA, and the Contras dramatically raised the costs of competition to the Soviet Union is countered by evidence that suggests it may have prolonged the superpower competition by increasing the perceived symbolic value of what was at stake. The INF treaty might seem to constitute a strong case for material capabilities, but Evangelista finds no support in Soviet archives, memoirs, or oral history that the NATO deployment of American Pershing-II and cruise missiles in the autumn of 1983 convinced the Soviet side to negotiate seriously. The transcript of the relevant Politburo meeting shows that every member who participated in the discussion about arms control expected the American missiles to be deployed despite the active opposition of the European peace movement. The differences among them in policy, which continued after the Western deployment, reflected their different ideas about security. The change in Soviet negotiating policy was a function of a new leadership with new ideas. Jacques Lévesque insists that the distribution of power did not make necessary or probable the kind of political changes that took place in Eastern Europe, and he finds no evidence that power considerations were paramount in Soviet calculations.

Lévesque's argument is an interesting variant of the liberal thesis, common in the literature, but otherwise unrepresented in our volume. It attributes the end of the Cold War and the wider decline of authoritarian regimes to the economic success and political tranquility of industrialized democracies. The liberal thesis is open to the same kind of criticism as its realist counterpart: failure to document the links between the few macro causes that move history and the many micro decisions that give it concrete shape. However, Lévesque and Evangelista in their two chapters, which build on the richer documentation provided in their books, base their case more on evidence than inference. The evidence is particularly rich in the case of Soviet policy toward Eastern Europe, and somewhat less so with respect to arms control. Even so, Evangelista maintains, there is enough evidence to cast serious doubt on materialist explanations and to provide a good foundation for an explanation based on ideas.[6]

Herrmann also argues that ideas were important, but relies more on inference than evidence. As additional documents become available, he suggests, it may be possible to establish the role they played in the specific decisions that led Gorbachev to back away from Soviet involvement in Third World conflicts. Herrmann cautions that it would still be necessary to show that ideas were not epiphenomenal, that they were not simply a response to the Soviet Union's economic decline. An important step in this direction is Robert English's recent book, which documents the extent to which new thinking in domestic and foreign affairs preceded economic decline and were an independent cause of foreign policy change.[7]

Synergism Among Causes

Our analysis of the end of the Cold War has broader implications for explanation in foreign policy and international relations. Our authors begin from different entry points, but all acknowledge the need to combine their preferred explanation with others to account for the timing, details, and consequences of their turning points. Going beyond an ad hoc historical narrative that draws together different explanations requires conceptual tools that bridge levels of analysis and permit a more rigorous framing of the problem of multiple causation.

The first step may be to consider the different forms that synergy can take. In a straight-forward, additive relationship, A is a necessary but insufficient condition for X, but A + B together produce that outcome. In a variant, A can cause X by itself but A + B (and perhaps C and D) tell us more about its timing, intensity, or consequences. The A + B formulation assumes a single causal chain. But turning point X could be brought about by other routes; it might be the products of B + C and C+ D as well as A + B. These several causal chains can be independent of one another or they can be connected if a cause is part of two or more chains or their products.

We also need to consider situations in which the synergistic interaction among variables can produce a result that is more than the sum of their independent values. When the value of one variable depends on the presence or state of another, it is impossible to predict or understand their consequences independently. The recall of Firestone ATX, ATX II, and Wilderness AT tires because they were involved in an unusual number of accidents illustrates this kind of synergy. These accidents have been traced to the propensity of the outer layer of rubber to detach from the steel belt underneath. Firestone, and some independent investigators, also blamed the problem on Ford, whose Explorer sports utility vehicle is very difficult to control in the case of a tire separation, especially at high speeds. The Firestone tires were standard equipment on the Ford Explorer, and this combination may have been responsible for a far greater number of accidents and fatalities than would have been the case if the same number of Firestone tires (on different vehicles) and Ford Explorers (equipped with different tires) had been on the road.[8]

An even stronger case of synergy occurs when a multiple stream of independent causes come together to produce an outcome that could not otherwise occur. In the case of Firestone-Ford, there were other conditions that contributed to the likelihood of a blowout. It was more likely to happen at high speeds in warm climates with fully inflated tires; all three conditions contributed to heat buildup in the outer rubber layer. Layer separation and blowouts were nevertheless still possible, although much less likely, at slow speeds in cold climates with underinflated tires. They were also possible with vehicles other than Ford Explorers. But consider the example of a house that goes up in smoke. Investigation reveals that the fire spread from a lighted candle that was left unattended on a window sill. The window was not completely sealed, and a draft blew one of the curtains close enough to the flame for it to catch fire. The smoke alarm, connected to the house security system, did not function because its battery was dead, and the fire department failed to receive the timely warning that might have permitted it to save the dwelling. What caused the house to burn down? The candle was the source of the fire, but it would not have been lit or placed on the window sill if it had not been the holiday season and had its owners not been following a neighborhood custom. If the window had not been warped, or the insulation around it had provided a better seal, the candle would not have started a fire. If the owners had been home, or if the smoke alarm had a charged battery, the house would not have burned down. No single factor was responsible for this disaster; all of them had to be present and interact in a particular way.[9]

How much and what kinds of synergism can be identified in these turning points? Archie Brown argues that A (new leader) + B (ideas) + C (accidents) combined to bring about fundamental domestic and foreign policy changes. He concedes that Viktor Grishin was the only other half-serious contender for the leadership, and backed Gorbachev to save his position when he recognized he could not win. While Gorbachev's appointment was uncontested, nobody in the Politburo expected him to transform the political system and end the Cold War. Gorbachev succeeded in doing this because the numerous past failures of the system had generated numerous proposals for reform and a cadre of officials who were sympathetic to at least the initial steps he took in opening the system and extending the olive branch to the West. However, he faced enormous constraints in moving further, but judiciously used his power of appointment to neutralize opponents and put key supporters in important positions. The nuclear accident in Chernobyl in April 1986 was an enormous stimulus in this regard, and Matthias Rust's unscheduled flight to Red Square in May 1987 provided the opportunity to purge the military and to replace Sergei Sokolov as Minister of Defense with the more complaint Dimitri Yazov. Gorbachev, for the time being at least, was able to sidetrack powerful opposition to change within the Ministry of Defense and KGB.

For Richard Herrmann, A (a costly war in Afghanistan) + B (ideas) + C (new leader) produced a turning point that none of these conditions could have generated singly. A debate had been underway for some time about Afghanistan, with some prominent policy experts in the institutes in favor of a negotiated withdrawal. But their position was a minority one, and while they were allowed to express their views in memoranda, these documents were never presented to the leadership. Serious consideration of their recommendations required a leader with an openness to new ideas and a willingness to experiment in foreign policy. Gorbachev qualified on both counts. He first escalated Soviet military involvement in the hope of compelling a political settlement, but then reversed himself and came to favor withdrawal when war failed to bring success. According to Herrmann and Brown, Gorbachev was the only candidate for the general secretaryship who for reasons of personality and politics was likely to embrace the radical option of withdrawal. But the espousal of withdrawal by foreign policy experts not only made the policy available to Gorbachev, it legitimated it within the policy process.

Adding domestic politics might provide an even more complete picture of Soviet policy toward Afghanistan. To maintain his governing coalition, Gorbachev had to outflank hard-line opposition. Important figures in the military, the Communist Party, and the KGB opposed withdrawal from Afghanistan, but their opposition could be minimized by demonstrating support for Najib's regime through continued military and economic support. This may explain why the flow of weapons and aid continued after withdrawal.

Could other chains of causation have led to roughly the same outcome? Herrmann's chapter gives us little reason for thinking so. An earlier resolution of Afghanistan would have required much earlier American willingness to accept a negotiated solution that would have left a pro-Soviet regime in power, at least as a transitional government. As late as 1989, Secretary of State James Baker's effort to terminate military supplies to anti-Soviet forces in Afghanistan, Angola, and Nicaragua met fierce opposition from important figures in the Republican Party, the national security community, and from Senator Jesse Helms. Later resolution to Afghanistan is a more realistic possibility. But this too would have required news ideas, new leaders, a favorable domestic political climate, and at least tacit American compliance.

Evangelista offers us another example of additive causation. In this case A (ideas) + B (new leader) were necessary to produce turning points (INF and the unilateral reduction in conventional forces). "New thinking" had slowly emerged as a new and idealistic approach to foreign affairs championed by those who were for the most part on the peripheries of power. To achieve the broader goals of Soviet reform, it was necessary to reach an accommodation with the West. This in turn required a resolution to the military issues that had exacerbated the insecurity of both sides. Gorbachev and Eduard Shevardnadze were essential to the implementation of new thinking; they responded favorably to overtures from *institutchiki* pushing for radical departures in arms control policy, and were willing to confront the establishment to implement these policies. In the INF decision, Shevardnadze's decisions generated sustained criticism from many of his veteran colleagues in the foreign ministry and the international department of the central committee, who accused him of pursuing a "capitulationalist line." Marshall Sergei Akhromeev felt so betrayed by the decision to give up the SS–23 "Oka" missile that he considered resigning his post as Chief of the General Staff. The evidence suggests that domestic politics was less relevant, as Gorbachev and Shevardnadze felt unconstrained by widespread opposition to their security policies.

Were there other routes to these outcomes? We have already noted Evangelista's counterfactual that Brezhnev could easily have had an INF agreement. But in his judgment, such an agreement would not have constituted a turning point. It seems inconceivable that Brezhnev or any other Soviet political figure likely to have followed him as general secretary would have carried out a unilateral conventional forces reduction in the face of an American arms buildup, the Strategic Defense Initiative, *and* strong opposition from the Soviet security establishment. Nor is it likely that the Cold War could have ended without having first removed the threat posed by the deployment of Soviet forces in Eastern Europe with the capability to conduct offensive operations against the West. This problem might have been addressed in a variety of ways if the United States had been a willing partner. But the Reagan administration, although not the President himself, was strongly opposed to arms control of this magnitude.

Consequently, dramatic, irreversible, and even unilateral actions on the Soviet side were probably necessary to jump start the process of accommodation.

Lévesque's turning point also seems to be explained by the A + B formulation of new ideas and a new leader. Gorbachev's policy toward Eastern Europe was another application of new thinking, based on the twin beliefs that the democratization of socialism was both advantageous and politically possible. Ideas were particularly important, Lévesque argues, because a communist Eastern Europe was much more central to legitimization of the Soviet Union and its ideology than arms control or the outcome of Third World conflicts. Hence a deeper change in beliefs was essential to move away from the Brezhnev Doctrine. Gorbachev was also essential given his subsequent, incremental path toward social democracy and related willingness to push for political reform in Eastern Europe. Gorbachev was important in a counterintuitive way: he was more inconsistent in his policies toward Warsaw Pact allies than he was in arms control and domestic political and economic reforms. Lévesque maintains that a more consistent and strategic leader might have been more successful in slowing the pace and scope of change in Eastern Europe.

Eastern Europe also presents a more complex picture because of the multiplicity of actors involved: the Soviet Union, the countries of Eastern and Western Europe, the United States, and important leaders, factions, and movements in each of these countries. Lévesque suggests nonlinear elements in their interaction.[10] One of the most important was the independent evolution of Eurocommunism in the West. Even under Brezhnev, the Italian, Spanish, and French parties were considered part of the world communist movement, although they were at the margin and subjected to strong criticism. The existence of Eurocommunism both inspired and gave legitimacy to Gorbachev and his new thinking. Many Soviet reformers—especially those associated with Oleg Bogomolov's Institute of the Economy of the World Socialist System—insisted that perestroika and new thinking would greatly strengthen the Italian communist party and the West German left and lead to a more convergent Europe. Change in Eastern Europe was a confluence of at least three independent factors—economic stagnation, Eurocommunism and the accession to power of Mikhail Gorbachev—and the particular ways in which they interacted.

Our final turning point is the unification of Germany. Here too the authors make the case for additive causation, but suggest that the outcome may have been equifinal with multiple causal pathways. A (Soviet economic decline) was the principal cause of unification. It encouraged the Soviet Union to retrench and seek accommodation with the West, and later, significantly shaped the bargaining outcome with the West when the DDR began to implode. Sooner or later, they contend, some Soviet leader would have come to regard retrenchment and accommodation as the only rational policy, and such a policy would have led ineluctably to the collapse of the DDR and some form of reunification of Germany. Davis and Wohlforth believe that the particular outcome realized in 1991–92 was the result of A (Soviet decline) + B (new thinking in the Soviet Union) + C (German and American domestic politics) + D (leaders). These additional factors influenced the timing and institutional structure of unification, but were not necessary to bring some form of unification about at some future time.

Interactions Among Turning Points

The individual turning points are important to explain specific outcomes but also because they are components in a complex chain that explains the end of the Cold War. To examine their cumulative impact and the interaction among turning points, we must move up a level of analysis. To explain the end of the Cold War, we need to know: (1) how many of the turning points were necessary to achieve this outcome; (2) how independent were these turning points from one other; and (3) how many different pathways could have led to the end of the Cold War?

At the outset of this chapter, we considered the relative importance of our several turning points and the extent to which they were necessary to terminate the Cold War. There is a consensus among our authors that *all* five turning points were necessary to end the Cold War, but that they could have come in different order. Davis and Wohlforth contend that there still would have been significant changes in Soviet foreign policy without Gorbachev, but acknowledge that the changes may have been less conciliatory or less far-reaching. The other authors put more weight on Gorbachev and are dubious that the Cold War would have ended in the 1990s if he had not become general secretary. So the coming to power of Gorbachev represents an important turning point because he enabled all of the others.

Most of our contributors agree that the Soviet retreat from Afghanistan, arms control, and troop withdrawals and encouragement of political reform in Eastern Europe were all linked and manifestations of new thinking. But a change in policy toward Afghanistan would have been possible without any of the other initiatives; it could have been carried out by a conservative leadership anxious to cut losses and shore up support at home. We can also imagine major changes in Eastern Europe leading to the collapse of communism and the unification of Germany prior to withdrawal from Afghanistan or any arms control agreements. Breslauer and Lebow create this scenario as one of many that might have occurred if Reagan had been assassinated and Gorbachev had as a result confronted a much more cautious and suspicious George Bush. However, the end of the Cold War almost by definition required a resolution of Afghanistan and some kind of arms control; competition in the Third World and military insecurity were major sources of East-West tensions. Presumably, an end to the division of Europe would have created strong pressures to deal with these issues.

What about a different set of turning points leading to more or less the same outcome? Or, could the same turning points have led to a different outcome? It is relatively easy to conceive of different routes to political change in Eastern Europe and the unification of Germany within NATO. Gorbachev or some other Soviet leader could have offered to let their Eastern European allies reform politically without Soviet interference in return for promises that they would remain members of the Warsaw Pact and continue to allow Soviet forces to be stationed on their territories. The United States might even have become a co-guarantor of such an agreement if an American president thought it necessary to bring about liberalization in Eastern Europe. In December 1988 Henry Kissinger pleaded with the incoming Bush administration to propose such a deal to Moscow.[11] It seems unlikely that such an arrangement could have endured in the long term—although Gorbachev might easily have convinced himself that it could—and when it began to unravel, the Soviet Union might have faced a situation roughly comparable to the one it did in 1990–91. In the aftermath, historians and political scientists might have argued that the de-Sovietization of Eastern Europe and the unification of Germany within NATO would have been impossible without this intermediary agreement.

Another possibility is a Soviet rejection of political change in Eastern Europe and the use of force to maintain the status quo. Military intervention in East Germany in 1953, Hungary in 1956, Czechoslovakia in 1968, and an internal coup in Poland in December 1981 succeeded in stabilizing or restoring to power pro-Soviet, communist regimes. The political culture of the communist world had evolved considerably since 1968, and Soviet military intervention in the 1990s, in Poland, for example, might have provoked widespread protests throughout the region and within the Soviet Union itself. Intervention could even have served as the unwitting catalyst for the unraveling of communism and, possibly, of the Soviet Union. In retrospect, the Polish revolution would have been regarded as a critical and necessary turning point for the end of the Cold War.

It is also possible to construct an alternative context in which many of the turning points we identified would still have taken place but not moved the Cold War toward resolution. According to Breslauer and Lebow, the most likely alternative to Gorbachev was a more conservative and cautious leader who might have pursued what they call "a kinder, gentler form of Brezhnevism." In foreign policy this might have led to a withdrawal from Afghanistan. A leader such as Yegor Ligachev might also have sought arms control agreements with the West and a broader disengagement from the Third World as a means of reducing tension, saving money, and building domestic support. But accommodation with the West might have stopped there, without major changes in Eastern Europe, in which case neither the retreat from Afghanistan nor arms control would have constituted turning points in a chain leading to the end of the Cold War.

It is more difficult to conceive of variation in the form of alternative endings to the Cold War. Given the Soviet Union's economic decline and the loss of appeal of ideology in Eastern Europe and at home, it seems unlikely that the Cold War could have ended in the manner envisaged by most Soviet and American participants in the Helsinki process: recognition and support of the status quo by both sides, with a commensurate decrease in tensions, military disengagement, and normalization of relations. This outcome required a prosperous and stable Eastern Europe with populations committed to preserving socialism and close ties with the Soviet Union. According to Lévesque, Gorbachev favored political reform in Eastern Europe in the erroneous expectation that it would serve this end. He pushed, unsuccessfully, for the follow-on disbanding of *both* NATO and the Warsaw Pact as a condition for German unification. In this outcome many of the same turning points would have led to a different outcome. A more far-fetched scenario would be the reverse of what actually transpired: a crisis of capitalism, collapse of American influence and NATO and the Sovietization of Western Europe. At the very least, this outcome would have required the double counterfactual of robust Soviet growth and dramatic Western decline.

How independent were our five turning points? Proponents of both the material and idea-based explanations for the end of the Cold War contend that they were tightly coupled and to varying degrees an expression of underlying changes in material capabilities or ideology. Even if this argument is accepted, it says little about possible interaction effects among the turning points and the extent to which the presence of one or more of them made others more or less likely. Taking Gorbachev's accession to power (A), our first turning point, as a given, there are obviously strong links between this turning point and everything that followed, but none of our authors argue that these turning points were inevitable after A, or that (B) withdrawal from Afghanistan and (C) arms control could not have happened without A. These latter events were turning points in part because they helped to establish Gorbachev's bona fides in the West, but they did not directly lead to (D) political change in Eastern Europe or (E) the unification of Germany within NATO. There are very strong links between D and E; it is almost inconceivable that German reunification—especially within NATO—would have been possible without the prior collapse of communist regimes in Eastern Europe and the ensuing collapse of the Warsaw Pact. Those events were set in motion by A, but, our authors contend, required other, independent and contributing causes. So too was the particular shape of these outcomes significantly influenced but not determined by Gorbachev's policies.

The preceding analysis suggests that there is little evidence for a monocausal explanation for the end of the Cold War (X). A was a necessary but insufficient condition for X, but A + B + C + D + E combined in additive *and* interactive ways to produce that outcome. Our counterfactual exploration suggests that A, B, C, and D might have been ordered differently, and more importantly, that there were other causal pathways that could have led to the same generic resolution of the Cold War. If we are dealing with an outcome that was at some point highly likely but could have been reached through multiple, additive pathways, we must consider the possibility that the pathway A + B + C + D + E was an accident of history.

A linear, additive world is generally unpredictable, and this problem is more acute in a nonlinear environment. Our authors have made the case for nonlinearity in the broadest sense. Realist and constructivist contributors concur that it took a decline in material capabilities *and* the triumph of new thinking to set in motion the changes that resolved the Cold War, and that these two factors had largely independent causation. Davis and Wohlforth, who make the strongest case for the determining role of material capabilities, acknowledge that the Soviet response to the decline in capabilities could have taken many different forms. Gorbachev's encouragement of reform in Eastern Europe and his subsequent refusal to consider the use of force to maintain pro-Soviet regimes can only be explained by his beliefs, goals, and expectations.

Most of the authors who privilege ideas credit the Soviet decline with creating the context in which Gorbachev came to power and chose his policies; they acknowledge that there would have been much less incentive for political and economic experimentation at home and in Eastern Europe if the Soviet economy had been robust.

Another form of nonlinearity is confluence, where a multiple stream of independent causes come together to produce an outcome that could not otherwise occur. A good case can be made that the end of the Cold War was the result of such a confluence. Some of our authors invoke material decline, new thinking, and the election of Gorbachev to explain turning points B through E, and, by extension, the end of the Cold War. Few realists would argue that the Soviet decline gave rise to new thinking and determined the election of Gorbachev. Our contributors acknowledge that these three developments are in some way linked, but in other ways independent of one other. They can imagine new thinking developing in the absence of Soviet economic decline, but in response to the arms race, competition in the Third World and their dangers, these developments may have been the most important catalysts of new thinking in foreign affairs. If someone like Gorbachev had come to power in the late 1970s, when the Soviet economy was still growing, albeit slowly, some kind of accommodation might well have been possible. Nor were Gorbachev and new thinking synonymous. If Gorbachev had come to power in the absence of new thinking, he would probably have pursued different domestic and foreign policies. Breslauer and Lebow contend that new thinking and material decline without Gorbachev would also have produced a different outcome.

New thinking in turn was made possible by Eurocommunism, and it was in large part a response to the economic boom in the West that produced a half-century of nearly constant growth. Some of our contributors also insist on the importance of Reagan and Kohl as distinct from other possible American and German leaders. Thus, at least some of the contributing causes for change in the Soviet Union were independent of anything that happened inside the Soviet Union. As all of these and earlier examples indicate, it was the confluence and interaction of a number of independent and quasi-independent conditions that brought about the end of the Cold War.

This finding suggests that the end of the Cold War, its timing, and details were all to varying degrees contingent. The Cold War could have led to a shooting war, conventional or nuclear, but there is a general consensus that this possibility declined sharply after peaceful resolution of the Berlin and Cuban crises and de facto and then de jure acceptance by the West of the postwar political and territorial division of Europe. A superpower crisis always remained a possibility, and many thoughtful people on both sides of the East-West divide worried about such a confrontation during Reagan's first term in office. However, over the decades, the two superpowers had become more cautious in practice, if not in rhetoric, and more skillful in keeping their differences from escalating into war-threatening crises. Peaceful Sovietization of Europe, the direct opposite of the actual outcome of the Cold War, had become a pipedream with the economic recovery of Western Europe and the decline and subsequent transformation of the French and Italian communist parties. The Helsinki-style solution based on preservation of socialism in a demilitarized Europe also became increasingly unlikely as a result of the growing economic disparity between East and West and the widespread loss of faith in Marxism-Leninism in the Soviet Union and Eastern Europe. To be sure, a clever Soviet leader might have negotiated such an end to the Cold War, but we doubt that it would have been stable in the long-term.

The important puzzle may not be the avoidance of superpower war or the collapse of socialism, or even the fragmentation of the Soviet Union, but the fact that the transformation of the Soviet Union was achieved in a relatively peaceful way. We and our authors have described various alternative, and much less pleasant, scenarios that might have come about with no more than minimal rewrites of history. Some, if not most, of these scenarios could have had tragic human consequences and have made the post–Cold War world much more difficult to manage than it has been. One need only look at the violent, troubled, and unstable Europe and Middle East that emerged at the end of World War I as a result of the breakup of the Austro-Hungarian, Russian, and Ottoman empires. Many of the conflicts that threaten the peace today date back, or were at least dramatically intensified, by the violence associated with these transformations.

Process

The end of the Cold War—indeed, any kind of accommodation—can be conceptualized as a process of bargaining in which the parties involved signal preferences, solicit information, and search for mutually beneficial agreements. Models of strategic interaction assume that the parties involved have predetermined and transitive preferences and bargain in a series of moves until they reach an agreement or deadlock. Games of incomplete information recognize that bargaining is also a search for information, and that new information may prompt parties to change their bargaining strategies or goals.[12] The end of the Cold War suggests that these assumptions may be inappropriate, and that these kinds of models may not capture important dynamics of the bargaining process and thus fail to predict or explain their outcomes.

The interactions that led to the end of the Cold War encourage us to problematize the concept of moves. It may usefully describe much of the signaling that occurs in bargaining, but the most important part of the process is that which determines how, by whom, and when moves are made. The negotiations that led to German reunification offer a telling example. Most of the Russian, American, and German policymakers we interviewed agreed that a different format, one, for example, that involved a vote by NATO members, would have resulted in a different outcome given the widespread opposition to unification by Germany's neighbors. While there was general agreement that Gorbachev had few degrees of freedom on the German question at the time of the Two-Plus-Four talks, several Soviet officials suggested that he might have been able to negotiate a better deal if he had broached the issue in 1987. Jacques Lévesque and Davis and Wohlforth offer supportive counterfactuals in their respective chapters. But Gorbachev equivocated, and despite his publicly voiced opposition to a reunified Germany within NATO, Kohl and Bush correctly judged that he could be coerced and persuaded to accept this outcome.

Nor does the concept of moves effectively capture the most important attributes of process. Process is often given impetus by deliberate initiatives of various parties and stimulated and given momentum by outside events. In the case of the Cold War, there were numerous developments (e.g., Chernobyl, Matthias Rust's flight to Red Square, the attempt by East German tourists in Hungary to flee to the West) that facilitated reforms and accommodation. The coverup of Chernobyl, to take only one example, drove home the lessons of openness and international cooperation to Gorbachev and made it easier for him to implement restructuring. It is worth speculating how a different set of random, or at least outside events could have retarded reform or accommodation or moved it along a different track. Would the Soviet Union have fragmented the way it did, for example, in the absence of an unsuccessful coup attempt? Would a successful coup attempt have ultimately led to a more violent breakup?

Game theorists might characterize superpower accommodation as the result of multiple, interacting games; each superpower leader was involved in a domestic bargaining game in addition to multiple international bargaining encounters.[13] Gorbachev and Reagan, and later, Bush, had to build a coalition in support of their foreign policy preferences. This was a more difficult challenge for Gorbachev, who was struggling to consolidate his power at the same time he implemented major initiatives in foreign and domestic policy. Moreover, his initiatives were radical departures from previous practice and antagonized powerful vested interests and influential individuals. Archie Brown argues that Gorbachev had to proceed slowly in incremental steps and convey assurances at almost every move that he did not intend to go any further. This long, and ultimately uncompleted, internal, political process that unfolded between 1985 and 1991 permitted Gorbachev to move ahead on both the domestic and foreign fronts. Success required major personnel changes, mobilization of public opinion, educational efforts, a learning process, consensus building within the leadership, emasculation of the communist party apparatus, and a general opening of state institutions.

A lengthy, largely public process also gave Gorbachev, Bush, and Reagan time to formulate their goals. Neither Gorbachev nor Bush had a clear idea of where they wanted to go when they began their interaction. Reagan was anxious to reduce the risk of war and entertained the vague hope that someday nuclear arsenals might be reduced or eliminated. Gorbachev had a more focused goal: a reduction in tensions that would allow the Soviet Union to become a member of "the common European home," and in the process become a more demo-cratic and productive society.[14] But Gorbachev was vague about the precise na-ture of the relationship he sought and the strategies that would achieve his objective. Ends and means took shape only slowly and through extensive con-sultation with key advisors, experts, and diplomats, interaction with Reagan, and repeated trial and error.

The summits and other high-level meetings served important functions in addition to supplying information that allowed leaders to reorder preferences. Most importantly, they generated trust. Early on, Gorbachev persuaded West-ern public opinion and some leaders—most notably British Prime Minister Margaret Thatcher—that new thinking and his interest in accommodation were genuine. But it took repeated personal encounters with Reagan to break through his cognitive wall of mistrust, and here, too, East-West rapprochement benefited from a process that spanned almost five years. By all accounts, face-to-face en-counters between Reagan and Gorbachev convinced the American President that his counterpart sincerely sought to end the Cold War and improve the lot of the Soviet people. The summits also allowed Reagan and Gorbachev, and later Bush and Gorbachev and Baker and Shevardnadze, to develop personal rela-tionships, based on mutual respect and trust.

Timing was also important because of the positive linkages it created among turning points. Herrmann suggests that by the late 1980s there were compelling reasons for the Soviet Union to disengage from costly involvement in Third World conflicts, and that this was widely recognized within the Soviet policy-making elite. However, it only became possible in the context of the broader dis-engagement from an ideological commitment to oppose Western influence everywhere in the world. New thinking provided the rationale for redefining na-tional security in a way that legitimized arms control concessions and other mea-sures that moved the superpowers toward rapprochement, and that in turn created the political context in which withdrawal from Afghanistan became fea-sible domestically.

The concept of "move" is itself problematic. Most strategic games treat moves as simultaneous or reciprocal, and as the principal source of information about preferences and resolve. The process that resulted in the termination of the Cold War indicates that one side can make repeated moves before the other makes any response that might be considered a move. Gorbachev made a series of unilat-eral gestures (e.g., easing restrictions of emigration, a unilateral moratorium in nuclear testing, acceptance of on-site inspection, reduction of Soviet involve-ment in Third World conflicts, a troop withdrawal from Eastern Europe, will-ingness to accept a one-sided, tongue-in-cheek American proposal to eliminate intermediate range ballistic missiles). In part these were to demonstrate his interest in accommodation to Western publics and leaders and to prod the Reagan administration into pursuing a more cooperative policy.

Games of strategic interaction rely on the ability of players to distinguish cooperation (tits) from defection (tats). Real-life bargaining calls these assumptions into question and shows how moves can easily be misinterpreted.[15] Reagan's principal advisors consistently misread Gorbachev's initial attempts to signal interest in accommodation. Gorbachev's rhetorical and policy moves were subjected to "worst case" analysis by many of Reagan's key advisors. They were understood as part of a clever strategy to divide Western Europe from the United States, compel the Reagan administration to accept some form of arms control it did not want, and buy time for the Soviet Union to restructure and emerge as a more powerful and confident challenger. Moreover, it took drastic, unilateral, and one-sided Soviet concessions to move the process forward. When George Bush became President in January of 1989, after three years of intensive East-West diplomacy and movement toward accommodation, he still doubted Gorbachev's interest in winding down the Cold War and thought that Reagan had gone too far to accommodate him. It was not until after their December 1989 Malta summit that Bush acknowledged that Gorbachev's initiatives "deserved" and "mandated" new thinking on the part of the West. Even then, there were influential figures within his administration who remained suspicious and on guard, and who advised a slowdown in the process of accommodation.

Noise can also be mistaken for moves. Several scholars have suggested that the catalyst for Reagan's commitment to reduce tensions was the Soviet Union's overreaction to the November 1983 ABLE ARCHER command-post exercise. Western intelligence received reports that the KGB worried that this exercise was a prelude to a real attack, and, not for the first time since Reagan had come to power, Moscow ordered a "surprise nuclear attack alert" as a precaution. Reagan was appalled that the Soviet Union could see him and the United States as a threat.[16] To the extent that this realization served as a catalyst for reestablishing better communications with Moscow and made the president more responsive to Gorbachev's subsequent overtures, noise was an important source of information, a catalyst for reassessing goals and possibly a turning point in the process that culminated in the end of the Cold War.

These several examples point to a second generic problem with strategic models: their reliance on Bayesian updating. Bayesian models assume that people make incremental changes in their beliefs or expectations in response to new information, especially when it is discrepant with prior beliefs or expectations. The behavior of key policymakers and their advisors were sharply at odds with this assumption. Reagan, his advisors, and academic experts varied enormously in how they responded to the same information about the Soviet Union and its new leader. To a lesser extent, the same was true of Bush and his advisors. Reagan is a particularly interesting case because his "updating," as Breslauer and Lebow show, stands in sharp contrast to both Bayesian models and the behavior of his principal advisors. His dramatic about-face was facilitated by his propensity—noted by many of his confidants—to reduce issues to personalities. Once he accepted Gorbachev as sincere, he worked with him to bring about the accommodation both men desired.

Gorbachev departed from Bayesian updating in a different way; he was often slow to recognize that his policies were not achieving the consequences he expected. Gorbachev was correct in his estimate that he could mobilize Western public opinion to put pressure on the American President to become more receptive to his overtures to reduce East-West tensions. Almost all his other estimates were flawed; neither his domestic nor foreign policies produced the consequences he anticipated. These reinforcing failures were attributable in large part to Gorbachev's set of overoptimistic and unwarranted assumptions. Chief among these were his beliefs that: (1) the communist party could be transformed through glasnost and made a vehicle for positive economic reforms; (2) he could shift his base of power from the communist party to democratic elements in the Soviet Union; (3) political change in Eastern Europe would bring "little Gorbachevs" to power who would be his natural allies; (4) the Cold War would end as a compromise between blocs, not with the disintegration of socialism and the socialist bloc; (5) democratization would strengthen, not weaken, the Soviet Union.

Gorbachev's misconceptions doubtlessly had many roots. Some of this myopia may have been the result of having spent a lifetime in an authoritarian political system. Without any experience of democratic politics, he was not the only reformer who believed that public opinion could be treated like a water tap: turned on and off at the political convenience of leaders. Most members of his inner circle had little understanding that public opinion, once mobilized, could not easily be channeled or restrained. They also failed to see the inherent political contradiction between their goals of democracy and a public pliant and responsive to their political will.

Gorbachev also displayed motivated bias. When leaders, for whatever reason, feel compelled to pursue a policy, they often convince themselves that it will succeed in the face of evidence to the contrary. For psychologists, wishful thinking of this kind is a form of "bolstering." People are most likely to bolster decisions that risk serious loss. They exaggerate the expected rewards of their chosen course of action and suppress their doubts about possible negative consequences. They may also try to avoid anxiety by insulating themselves from information that indicates their choice may lead to serious loss. Bolstering serves a useful psychological purpose by helping people move toward commitment and cope with the doubts and internal conflicts that risky decisions generate. It is detrimental when it discourages careful evaluation of alternatives or realistic risk assessment. It lulls people into believing that they have made good decisions when they have avoided a careful appraisal of the options. People who bolster become overconfident and insensitive to information that is critical to the evaluation of their policy.[17]

An examination of Gorbachev's pattern of decision making suggests strongly that he engaged in wishful thinking. As numerous analysts have observed, he was remarkably late in grasping the extent of the resistance in the communist party to glasnost and perestroika, the rise of separatist nationalism within the Soviet Union, the failure of his economic reforms, the opposition of Eastern European regimes to political reform, the impending collapse of communism in Eastern Europe, and the growing opposition to him in the military, KGB, and party that culminated in the coup attempt in August 1991. On all these issues, Gorbachev denied, distorted, or reinterpreted information that suggested that his policies were producing negative consequences. Throughout the spring of 1991, he repeatedly brushed aside warnings from his foreign minister that a coup was imminent.

The behavior of Reagan and Gorbachev calls into question the third assumption of strategic interaction models: transitive preferences. At a minimum, actors are assumed to have a priority of preferences that can be ranked ordinally. They are expected to see, within reason, the connection between their preferences, their consequences, and the choices across alternative outcomes. While very different in their personalities and policymaking styles, Gorbachev and Reagan shared a pronounced reluctance to make hard choices.

Reagan believed he could reduce the size of the government and its deficit and finance a massive military buildup. He allowed himself to be persuaded that "supply side" economics would resolve the contradiction. He pursued SDI and arms control, and once again convinced himself that the two were consistent; both would reduce the danger of nuclear war. Gorbachev's failures to face hard choices are legion. We have previously noted his expectations that he could maintain the primacy of the communist party and reform the Soviet economic and political system, encourage democracy and discourage nationalist agitation, foster reform in Eastern Europe and preserve socialist regimes, and end the Cold War on the basis of mutual compromises that would strengthen socialism and the Soviet Union. In almost all of these cases, ample information was available to leaders to suggest that their goals were contradictory and required difficult choices among them. But they chose to ignore this information and convinced themselves that their multiple objectives were not only compatible but reinforcing.

Motivated bias has often been found to be a principal cause of miscalculations that leads to war, or at least to serious confrontations. But the end of the

Cold War, and other recent accommodations, suggest that motivated bias may not be uniformly negative in its implications. Leaders committed to break out of long-standing patterns of conflict confront enormous challenges. They must generally convince strongly distrustful adversaries of their sincerity, build and maintain domestic and allied coalitions in favor of territorial or other sacrifices that peace entails, and survive attempts by opponents of accommodation on one or both sides to sabotage accommodation, often through the use of violence. The chance of success is not high—there are more instances of failure than success—and even successful attempts may entail an enormous political or even personal price for the leaders who try to reach accommodation.

It requires extraordinarily driven and self-confident leaders to assume these kinds of risks, especially when initial attempts, some irreversible, are rejected. They need to convince themselves, against all odds, that their efforts will succeed. High-risk commitments of this kind prompt motivated bias to reduce anxiety and allow leaders to move toward decision and commitment. Motivated bias may thus serve an important, perhaps even necessary role, in the search for accommodation. It provides a psychological prop for risky decisions, but also blinds leaders to many of the dangers they confront.

Structural explanations of all kinds assume that leaders are more or less interchangeable—that national leaders who confront the same combination of constraints and opportunities will respond in similar ways. The process that ended the Cold War indicates enormous variation. Brezhnev and Gorbachev both recognized the need to reinvigorate the Soviet economy, but implemented strikingly different reform programs and related foreign policies. So too did Reagan respond differently to Gorbachev than did Eisenhower to Khrushchev. These differences cannot be attributed only to changed circumstances.

Summing Up

Our discussion of context highlights another way in which the outcome of the Cold War was contingent. Mutual commitment to goals by Soviet and American leaders was not enough to bring these conditions or agreements about. The two leaders had to build internal, and often allied, coalitions in support of their goals and to negotiate with one another through trusted—and not so trusted—advisors and officials. On occasion, these interactions side-tracked, postponed, altered, or transformed the goals sought by one or both sides. Our contributors document two dramatic examples—the negotiations over arms control and the future of Germany—both of which illustrate the independent role of process.

Our emphasis on contingency challenges not only structural theories but the seeming beliefs of policymakers. As we noted in the introduction, one of the most striking findings of the conferences we and our European collaborators ran at the Mershon Center and Wildbad Kreuth is the extent to which participants from the policy world, independent of their country or ideology, saw the end of the Cold War, the unification of Germany, and the collapse of the Soviet Union as more or less inevitable. At the same time, almost all of these officials confessed their utter surprise—and even incredulity—as these events unfolded. The contradiction in their belief systems was made further apparent by the insistence of almost every official we interviewed that the outcome of any decision or negotiation in which they participated was highly contingent. In conference discussions and conversations over drinks or coffee, they told amusing stories of how clever tactics, the nature of the personal relationship between them and their opposites, or just sheer coincidence, played decisive roles in shaping the outcome of negotiations.

Some policymakers, including a few who characterized the end of the Cold War, the unification of Germany, and the dissolution of the Soviet Union as inevitable, proved responsive to counterfactual suggestions that process and outcome might have been different. At Wildbad Kreuth, there was widespread agreement that there was nothing foreordained about the Two-Plus-Four format for negotiations over the future of Germany. When pushed, Russian, American, and German policymakers on the whole agreed that a different format, say one that involved more European countries as participants, might well have resulted in a different outcome given the widespread opposition to unification by Germany's neighbors. While there was general agreement that Gorbachev had little freedom to maneuver on the German question at the time of the Two-Plus-Four talks, several Soviet officials suggested that he might have been able to negotiate a better deal if he broached the issue in 1987.

It seems likely that policymakers and scholars alike are susceptible to what Baruch Fischoff has called the "certainty of hindsight" bias. Experiments that he and others have conducted demonstrate that "outcome knowledge" affects our understanding of the past by making it difficult for us to recall that we were once unsure about what was going to happen. Events deemed improbable by experts (e.g., peace between Egypt and Israel, the end of the Cold War), are often considered "overdetermined" and all but inevitable after they have occurred.[18] There is also experimental evidence that priming people with counterfactuals makes them more responsive to suggestions of contingency and may counteract in part the hindsight bias—and certainly, our experience in Wildbad Kreuth provides additional anecdotal evidence.[19]

Given the reinforcing tendencies of the hindsight bias and intellectual predilections of social scientists for parsimonious theories, it is difficult but all the more essential to make the case for contingency, as we have tried do. This said, we must be careful not to reject one extreme position in favor of another. We are not suggesting that the end of the Cold War was the result of an entirely stochastic process, like that responsible for many kinds of accidents. In this connection, it is useful to return to the suggestion made by Davis and Wohlforth in their chapter that scholars who work on questions with complex causes must establish *levels* of indeterminacy and use them to assess the relative merit of competing explanations. Such levels might also be used to assess contingency. At the most fundamental level, the collapse of communism may have been close to inevitable. So long as the West remained economically vibrant and politically secure, and the command economies of the communist bloc stagnated, tremendous pressures were bound to develop in East Europe and the Soviet Union itself for radical political change. But such pressures did not determine the nature, the timing, or the process of change—or its implications for the international system. The more specific we become about any of these outcomes (e.g., peaceful demise of the Communist Party and the Soviet Union versus national resistance, internal rebellion and civil war, or negotiated versus forced withdrawal of the Soviet Union from Germany and Eastern Europe), the more contingent they become.

Our study of the Cold War suggests the broader conclusion that underlying causes, no matter how numerous or powerful, rarely make an outcome inevitable, or even highly probable. Their effects may depend on fortuitous coincidences in timing of multiple causal chains, the independent actions of people even on accidents unrelated to any underlying cause. The Cold War case suggests that system transformations—and many other kinds of international events—are unpredictable because their underlying causes do nothing more than create the *possibility* of change.

The nonlinear nature of the processes we have described often led to unintended consequences—the collapse of communism in Eastern Europe is a case in point. Unintended consequences are often described as emergent properties of systems.[20] As presently used in the international relations literature, the concept of emergent properties elides two significantly different consequences. The first, and most common, are the unanticipated outcomes we would expect in a stable system. Examples include arms races, runs on banks, or the 1990s Asian financial crisis. These phenomena are the aggregated, unintended, and counterproductive result of individual behavior based on instrumentally rational calculations of self-interest. The second kind of consequence, and the one relevant to the end of the Cold War, are those that are *doubly* unintended. Here, behavior has unintended consequences for the actors and their strategic interaction, and also for the system as a whole. It sets in motion a chain of events that leads to the system's transformation. None of our theories, as presently constituted, can account for this outcome.

Niklas Luhmann suggests that systems are repertories of codes, and that outside influences must be translated by the logic of the system to have an effect upon its operation.[21] Outside influences in economics, for example, are translated into prices. Simple structural theories like that of Kenneth Waltz completely ignore outside effects. Waltz acknowledges that an international system can change, but says nothing about how such change might come about. More evolutionary approaches to systems—Robert Jervis makes the case for them in his recent book—acknowledge that the structure and operating principles of systems undergo fundamental shifts in response to *outside* stimuli. World War I and the end of the Cold War indicate that systems can also be transformed through their *internal* operations.[22] These cases point to the existence of a self-referential loop by which actors change their understanding of themselves, the system, and how it operates.

The possibility of system change through actor learning has important implications for the study of international relations. It suggests that structural change may be the *product,* not the cause, of behavior—the opposite of what most realist theories contend. It also directs our attention to the understandings actors have of each other and of their environments, and how these understandings evolve and become shared, an underlying premise of constructivism. Finally, it constitutes a possible conceptual bridge between scholars in the neopositivist tradition who privilege structures, and those in the constructivist tradition who privilege ideas.

Notes

1. Alexander Gerschenkron, *Economic Backwardness in Historical Perspective, A Book of Essays* (New York: Praeger, 1965).
2. In support, Brown cites Alexander Yakovlev's view that "a totalitarian regime" could only be dismantled from inside, and that this would have been "impossible" without Gorbachev. BBC interview, March 11, 1997.
3. Jacques Lévesque email to the author of October 16, 2000.
4. For a fuller elaboration of this argument, see Randall L. Schweller and William C. Wohlforth, "Power Test: Evaluating Realism in Response to the End of the Cold War," *Security Studies* 9 (Spring 2000), pp. 60–107.
5. Schweller and Wohlforth, "Power Test," pp. 75–76; John Kurt Jacobs, "Much Ado About Ideas: The Cognitive Factor in Economic Policy," *World Politics* 47 (January 1995), pp. 283–310.
6. Jacques Lévesque, *The Enigma of 1989: The USSR and the Liberation of Eastern Europe,* trans. Keith Martin (Berkeley: University of California Press, 1997); Matthew Evangelista, *Unarmed Forces: The Transnational Movement to End the Cold War* (Ithaca, NY: Cornell University Press, 1999).
7. Robert D. English, *Russia and the Idea of the West: Gorbachev, Intellectuals and the End of the Cold War* (New York: Columbia University Press, 2000).
8. Jennifer Bott, "The Big Blowout: Maneuvering by Bridgestone/Firestone, Ford May Have Made a Bad Situation Worse," Auto.com (Detroit Free Press), October 5, 2000, pp. 1–10; Dan Keating and Caroline E. Mayer, "Explorer has Higher Rate of Tire Accidents," *Washington Post,* October 9, 2000, p. Al; Dan Keating, "Examining Data on Traffic Accidents," *Washington Post,* October 9, 2000, p. A 10.

9. J. L. Mackie, "Causes and Conditions," in Myles Brand, ed., *The Nature of Causation* (Urbana: University of Illinois Press, 1976), pp. 308–44; Roy Bhaskar, *The Possibility of Naturalism. A Philosophical Critique of the Contemporary Human Science* (Brighton, UK: Harvester Press, 1979); Rom Harré and Peter Secord, *The Explanation of Social Behaviour* (Oxford: Basil Blackwell, 1973); Heikki Patomäki, "How to Tell Better Stories about World Politics," *European Journal of International Relations* 2 (March 1996), pp. 105–34.

10. Email communication to the author, October 1, 2000.

11. Michael R. Beschloss and Strobe Talbot, *At the Highest Levels: The Inside Story of the End of the Cold War* (Boston: Little, Brown, 1993), pp. 13–17, 19–21, 45–46.

12. Barry Nalebuff, "Brinkmanship and Nuclear Deterrence: The Neutrality of Escalation," *Conflict Management and Peace Science* 9 (1986), pp. 19–30; Robert Powell, "Nuclear Brinkmanship with Two-Sided Incomplete Information," *American Political Science Review* 82 (March 1988), pp. 155–78; Steven J. Brams, *Superpower Games* (New Haven, CT: Yale University press, 1985), pp. 48–85, and *Negotiation Games* (London: Routledge, 1990), pp. 101–37; R. Harrison Wagner, "Nuclear Deterrence: Counterforce Strategies and the Incentive to Strike First," *American Political Science Review* 83 (September 1991), pp. 727–49; Frank Zagare and Marc Kilgour, "Asymmetric Deterrence," *International Studies Quarterly* 37 (March 1993), pp. 1–27; Cédric Dupont, "Domestic Politics and International Negotiations: A Sequential Bargaining Model," in Pierre Allan and Christian Schmidt, eds., *Game Theory and International Relations: Preferences, Information and Empirical Evidence* (Aldershot: Edward Elgar, 1994), pp. 156–90.

13. Robert D. Putnam, "Diplomacy and Domestic Politics: The Logic of Two-Level Games," *International Organization* 42 (Summer 1998), pp. 427–60.

14. Mikhail S. Gorbachev, "Vystuplenie pered chlenami parlamenta Velikobritanii," December 18, 1984, in *Izbrannye rechi i stat'i* (Moscow: Politzdat, 1987), II, pp. 109–16.

15. Richard Ned Lebow, *The Art of Bargaining* (Baltimore: Johns Hopkins University Press, 1996), ch 12, and "Beyond Parsimony: Rethinking Theories of Coercive Bargaining," *European Journal of International Relations* 4 (1) (1998), pp. 31–66.

16. Beth A. Fischer, *The Reagan Reversal: Foreign Policy and the End of the Cold War* (Columbia: University of Missouri Press, 1997); Jack F. Matlock, Jr., *Autopsy on an Empire: The American Ambassador's Account of the Collapse of the Soviet Union* (New York: Random House, 1995); Don Oberdorfer, *The Turn: From The Cold War to A New Era* (New York: Poseidon Press, 1991), pp. 65–68.

17. Irving L. Janis and Leon Mann, *Decision Making: A Psychological Analysis of Conflict, Choice and Commitment* (New York: Free Press, 1977), esp. pp. 55–58, 74, 107–33. Richard Ned Lebow, *Between Peace and War: The Nature of International Crisis* (Baltimore: Johns Hopkins University Press, 1981); Robert Jervis, Richard Ned Lebow and Janice Gross Stein, *Psychology and Deterrence* (Baltimore, MD: Johns Hopkins University Press, 1985); and Richard Ned Lebow and Janice Gross Stein, *We All Lost the Cold War* (Princeton, NJ: Princeton University Press, 1994), ch. 4, for applications to international relations.

18. Baruch Fischoff, "Hindsight is not Equal to Foresight: The Effect of Outcome Knowledge on Judgment under Uncertainty," *Journal of Experimental Psychology: Human Perception and Performance* 1 (2) (1975), pp. 288–99; S. A. Hawkins and R. Hastie, "Hindsight: Biased Judgments of Past Events after the Outcomes are Known," *Psychological Bulletin* 107 (3) (1990), pp. 311–27. The tendency was earlier referred to as "retrospective determinism" in comparative-historical studies by Reinhard Bendix, *Nation-Building and Citizenship* (New York: Wiley, 1964). See also Philip E. Tetlock and Aaron Belkin, "Counterfactual Thought Experiments in World Politics: Logical, Methodological, and Psychological Perspectives," in Tetlock and Belkin, *Counterfactual Thought Experiments in World Politics*, pp. 15–16.

19. L. Ross, M. R. Lepper, F. Strack and J. Steinmetz, "Social Explanation and Social Expectation: Effects of Real and Hypothetical Explanations on Subjective Likelihood," *Journal of Personality and Social Psychology* 35 (1977), pp. 817–29; Philip E. Tetlock and Richard Ned Lebow, "Poking Counterfactual Holes in Covering Laws: Cognitive Styles and Political Learning," *American Political Science Review* 95 (December 2001), pp. 829–43

20. Kenneth N. Waltz, *Theory of International Politics* (Reading, MA: Addison-Wesley, 1979); Jervis, *System Effects;* Lars-Erik Cederman, *Emergent Properties in World Politics: How States and Nations Develop and Dissolve* (Princeton, NJ: Princeton University Press, 1997).

21. Niklas Luhmann, *Die Gesellschaft der Gesellschaft,* 2 vols. (Frankfurt am Main: Suhrkamp, 1998) I, ch. 2.

22. On the World War I case, see Richard Ned Lebow, "Contingency, Catalysts, and International System Change," *Political Science Quarterly* 115 (Winter 2000–01), pp. 591–616.

Chapter 9

Learning from the End of the Cold War

Richard K. Herrmann

Introduction

There is no doubt that policymakers and scholars alike will draw lessons from the end of the Cold War: it was that type of historically relevant event. It ushered in revolutionary change in the status of states, the independence of nations, and the policy agendas and priorities of many countries around the world. Of course, just because the Cold War has all of the characteristics of the sort of historical event people learn the most from, there is no guarantee that the lessons that will be drawn are appropriate or wise.[1] People have routinely drawn inappropriate lessons from the past and they are likely to do so again.

Reviewing the track record on learning from major historical events, Robert Jervis paints a bleak picture.[2] He finds that people tend to engage in a quick and oversimplified search for causes and to make few attempts to consider the comparisons that are necessary to render in a logical way the causal efficacy of specific variables. In this rather "sloppy" search for causes, Jervis reports that people tend to slight the importance of specific conditions and circumstances and stress instead the overriding importance of a few variables and simple connections between them. Philip Tetlock's more recent experimental study of how scholars learn from the Cold War has produced results quite parallel to Jervis's earlier conclusions about how lessons from history are typically drawn.[3] Tetlock concludes that belief system defense mechanisms that work against learning are sufficiently robust so that, to a quite disturbing degree, scholars and policymakers alike are prisoners of their preconceptions. They use ideological theory-driven connections to interpret the meaning of the past and allow contemporary concerns to motivate their historical reconstructions.

The end of the Cold War has already led people to draw lessons and in many cases the patterns described by Jervis and Tetlock are evident. Jervis suggests that people tend to exaggerate the impact of constant factors and see the new situation and the historical path leading to it through the lenses of their old beliefs.[4] This was true in many accounts of the end of the Cold War provided to us by former officials directly involved in the process. Just as Jervis would expect, people were especially reluctant to adjust their beliefs about specific actors and the motives that drove them. When the outcome was judged to be a failure, as is common among former Soviet hard-liners, there was a fairly quick conclusion that other policies would have produced more success and at less expense. On the other hand, for those who judged the outcome of the Cold War as a success, there is a tendency to assume that the actions they took were the cause of the success and that these actions represent the most efficient path to the successful outcome that was possible. Failure, Jervis finds, in general leads to a more aggressive search for alternatives, while success often produces little learning at all, reinforcing preexisting conceptions.

Although history is a very powerful teacher, unfortunately it is not a very good one. Its lessons are controversial, typically hard to decipher, and are dependent on a good deal of prior knowledge. Moreover, the so-called historical lessons history teaches are the result of competitive current political processes and are influenced by a host of ideational and material motivations. The lessons being drawn from the end of the Cold War, for instance, are affected not only by the cognitive, logical, and evidentiary limits facing any historical analysis, but also by current political interests. This includes both the efforts to take credit and assign blame for the good and bad aspects of the Cold War's end and the use of history to argue in favor of contemporary policy preferences. Beyond motivated biases, the lessons being drawn from the Cold War also reflect the projection backward of ideas about world affairs that are popular today. For instance, contemporary thinking about globalization and economic considerations often figure prominently in the logic explaining the Cold War's end and in the process of deriving lessons from it.

Given the track record of learning from the past and the current contest already underway regarding the interpretation of the Cold War's end, what can be done to advance learning? Is there any way to improve the process? The process of drawing lessons can be made more systematic and transparent, and multiple explanatory factors can be considered simultaneously. We aimed to unearth and confront new evidence and to use counterfactual thought experiments to partially address the limitations inherent in historical interpretation. We did not expect to determine once and for all the true explanation, but rather to improve the process by which substantive conclusions are drawn and to better calibrate how confident people should be in the conclusions they reach.

This chapter begins with a discussion of learning in general and the lessons being drawn from the end of the Cold War in particular. After discussing the lessons and processes of learning that appear to be underway, this chapter turns to a discussion of the research strategies employed in our study. Part 2 looks at the strategies authors in this study used to defend the casual inferences they drew. Part 3 offers ideas regarding how the inferences and lessons drawn might be tested in the future and how this may improve our understanding of the past.

Part 1: Lessons Being Drawn from the End of the Cold War

Learning is a popular concept but one that is defined in different ways.[5] Learning may refer to the substantive conclusions that people draw regarding how A produces B, and it may also involve the confidence a person has that A does in fact produce B. For our purposes, we define learning as change in either substantive causal beliefs or change in the confidence with which these beliefs are held. With this definition, people can learn they were wrong and change their belief that A causes B, and people can learn they were correct and simply update the confidence they have in the causal connection between A and B.

Lessons Being Drawn

One popular lesson being drawn in the United States is that U.S. military and economic power triumphed over the Soviet Union. In this picture, the United States, by moving the competition into the high frontier of military technology, compelled the Soviet Union to retreat. Moscow, due to its totalitarian system, was unable to compete in the scientific and engineering realms and could not fuel an economy capable of sustaining competitive military deployments. The lesson often drawn is that peace was produced through strength and that containment and deterrence worked. No new substantive beliefs are prominent in this picture, rather the learning is almost entirely in the domain of increased confidence in preexisting beliefs. The learning also applies to the generalization of the lesson. Containment throughout the 1990s was the logic for dealing with Iran and Iraq and was a candidate strategy for U.S. policy toward China as well.

The triumphal lesson comes in a softer version that places less causal significance on the actions of the United States and more significance on the structural constraints imposed by the globalizing world economy. In this story, the Soviet Union was compelled to retreat because it could not remain isolated from the world economy without suffering huge costs in terms of quality of life, and it could not engage the world economy without changing its domestic political and commercial systems. This view is represented in our book by Davis's and

Wohlforth's study of German unification. The lessons that follow are that economic production is the cornerstone of international power, and, in a globalized world, states have only limited room for maneuver with regard to diverse political and commercial practices. Sometimes an additional lesson is drawn, which is that given the importance of economic factors in strategic competition, the United States, as the world's dominant economy, can expect to enjoy a period of superiority during which it can move in world affairs with substantial latitude.[6]

Stories that explain the end of the Cold War by referring to Moscow's economic constraints in a globalized world can also reinforce the belief that engagement is an effective strategy. The reform leaders who came to power in Moscow can be seen as the product of earlier periods of detente and the Soviet Union's partial connection to the Western world in the 1970s and 1980s. The process of increasing West German–Soviet trade, for instance, can be seen as an important factor in promoting the development of a new set of elites in Moscow who had both vested interests in better relations and growing appreciation for the benefits of reform. Here the lesson drawn is that engagement works, by increasing the material gain from cooperation while reassuring countries that they are not threatened. Some U.S. leaders suggest that this lesson be applied to contemporary U.S. policy toward Iran and China.

In Moscow, former Soviet leaders who came to oppose Gorbachev and who doubted that the Cold War had ended drew the lesson that the Cold War was always fueled by an American desire to destroy the Soviet Union and Russia as potential competitors. This, of course, was the belief they had during the Cold War, and for them it was clearly reaffirmed by how it ended. They insisted that although the bipolar era had ended, the Cold War that Washington was directing toward Moscow was still underway. For them, Gorbachev's idea that the Cold War was a spiral of mistrust was wrong, and his expectations accommodative Soviet policies would lead to accommodative U.S. policies was at best naive. More likely, they insisted, Gorbachev was a traitor or under the influence of traitors. In any case, the lessons they draw for contemporary Russian foreign policy is to stiffen resistance to the United States and that only countervailing power will stop otherwise unending Western demands, a lesson that may also have popularity in Beijing.

The Politics of History

Clearly the stories of the past and the lessons that are said to follow are part of political debate in the present. As Hegel explained, arguments made about the cause of events in the past affect the way future events unfold.[7] This happens in two different ways. In the first way, the patterns in the past are thought to reflect laws of nature that cannot be ignored. Historical analysis thus reinforces behavior that conforms to the prescriptions and proscriptions of these presumed laws. This persistence of behavior produces increased confidence in the correctness of the laws and a behavior pattern more clearly consistent with them in the future: That is, adherence to the "laws" reinforces them. In the second way, explanations of the past can challenge the causal significance of factors that over time have become accepted as natural and unalterable. In this case, the discovery of new possibilities emancipates people from the mental straight-jackets that had been imposed by their prior beliefs, which had been taken to be laws, and contributes to changes in the behavior of actors and the dynamic of future relationships. Causal understanding of the past thus enables change, making that causal understanding out-of-date in the future.

Knowledge created about historical and social phenomena is affected by political motivations and extant beliefs popular in society. Because the lessons drawn change the subject matter itself and change future behavior, they become the objects of political contest. Philip Tetlock and Penny Visser find that the explanations for the end of the Cold War that U.S. scholars accept as persuasive are closely associated with the beliefs they had about what caused the Cold War.[8] Hawks are substantially more inclined to believe the material explanation. Doves are more inclined to accept the ideational and leadership story. If the association between prior political view and subsequent interpretation of the end of the Cold War was not so strong, we might dismiss the correlation as coincidence. It appears, however, that two sources of bias are at work. The first is the desire to believe that one's past interpretation was correct and that subsequent history has confirmed one's knowledge. The other is the inclination to blame others for bad outcomes and to take credit for good outcomes.[9]

In the case of the Cold War, this means that for those who saw the Soviet Union as aggressive and bent on expansion, the change in Soviet policy should be attributed not to a change in motives or guiding ideas but to dire necessity and material compulsion. For those who saw the Soviet Union as mostly defensive, on the other hand, change should be explained by referring to the rise of ideas about the stability of mutual assured destruction, the sensibility of pursuing mutual security, and the willingness to test whether a spiral security dilemma could be de-escalated. The biases are also evident among Soviet writers who described an aggressive United States and defensive Soviet Union and attribute the end of the Cold War to Gorbachev's ideas. Depending on how aggressive they believe the United States was, they see these ideas as wise, naive, or treasonous. Soviet intellectuals who hated the Soviet system and saw it as oppressive at home and aggressive abroad are attracted to the same storyline emphasizing material constraint and dire necessity as hawkish-minded Americans.

Of course, if there were clear tests of the alternative arguments, it might be harder for competing points of view to stay on the field; some would be proved right, others wrong. Our tests of competing arguments, however, are at best ambiguous and rest on a host of assumptions that can be controversial. The result is that scholars and leaders alike can define the terms of the test in ways that lead to whatever conclusion keeps their preconceptions about state motivation and policy efficacy intact. For example, central to the material compulsion versus ideas debate is the concept of dire necessity. Nowhere, however, is this concept defined. Clearly, in the 1980s neither the Soviet Union nor the United States faced the sort of material constraints the conquered and occupied Germany and Japan did in 1945. Short of this sort of physical compulsion, it is hard to know what necessity is. What level of poor living standards would lead to a collapse of the state? What military threats that it could not deter would cross the threshold and compel retreat? Because we cannot establish such thresholds a priori, both hawks and doves can retroactively explain any outcome.

Paul Krugman argues that from an economic perspective nations are not competitors the way firms are.[10] They are not locked into zero-sum negative interdependence in which at the extreme survival of one means the destruction of the other. According to Krugman, the popularity of the competition metaphor in the economic realm of interstate relations is more a product of nationalist ego, desire for prestige and self-serving romance than it is connected to economic reality. Nations can persist with quite different standards of living that depend on a host of social values and choices made domestically. Although this is generally recognized, and thus qualifies arguments about dire necessity, it often gets buried in the heat of a polemical debate. Because the concept of economic necessity is so elastic and difficult to define short of physical catastrophe, it is quite easy for scholars to employ it in a way that protects their prior motivational belief.

Besides the motive to confirm prior beliefs, more overtly political considerations can also bias the interpretation of the past. Taking credit and laying blame for historical developments is a case in point, especially when these assignments of past responsibility are linked to present obligations and debts. Many Russians, for instance, are keen to take credit for having made the compromises that ended the Cold War. They argue that in return for this the United States should now provide compensation and aid to Russia. Former U.S. officials give credit to President Reagan and deflect any notion that Washington owes something to Moscow. In the story popular with American officials, Moscow had caused the Cold War, and decades of containment combined with Reagan's firm line finally compelled it to retreat from its transgressions. Among Russians, a more popular story distributed blame for the Cold War to either the United States, emphasizing its imperial aspirations, or to both sides, emphasizing the hostility perpetuated by military-industrial interests. Often the argument that Gorbachev's enlightenment ended the Cold War is coupled with a notion that in return the

United States has an obligation to reciprocate and also pull back from its imperial behavior.

Of course, just as it is easy to construct different motivational stories for states, it is easy to speculate on the motivational sources of a scholar's beliefs. People invest an important part of their self-identity in national communities, and, therefore, a host of ego-defensive motives may affect how they recall and write history. Ethnocentric and in-group biases are well established and need not be discussed here.[11] At times, victors are said to write history to justify their supremacy, losers to establish their victimhood. Regardless of why people find a triumphalist story appealing or a story of heroic enlightenment gratifying, the main point I want to stress here is that disentangling the writing of history, and especially the drawing of lessons, from the contemporary political scene is very difficult.

Part 2: Strategies for Learning from the Past

Recognizing that history is a powerful but not very good teacher, it is important to examine in detail the competing interpretative explanations of the end of the Cold War and to interrogate the conclusions that are becoming part of the conventional wisdom in both American and Russian society. To do this, a number of procedures might help to improve the process of interpretation, and, at a minimum, better calibrate the confidence placed in explanations and the applicability of lessons drawn.

One reason it is hard to learn from history is that we cannot rerun history to test if the causal inferences we are drawing are the right ones. In the physical sciences, the experimental method is well developed and relies on the ability to repeat procedures in controlled settings to see if, when all else is held constant, the single factor under consideration leads repeatedly to a specific outcome. By rerunning the experiment many times, scientists can establish not just if the association is evident but also how often it appears and what the probability is that in any single run the general pattern will occur. In research based on history, we do not have the luxury of running controlled experiments. We also cannot rerun history and test definitively whether A is associated with B, and if so, with what probability.

Aware of the logical limits facing the identification of even strict correlation, much less causation, in history, we adopted several research strategies to promote careful inferential assessment. The first of these strategies was to insist that all authors of the turning point chapters consider at least the four explanatory factors we identified as prevalent in the contemporary debates about the end of the Cold War. Our intent was not to compel authors to think in terms of mutually exclusive alternative interpretations, but rather to promote a broader search for new evidence and more thoughtful and complex causal explanations.

The second strategy was to divide the end of the Cold War into discrete turning points. The aim was to direct attention to more detailed analyses and toward the process of change. By subdividing the overall story into multiple cases, we are able to evaluate the role four different factors play in each turning point and to draw generalizations on this multicase foundation. In other words, by unpacking the interpretative task into smaller endeavors for which we could acquire new empirical information, we can determine whether particular explanations hold in one turning point as an exception or as a general rule.

The third strategy we introduced to the initial design of the project was the production of counterfactual thought experiments. Although this may strike many readers as a strategy that is inherently inconclusive, we argue that all causal claims that rest on historical evidence ultimately rely on a counterfactual argument.[12] We asked each of our authors to conduct counterfactual thought experiments as a way to evaluate the persuasiveness of alternative causal stories. Our authors employed three additional strategies for identifying causal relationships in history and for making causal stories persuasive to readers. These three strategies are: (1) establishing a sequence in history showing that one factor changed prior to an outcome; (2) establishing that one factor varied and thus could be related to the changed outcome while establishing that other possible causal factors remained constant and thus are unlikely to explain change; and (3) establishing a causal mechanism that links the presumed causal factor to the outcome in a way that draws on auxiliary knowledge that is taken to be true. None of these strategies can overcome completely the limits inherent in the task of drawing causal inferences in historical studies, but, as evidenced in our turning point chapters, they are quite common. They also can be more convincing on a rhetorical level than on a strictly logical level. They are worth considering in some detail.

Establish a Sequence

The most common strategy for making a causal argument about the end of the Cold War is to establish a sequence of events. Here the argument is that a change in one factor preceded and, therefore, could have caused a change in another factor. For example, Archie Brown argues that the top leadership in the Communist Party was not considering major change and did not select Gorbachev because they thought he would bring about radical change. Brown makes a case for Gorbachev's importance by establishing this relatively steady state in Soviet politics, then introduces Gorbachev to the scene and tracks the changes that followed. Brown argues that Gorbachev as leader was more important than new ideas alone by showing that new ideas were evident in some circles before Gorbachev rose to office and consolidated his power, but that the scholars and politicians who advocated them had little impact on the system prior to Gorbachev's ascension.

I develop a similar causal argument in my study of regional conflicts. At a tactical level, in each regional case I identify when each superpower escalated its delivery of weaponry and then look at subsequent actions on the part of the other superpower and the regional protagonists. By showing that escalation typically met counterescalation and that the sequencing story was one of tit-for-tat reciprocity and not peace-through-strength, I cast doubt on the causal plausibility of material power explanations.

Matthew Evangelista similarly argues that the deployment of U.S. cruise and Pershing II missiles were followed by reciprocal Soviet countermeasures. By demonstrating that a robust pattern of tit-for-tat competition prevailed prior to Gorbachev's consolidation of power, Evangelista makes the case for the causal importance of Gorbachev and his ideas by showing that previous attempts to change the material balance were not followed by change in policy and that only changes in leadership and ideas were followed by change in policy.

James Davis and William Wohlforth make a different causal argument, but employ a similar sequencing strategy. They argue that the Soviet economy was doing well in the 1950s and 1960s, faltered in the 1970s, and entered an acute crisis phase in the 1980s. Davis and Wohlforth argue that the clear downturn in Soviet economic fortunes preceded subsequent changes in Soviet strategic thinking. They give interpretative weight to material necessity rather than free-willed enlightenment.

Jacques Lévesque argues that material conditions affected the evolution in Gorbachev's visions for socialist renewal and mutual security, but were not solely responsible for them. Lévesque describes a feedback loop between ideas and material circumstances, in which Gorbachev demonstrated substantial flexibility, even inconsistency, in his thinking and behavior. A sequential storyline can be quite persuasive, but there are several important problems with this sort of causal logic. There is always a historical antecedent, and as Davis and Wohlforth point out, where scholars decide to cut into the story affects significantly what sort of causal sequence will appear. For instance, while Brown attributes important causal significance to Gorbachev, a popular storyline in the United States argues that the Reagan buildup and return to hard-line foreign policy in the early 1980s caused many of the negative changes in the Soviet material bargaining situation that Gorbachev had to address.[13] As previously noted, advocates of engagement argue that engagement had laid the causal foundation for the emergence of a Westernizing elite in Moscow and the evolution of Gorbachev's thinking regarding a common European home.

The problem is that as we move away from the field of contemporary action, the possible causal stories become endless and our ability to evaluate them disappears. Gorbachev's ideas in the mid-1980s can be attributed to material conditions then, and those conditions attributed to the ideas about advanced socialism enacted by Brezhnev, and those ideas shaped by the material experience under Khrushchev, and that experience shaped by the ideas imposed by Stalin, and so on. Just as Freudian psychologists could look back across a long lifespan and pick out all sorts of factors that they claim are responsible for actions taken many years later, so could historical analysts look back across time and pick out their favorite factors and claim these factors are the causal antecedents of contemporary behavior. Of course, Freudian logic lost most of its persuasive power in contemporary psychology to theories that focused on more immediate forces in the temporal environment. The historical antecedent strategy may be vulnerable in historical studies to a similar focus on immediate forces.

Not all causal claims that rely on a sequencing strategy are equal. Sometimes we have auxiliary theories and knowledge that make the connecting storyline more persuasive. For instance, our understanding of how the Soviet system worked makes Brown's argument about the importance of Gorbachev's ascension more compelling. Knowing that the General Secretary's office carried influence over personnel appointments and that the people Gorbachev appointed favored and implemented substantial change, gives significant weight to the argument that Gorbachev's ascension to power caused these appointments, which in turn accelerated reform. Other arguments—for example, that Gorbachev's unilateral test moratorium fueled the U.S. peace movement, which in turn constrained Reagan, or that economic growth rates declined and created new commercial incentives, which in turn caused foreign policy retrenchment—do not rest on commonly accepted auxiliary knowledge and thus are not as persuasive.

Other sequential-based arguments rest on claims about the motivation behind a leader's decision. For instance, Davis and Wohlforth argue that Gorbachev was motivated to retrench because he faced dire economic necessity, and Sarah Mendelson, in a study of the Soviet decision to leave Afghanistan, argues that Gorbachev's desire to consolidate his domestic coalition motivated him to construct a picture of Afghanistan and the United States that was naive.[14] The auxiliary assumptions that are needed to sustain these claims of motivated misperception are typically complicated and not widely shared.

Establish Variation and No Variation

A second common strategy for creating a causal storyline builds on the basic logic of sequence but goes a step further. It argues that one factor varies and thus could explain variation in the outcome and that other plausible causal factors do not vary, and, therefore, are not likely explanations. This strategy aims essentially to falsify the alternative causal propositions, leaving only one standing. It does not prove that the remaining factor is the causal explanation, but presents it as the most likely candidate.

Running through the turning point studies is an argument about how much the material circumstances changed compared to how much ideas varied. The most common way to make the case for the importance of ideas and leaders is to argue that there was significant disagreement among leaders regarding what options were available and wise to choose. The case for the importance of material factors questions the amount of variation in the ideas different leaders had and emphasizes the change in relative power.

Davis and Wohlforth, for example, argue that once decline and the costs of competition were understood in Moscow, nearly everyone agreed with Gorbachev's agenda, including most "old thinkers." They contend that Gorbachev's reform and detente package was the default option for most party officials, including conservatives. By making this claim about the empirical situation, Davis and Wohlforth suggest that material considerations had a decisive impact on all leaders, moving them essentially in the same direction. Arguing that Soviet leaders agreed on the implications of the material situation, Davis and Wohlforth conclude that these material factors were the central drivers and that the ideational and leader-specific factors were secondary.

Archie Brown and Matthew Evangelista disagree and make their case by arguing that Davis's and Wohlforth's characterization of the consensus among Soviet leaders is empirically false. Brown contends, for instance, that to claim that the idea of reform was a general consensus among a majority of party leaders is "extraordinarily wide of the mark." Evangelista makes a parallel argument describing in some detail the "enormous" debate within the party and military leadership at nearly every step of the arms control story. He draws special attention to Marshal Sergei Akhromeev and Valentin Falin as indicative of the opposition Gorbachev faced. Rather than consensus about available options and best choices, Brown and Evangelista emphasize the different perspectives on what choices Moscow had available and ought to take. In this way, they make the case for the importance of Gorbachev and the ideas he empowered.

Jacques Lévesque agrees with Brown and Evangelista and describes a wide range of perspectives in Moscow on what could and should be done with regard to Eastern and Central Europe. In Lévesque's picture of the political scene in Moscow, Gorbachev is a centrist, facing pressure from leaders on one side, who want to intervene and retain control, and those on the other side, who want to promote reform even more quickly. Rather than material circumstances producing a consensus, in this picture the range of viewpoints is quite wide. Lévesque contends that when Gorbachev repudiated the Brezhnev Doctrine in late spring 1989, he was not adopting a default consensus position but rather was defying the advice of the majority of the top Soviet leadership. Conservatives, Lévesque explains, saw Gorbachev's move as nothing short of treason. They could imagine no material reason for doing this. They concluded, consequently, that because Gorbachev was passing by so many preferable alternative options that were readily available, he must be either a traitor or under the influence of foreign agents. The strategy of arguing that a certain variable varies, and that the alternatives do not, often makes a more persuasive rhetorical story than is warranted on logical grounds. There is the obvious problem that even if a specific variable is the only one of the set considered that varies, this does not mean it is correlated with the outcome, much less that it caused it: we can never be sure that some third factor not in the set considered is the really important driving factor.

Problem of Interpreting Meaning

In establishing sequence and variation in the historical record, we face several problems that should not be overlooked. First, it is difficult to establish whether most people in a leadership group have the same idea or not. The debate between on the one side, Brown, Evangelista, and Lévesque, favoring ideas, and on the other, Davis and Wohlforth, favoring material capabilities, ought to be amenable to empirical resolution based on whether there was a consensus for reform and detente. This, however, requires agreement on what is meant by reform and detente. At our meeting in Moscow with the key former conservative Soviet leaders, we asked if they had believed in reform and detente. They said yes, as Davis and Wohlforth would expect; however, as we began to unpack what they meant by reform and what actions they thought were consistent with detente, it became obvious almost immediately that these words meant something entirely different to them than they did to Gorbachev, much less to us as Westerners. The ideas of reform and peaceful coexistence had been standard ideological lines in Soviet propaganda for decades. They were used at the polemical level by everyone. These words, however, were filled with very different practical content by different leaders. This greatly complicates the identification of any individual leader's point of view and the task of determining how widespread agreements or disagreements are.

Second, not only are the labels poorly defined in terms of content, so too is the baseline for measuring change. What were the Soviet beliefs that Gorbachev changed? Were these beliefs in the doctrinaire communist platforms of the 1930s, or Khrushchev's reformist ideas of the early 1960s, or the bureaucratized ideas associated with Brezhnev and stagnation? Was Gorbachev overturning a revolutionary foreign policy of expansion? Or was he revising a geopolitical bipolar realist mindset that had abandoned revolutionary ideas decades earlier and was quite complacent and cautious in a well-established and routinized superpower stalemate? Another former baseline relates to perceptions of the balance of power. Soviet leaders, for instance, spoke often about the correlation of forces shifting in their direction. They always started, however, from the assumption that the Soviet Union was behind, and they argued it was catching up. This is very different than saying they were ahead of or superior to the United States. In defining the baseline, this distinction is important. If Moscow was always behind and in the 1980s faced a slowdown, a reversal in the rate at which they were catching up, this would simply have left them behind and falling back to where they had traditionally been. On the other hand, it could be that the rate of catching up was what really mattered to Soviet leaders and that the baseline, therefore, should not be the absolute balance that was always in Washington's favor but the downturn in the shift. This decision about the baseline, however, requires additional assumptions about what dimensions of power really matter.

Third, the concepts of power and ideas are multidimensional. During the Cold War, for example, the nuclear and military balance that assured mutual destruction drew the most attention. On these dimensions of power there was no fundamental change. There also was no prospect that it would change.[15] Washington's Strategic Defense Initiative was far from deployable and Moscow had several countermeasures that it could take. Davis and Wohlforth draw our attention to a different dimension of power that is based on a high-tech economy and advanced engineering. Brooks and Wohlforth argue elsewhere that it is this dimension of power that really mattered, not the military balance.[16] Although this may be true, it is hard to evaluate because we could not judge the importance of each dimension of power until after the fact. We preserve our faith in the importance of power by redefining the measure of power to fit the outcome.

Ideas about what dimensions of power matter most are essentially just ideas. Conservative former Soviet leaders, who eventually opposed Gorbachev, thought it was safe to experiment with domestic reform (as they defined this) even though in their view Washington was trying to destroy communism. They felt this way because no one in Moscow doubted the robustness of the Soviet military deterrent. They knew Washington had no military option for compellence and could not move against them militarily. Convinced that the core defense of the nation was secure, they explained that some latitude for experimentation at home was available. They also said that the motivation behind reform at home had nothing to do with the United States. It had everything to do, they said, with improving the quality of life for the people living in the Soviet Union. Essentially, they were directing attention away from arguments about sequences and variation and toward a discussion about the mechanisms and motives that explain the decisions to change course.

Establish a Mechanism

The relationship between temporal sequencing and variation can be composed into a causal story with the construction of a connecting mechanism. For example, Gorbachev's failure to introduce change right away in the mid-1980s might be taken as evidence that he did not bring new ideas to power. Archie Brown argues against this interpretation by introducing the causal mechanism of serious institutional constraint. Brown argues that Gorbachev was constrained in foreign policy by the strength of the Ministry of Defense and the KGB. In Brown's study, it was necessary for Gorbachev to consolidate his power over the bureaucracy before he could introduce major change.

In my study of regional conflicts, I draw attention to the facilitating mechanisms that were operating abroad. For instance, I reject the argument that only a conservative U.S. president, like Reagan, could have led the United States out of the Cold War. I suggest that the mechanism that allowed a U.S. president to change course and retain public approval was the change in Soviet behavior and the perception of many leaders in the United States that regional wars had predominately indigenous roots.

Matthew Evangelista also focuses on a mechanism to explain Gorbachev's presentation at the United Nations in December 1988. Here the causal mechanism was not American pressure, but instead, Evangelista argues, the central ideas of the leaders of the transnational peace movements that had met with Soviet officials. The same sort of logic holds in Evangelista's contention that Gorbachev's response to SDI was not the result of an appeasement mechanism but rather a product of the dialogue among concerned scientists and their notion of how to deflate public support for SDI and strategic escalation in the United States.

Of course, as already discussed above, identifying the motives that give rise to a leader's perception and to their decision is very difficult. We cannot rest these inferences on the consequences that follow from the decision. As Jacques Lévesque points out, many of the consequences in Eastern Europe were unintended. In fact, Lévesque argues that the most important mechanism explaining the course of events was Gorbachev's misunderstanding of the situation and the mistakes he made, some of which were the result of motivated bias. In Lévesque's study, Gorbachev, far from responding to material incentives, committed himself to ideas about the prospects for freedom, stability, and socialism in Eastern Europe that were unrealistic. Although Gorbachev in many ways was flexible and adjusted his views, his rather stubborn commitment to core beliefs and principles about Eastern Europe, according to Lévesque, was the factor that best explains the surprising Soviet retrenchment.

The problems inherent in attributing motives to foreign policy behavior are not new. They are well known and have been discussed quite often.[17] Many motives can explain a single action and any single motive can be connected to many different actions. The persuasiveness of motivational arguments typically relies on a claim that in a given situation an actor with motive X would have done A, while an actor with motive Y would have done B. Quite often, alternatives are not considered in any detail and the claim that people with motives X would do A is simply asserted as an obvious fact. Of course, whether the situation really is as asserted and whether all of the instrumental assumptions about how doing A would really satisfy motive X is left unexplored. As soon as the causal story is unpacked in detail, the host of auxiliary assumptions that cannot be easily defended become all too obvious.

Returning to underlying motives as the basis for establishing the heart of a causal mechanism is a common strategy, but one that only takes us back to the inherent political nature of writing history. It probably surprises no one that Americans favor the stories that feature a Soviet leadership motivated by expansionist motives that was compelled to retreat and that Russians close to Gorbachev prefer stories that feature a Soviet leadership motivated by security and peace that was testing new ideas about mutual security. Arguments that ultimately rest on self-serving and ethnocentric motivations become as much statements of faith and political ideology as claims based on evidence.

Pointing out the constraints of each of the strategies employed in our study is not intended to undermine the importance of the historical research conducted. Rather, it is to remind us that none of these inferential strategies is perfect and that drawing conclusions with certainty and lessons with confidence is potentially dangerous. As Lebow and Stein point out, in every turning point chapter all four factors play a role and in none of the cases does a single factor explain enough of the story to merit exclusive billing. Moreover, in most of the turning point stories, the combination among the four key factors is important. Consequently, drawing the lesson that any one factor would produce predictable outcomes in the future would be quite misguided. Our study of the past suggests that the context, path sequence, and interaction of factors is important. Therefore, drawing simple one-to-one lessons, for example, that change in power produces retrenchment or that changing ideas produce new policies is a mistake. In fact, looking into the future may be a useful strategy for evaluating the conclusions and lessons that we draw from the past.

Part 3: Learning from the Future

There is a tendency when looking backward into history to forget what we thought was going to happen and to focus instead on what did happen. This makes the narrative storytelling easier, but has a deleterious effect on the process of drawing lessons. This is because simplifying the past scene to include only what did happen, leaving aside everything else that might have happened, creates an excessively simple picture from which to draw causal lessons.[18] This can lead to overconfidence and retrospective explanations that are tautological. For instance, knowing that the Soviet Union did not intervene in the Gulf, Americans forget that in the 1980s they thought Moscow could and would. Because Moscow did not, they conclude that the reason was because it could not—a conclusion inconsistent with earlier assessments of Soviet capability. In hindsight, we reevaluate how we measured power, rather than rethink basic assumptions about Moscow's motives.

There is good reason to be skeptical of theories that explain the past but have no predictive power about the future. If we understand and can explain what factors caused outcomes in the past, then we ought to be able to anticipate that these general patterns will hold in the future as well. If they will not, then we ought to be able to specify why not and what conditions or auxiliary factors are different than they were in the past and will, therefore, offset the effect of the causal factor. Looking forward into the future and considering whether our causal claims about the past will hold up, draws attention to contingencies and alternative combinations that we remove from our vision of the past by looking only at the outcome that actually occurred. This leads to three concluding suggestions for how to proceed.

(1) Use Turn-around Tests

One lesson that emerges from our effort to interpret the end of the Cold War is that we ought to apply any general causal lessons we draw to two turn-around tests. The first concerns turning around and looking at the future, the second concerns turning around and considering whether we draw comparable inferences across actors. Neither turn-around test is difficult to understand or apply, but both require a bit of elaboration.

First, let us consider looking into the future. If we conclude that material weakness in the form of economic constraint and dire need to address domestic hardship caused Soviet retrenchment, then we ought to ask if this same pattern will hold in the future. As Archie Brown points out, since the end of communism Russian production has dropped by 50 percent, Russia still sells mostly raw materials and depends on loans while social problems escalate. If the material realities and globalization in the 1980s compelled Moscow to retreat, then should we anticipate that the continued, even accelerated, globalized economic processes of the 1990s coupled with still further Russian decline will compel Russia to retreat even further? If we are confident about the causal power of material factors, then we ought to be confident that Putin or any other Russian leader will make little difference and that the ideas that become popular in Russia, say, nationalism and anti-Americanism, will also not affect future behavior.

It is not only our confidence in material determinism that may be shaken when we look forward and make predictions as opposed to looking backward and constructing post hoc explanations. Excessive confidence in the determinative power of ideas or leaders can also be undermined. For example, if we conclude that the collapse of communist ideology was the main engine behind the end of the Cold War, are we confident that non-communist Russian foreign policy will look radically different in the future? This, of course, requires that we define carefully what ideas are thought to have changed. During the Cold War it was not clear if pan-national communist ideas or Russian nationalist ideas drove Soviet policy.[19] As we look forward, it is necessary to clarify just what ideas changed, in this case communist internationalism or geopolitical realpolitik, and what ideas currently prevail. Moreover, it compels us to consider what options leaders with radical new ideas would have and how much change they could introduce.

Second, it also makes sense to turn the tables on the players. For instance, if we conclude that material weakness is the proper explanation for Soviet retreat after Afghanistan, should we conclude the same about U.S. capabilities after Vietnam? In other words, do we explain retreat on the Soviet side as a product of compulsion, and retreat on the American side as a product of the same thing? Or do we see the Soviet retreat as indicative of compulsion and the American retreat as an act of free will? If we conclude that Gorbachev was motivated by dire necessity and domestic need to pull back, should we conclude that George McGovern and other anti–Vietnam War leaders in the United States were motivated by the same things? If, on the other hand, we conclude that McGovern and William Fulbright and leaders in Washington who opposed the Vietnam War were motivated by changed understandings of the nature of the war, the competition with Moscow, and the character of global interdependence, then do we draw similar inferences about the factors that motivated change in Soviet policy? If we make entirely different inferences from similar patterns for U.S. and Soviet leaders, does this emanate from defensible empirical evidence or from political bias?

(2) Indeterminacy Empowers Ideas

When looking forward in time, the indeterminacy of many causal theories is evident. The turn-around tests draw attention to the lack of clearly defined, measurable variables and to the role of sequences, contingent moves, and stochastic events. Given substantial indeterminacy, post hoc explanations rely on reconceptualizations of key variables, remeasurement, and new interpretative causal conjectures. For example, after the Cold War, notions of which dimensions of power mattered and claims about the prevailing ideas in Moscow differed from analogous notions during the Cold War. This can include, in retrospect, focusing on economic dimensions of power rather than military dimensions and focusing on ideas about Russia's geopolitical interests as distinct from communist internationalist ideas. In both cases, it is our ideas about the causal concepts that is central to our interpretative theory—both during and after the Cold War.

When theories are indeterminate it is often because our ideas about the key causal factors in the theory are poorly defined and/or quite complicated. Theories that rely on power have been plagued by this problem for years. The problems inherent in identifying a leader's true ideas are equally well known. In both cases, the multidimensional nature of the concept and the many various combinations of different dimensions of power or compounds of ideas allow great flexibility in post hoc explanation. Because our causal theories are based on these subsidiary ideas about causal factors, it is very difficult to push the importance of mental constructions or ideas into a secondary status. The very meaning of what constitutes material power is an ideational construction.

(3) Calibrate Confidence and Use Diplomacy to Test

Drawing overconfident conclusions about what caused the past to unfold as it did can be dangerous. Policymakers and scholars alike should calibrate their confidence about how well they understand the past by their ability to predict the future. Making near-term predictions about the future, and making them quite explicit and clear, can facilitate learning and better policy making. For instance, it can reveal how confident we ought to be about our causal theories. Experience with making predictions and facing the unexpected outcomes, not with defensiveness and embarrassment, but rather with open-mindedness, can teach us how often we are right and under what circumstances we are likely to be wrong and when we are simply unable to gauge how far off we are likely to be. Knowing when to hedge and when to be more confident would be a valuable contribution.

At times, diplomatic probes can consist of emerging personal relationships among leaders and negotiators. Other times, probes can simply be initiatives designed to elicit a response from the other side. The use of diplomacy to explore uncertainties is a valuable and commonly used tool that should be employed more often. It should also be used to examine the validity of the assumptions taken for granted, especially, for instance, assumptions about the other side's motivations. Although probes were essential to the process of ending the Cold War, most policymakers felt not enough was done to explore the underlying and unchallenged assumptions. There, of course, were propaganda initiatives designed to embarrass or outflank the opponent in the contest over public opinion, but these were not real probes deriving from recognized uncertainty and a felt need to test.

Of course, admitting uncertainty is not always easy in the political realm, where certitude and confidence often sells. Simple heuristic lessons, like "strength produces peace" and "appeasement breeds aggression," are often attractive. People appear to want clear and simple answers to problems, and evidently also enjoy feeling highly confident and free from the anxiety uncertainty provokes. It is easy to understand why patients may be tempted by confident-sounding physicians who announce they know exactly what to do and how to cure the patient's cancer, and why the same patients may be frustrated or even nervous with physicians who say that the causes of the cancer are multidimensional, the results of treatment uncertain, and the best course of action careful and limited treatments along with substantially more testing. Of course, what sells and makes us feel good momentarily is not always the same thing as what is prudent, appropriate given our level of understanding, and the smart way to proceed.

The major lesson from this book is not a confident substantive conclusion about the causal importance of material factors, ideas, domestic politics, or leaders. Instead, our main conclusion is that locking into excessively confident conclusions about these things is a mistake. More than just an academic mistake: it is a political mistake that can have negative and very costly consequences. Gorbachev showed that the lessons of the past did not need to be accepted as unalterable truths or even as accurate causal claims about the past. They could be straight-jackets constraining thinking about the future, but they need not be. Conflicts, like the Cold War, that are taken to be inevitable might just be susceptible to change, and, to the great surprise of everyone, they might end.

The conclusion we end with is that it was a mistake to believe that the Cold War was inevitable and could not be ended; it would be equally a mistake to believe that its end was inevitable and that the lessons drawn from how it ended provide certain guides for the future. Our best bet is to draw, from the past, propositions about causal relations, not lessons. As we approach the future, these propositions may help us to establish tests, and incremental treatments as similar propositions have in the medical sciences, but should not delude us into thinking that we have discovered general laws and silver-bullet cures that can be applied across time and circumstance without the most careful continuous testing, evaluation, and readiness to rethink and change.

The twentieth century was filled with political movements arguing that science meant certitude and the discovery of general laws and that the more of these laws that were found and applied to the social world, the better off humankind would be. The horrors that followed hardly need to be recounted here.

Hopefully, in the twenty-first century, a more sophisticated understanding of science will guide the political world and lead to more modest, probabilistic, and qualified claims, more open-minded inquiry, and a greater appreciation for uncertainty and the myriad ways the path of history and human creativity can develop.

Notes

1. Robert Jervis, *Perception and Misperception in International Politics* (Princeton, NJ: Princeton University Press, 1976), pp. 239–70.
2. Ibid.
3. Philip Tetlock, "Theory-Driven Reasoning about Plausible Pasts and Probable Futures in World Politics: Are We Prisoners of Our Preconceptions?" *American Journal of Political Science* 43 (2) (April 1999), pp. 335–66.
4. Robert Jervis, *Perception and Misperception in International Politics,* pp. 271–81.
5. See Jack Levy, "Learning and Foreign Policy," *International Organization* 48 (2) (Spring 1994), pp. 279–312; Philip E. Tetlock, "Learning in U.S. and Soviet Foreign Policy: In Search of an Elusive Concept," in George Breslauer and Philip Tetlock, *Learning in U.S. and Soviet Foreign Policy* (Boulder, CO: Westview, 1991), pp. 20–61. Also see Lloyd Etheredge, *Can Governments Learn?: American Foreign Policy and Central American Revolutions* (Elmsford, NY: Pergamon Press, 1985).
6. William Wohlforth, " The Stability of a Unipolar World," *International Security* 24 (1) (Summer 1999), pp. 5–41.
7. Georg W. F. Hegel *Philosophy of Right.* Translated by T. M. Knox (London: Oxford University Press, 1952).
8. Philip Tetlock and Penny Visser, "Thinking about Russia: Plausible Pasts and Probable Futures," *British Journal of Social Psychology* 39 (2000), pp. 173–96.
9. Robert Jervis, op. cit., pp. 271–81.
10. Paul Krugman, *Competitiveness* (New York: Council on Foreign Relations, 1997).
11. Marilynn Brewer and Norman Miller, *Intergroup Relations* (Pacific Grove, CA: Brooks/Cole Publishing, 1996).
12. Philip Tetlock and Aaron Belkin, *Counterfactual Thought Experiments in World Politics: Logical, Methodological, and Psychological Perspectives* (Princeton, NJ: Princeton University Press, 1996); and Richard Ned Lebow, "What's So Different about a Counterfactual?" *World Politics* 52 (4) (July 2000), pp. 550–85.
13. Jack F. Matlock, *Autopsy on an Empire : The American Ambassador's Account of the Collapse of the Soviet Union* (New York: Random House, 1995).
14. Sarah E. Mendelson, *Changing Course: Ideas, Politics and the Soviet Withdrawal from Afghanistan* (Princeton, NJ: Princeton University Press, 1998).
15. Robert Jervis, *The Meaning of the Nuclear Revolution: Statecraft and the Prospect of Armageddon,* (Ithaca, NY: Cornell University Press, 1989).
16. Stephen G. Brooks and William C. Wohlforth, "Power, Globalization, and the End of the Cold War: Reevaluating a Landmark Case for Ideas," *International Security* 25 (3) (Winter 2000/01), pp. 5–53.
17. Hans, J Morgenthau, *Politics Among Nations: The Struggle for Power and Peace,* 5th edition (New York: Alfred Knopf, 1973) and Richard Cottam, *Foreign Policy Motivation: A General Theory and a Case Study* (Pittsburgh: University of Pittsburgh Press, 1977).
18. Robin Dawes, "Prediction of the Future Verus an Understanding of the Past: A Basic Asymmetry. *American Journal of Psychology* 106 (1) (1993), pp. 1–24.
19. Vernon Aspaturin, *Process and Power in Soviet Foreign Policy* (Boston: Little, Brown, 1971) and J. Triska and D. Finley, *Soviet Foreign Policy* (New York: Macmillan, 1968).

Contributors

GEORGE W. BRESLAUER is Professor of Political Science and Dean of Social Sciences at the University of California at Berkeley. He is the author of *Krushchev and Brezhnev as Leaders* (London: Allen and Unwin, 1982), and *Gorbachev and Yeltsin as Leaders* (Cambridge: Cambridge University Press, 2002).

ARCHIE BROWN is a Fellow of St. Antony's College, Oxford, and Professor of Politics at Oxford University. He has been a Fellow of the British Academy since 1991 and was elected a Foreign Honorary Member of the American Academy of Arts and Sciences in 2003. His book, *The Gorbachev Factor* (Oxford: Oxford University Press, 1996), won the W. J. M. Mackenzie Prize of the Political Studies Association of the UK and the Alec Nove Prize of the British Association for *Slavonic and East European Studies*.

JAMES W. DAVIS is Associate Professor of International Politics at the Geschwister-Scholl-Institut of the Ludwig-Maximilians-Universitäät in Munich, Germany, and Associate Editor of the *European Journal of International Relations*.

MATTHEW EVANGELISTA is Professor of Government and Director of the Peace Studies Program at Cornell University. He is the author of *Innovation and the Arms Race* (Ithaca, NY: Cornell University Press, 1988); *Unarmed Forces: The Transnational Movement to End the Cold War* (Ithaca, NY: Cornell University Press, 1999); and *The Chechen Wars: Will Russia Go the Way of the Soviet Union?* (Washington, DC: The Brookings Institution, 2002).

RICHARD K. HERRMANN is Director of the Mershon Center and Professor of Political Science at The Ohio State University. He is the author of *Perceptions and Behavior in Soviet Foreign Policy* (Pittsburgh, PA: University of Pittsburgh Press, 1985). and numerous articles on international relations.

RICHARD NED LEBOW is James O. Freedman Professor of Government at Dartmouth College. His most recent book is *The Tragic Vision of Politics: Ethics, Interest, Orders* (Cambridge: Cambridge University Press, 2003).

JACQUES LÉVESQUE is Professor and Dean of the Faculty of Political Science and Law at the Université du Québec à Montréal. He is the author of *The Enigma of 1989: The USSR and the Liberation of Eastern Europe* (Berkeley: University of California Press,

1995), and co-author of *La Russie et son ex-empire: la reconfiguration géopolitique de l'ancien espace soviétique* (Paris: Presses de la Fondation Nationale des Sciences Politiques, 2003).

JANICE GROSS STEIN is the Belzberg Professor of Conflict Management and the Director of the Munk Centre for International Studies at the University of Toronto. She has recently been appointed a Trudeau Fellow. Her latest publications include *The Cult of Efficiency*, delivered as the Massey Lectures in 2001 and *Street Protests and Fantasy Parks: Globalization, Culture and the State* (Vancouver: University of British Columbia, Press, 2002)

WILLIAM C. WOHLFORTH is Associate Professor of Government at Dartmouth College. He is the author of *Elusive Balance: Powers and Perceptions during the Cold War* (Ithaca, NY: Cornell, 1993) and editor of *Witnesses to the End of the Cold War* (Baltimore, MD: Johns Hopkins University Press, 1996) and *Cold War Endgame* (University Park: Pennsylvania State University Press, 2003).

Name Index

Subject Index